Proclaiming Christ to the Nations

100 Sermon Outlines on Spirit-Empowered Mission

Denzil R. Miller
Editor

A Decade of Pentecost Publication

Proclaiming Christ to the Nations: 100 Sermon Outlines on Spirit-Empowered Mission. © 2017, AIA Publications. All rights reserved. No part of this book may be reproduced, stored in a retrieval system, or transmitted in any form or by any means—electronic, mechanical, photocopy, recording, or otherwise—without prior written permission of the copyright owner, except brief quotations used in connection with reviews in magazines or newspapers.

All Scripture quotations in this book, unless otherwise indicated, are from the Holy Bible, New International Version. Copyright © 1973, 1978, 1984 by International Bible Society. All rights reserves.

Scripture citations noted ESV are taken from The Holy Bible, English Standard Version®, Copyright © 2001 by Crossway, a publishing ministry of Good News Publishers. All rights reserved.

Scripture citations noted KJV are taken from the Authorized (King James) Version. All rights reserved.

Scripture citations noted NKJV are taken from the New King James Version®. Copyright © 1982 by Thomas Nelson. All rights reserved

Library of Congress Cataloging-in-Publication Data
Miller, Denzil R., 1946–
Proclaiming Christ to the Nations: 100 Sermon Outlines on Spirit-Empowered Mission / Denzil R. Miller

ISBN: 978-0-9903008-7-8

1. Bible. 2. Practical Theology: Homiletics. 4. Missions 5. Pentecostal. 6. Holy Spirit.

Printed in the United States of America
AIA Publications, Springfield, MO, USA
© 2017

A Decade of Pentecost Publication
Websites: www.DecadeofPentecost.org
          www.ActsinAfrica.org

Books of the Bible
~ Abbreviations Used in This Book ~

Old Testament

Genesis	Ge
Exodus	Ex
Leviticus	Le
Numbers	Nu
Deuteronomy	Dt
Joshua	Jos
Judges	Jdg
Ruth	Ru
1 Samuel	1Sa
2 Samuel	2Sa
1 Kings	1Ki
2 Kings	2Ki
1 Chronicles	1Ch
2 Chronicles	2Ch
Ezra	Ezr
Nehemiah	Ne
Esther	Es
Job	Job
Psalms	Ps
Proverbs	Pr
Ecclesiastes	Ec
Song of Solomon	So
Isaiah	Is
Jeremiah	Je
Lamentations	La
Ezekiel	Eze
Daniel	Da
Hosea	Ho
Joel	Jl
Amos	Am
Obadiah	Ob
Jonah	Jnh
Micah	Mic
Nahum	Na
Habakkuk	Hab
Zephaniah	Zep
Haggai	Hg
Zechariah	Zec
Malachi	Mal

New Testament

Matthew	Mt
Mark	Mk
Luke	Lk
John	Jn
Acts	Ac
Romans	Ro
1 Corinthians	1Co
2 Corinthians	2Co
Galatians	Ga
Ephesians	Ep
Philippians	Phi
Colossians	Col
1 Thessalonians	1Th
2 Thessalonians	2Th
1 Timothy	1Ti
2 Timothy	2Ti
Titus	Tit
Philemon	Phm
Hebrews	He
James	Ja
1 Peter	1Pe
2 Peter	2Pe
1 John	1Jn
2 John	2Jn
3 John	3Jn
Jude	Jd
Revelation	Re

Table of Contents

Books of the Bible 3
Table of Contents 5
Sermon Author Index 9
Introduction 13

SECTION 1: PROCLAIMING THE GOSPEL

1   Proclaiming Christ to the Nations 20
2   Tears of the Harvest 22
3   Proclaim Christ to All Creation 24
4   Declare to the Nations 26
5   Preach the Gospel 28
6   Jesus, the Model Soul Winner 30
7   Four Necessities for the Harvest 32
8   This Gospel Shall Be Preached 34
9   We Will Not Stop Proclaiming 36
10 Fully Proclaiming the Gospel of Christ 38
11 One Hope for the World 40

SECTION 2: THE GREAT COMMISSION

12 Great Commission Mandate 1: "Pray!" 44
13 Great Commission Mandate 2: "Go!" 46
14 Great Commission Mandate 3: "Preach!" 48
15 Great Commission Mandate 4: "Witness!" 50
16 The Great Commission Never Ends 52
17 Finding Your Place in the Great Commission 54
18 Living the Great Commission 56
19 Go and Make Disciples 58
20 Fulfilling the Great Commission 60
21 Don't Leave Home Without It 62
22 Understanding the Great Commission 64
23 Obeying the Great Commission 66
24 Four Superlatives for the Harvest 68
25 "Great Comissioners" 70
26 Perspectives on the Great Commission 72

SECTION 3: PASSION FOR THE LOST

27 Mastered by the Cross 76
28 God's Mission—Our Mission... 78
29 What Time Is It? 80
30 Buying Fields When It Makes No Sense 82
31 Motivated for Mission 84
32 Three Foundation Stones for Missions 86
33 It's Harvest Time: Let's Get Involved 88
34 Ripe for Harvest 90
35 God's Desire for the Nations 92
36 Rekindling Our Passion for the Lost 94
37 Partnering with God in His Mission 96
38 The "Insignificant" Woman 98
39 The Seeking God 100
40 The Heartbeat of God for Lost People 102
41 Missions, the Heart of God 104
42 Four Great Facts about the Harvest 106
43 Committed to the World 108
44 Kingdom Treasures 110
45 The Priority of the Harvest 112

SECTION 4: THE HOLY SPIRIT AND MISSIONS

46 The Pentecost Question 116
47 Spirit-Directed Missions 118
48 God's Will for You 120
49 Empowered to Speak 122
50 The Missionary Signs of Pentecost 124
51 Dependence on the Spirit in Missions 126
52 You Will Be My Witnesses 128
53 The Spirit Says, "Go!" 130
54 Keep the Fire Burning 132
55 Compelled by the Spirit 134
56 Your Power to Witness 136

SECTION 5: THE CALL OF GOD

57	Beautiful Feet	140
58	Jesus is Calling	142
59	Christ's High Calling to be Fishers of Men	144
60	The Savior Who Sends	146
61	Blessed to Obey	148
62	Christ's Sent Ones	150
63	The God Who Calls	152
64	Chosen for His Mission	154
65	Deep Convictions about Missions	156
66	God is Calling! Are You Listening?	158
67	The Call of God	160
68	Called to Work for the Kingdom	162

SECTION 6: MOBILIZING FOR MISSIONS

69	Following the Example of Jesus	166
70	Five Important Elements of Missions	168
71	Three Strategic Functions of Missions	170
72	The "World of Unless"	172
73	The Power of One	174
74	Two Great Missionary Challenges	176
75	God's Missionary Plan	178
76	A Missionary Psalm for Everyone	180
77	The Gospel Spread Unhindered	182
78	God's Great Destiny for Africa	184
79	The Measure of a Missionary Church	186
80	A Motto for Missions	188
81	Nine Steps to the Mission Field	190
82	Reaping the Nations: What It Will Take	192
83	Seedtime and Harvest	194
84	The Sending Mission of the Church	196
85	How Can They Hear?	198
86	By All Possible Means	200
87	Four Principles of the Harvest	202
88	Seventy-two Plus You	204
89	Becoming a Global Christian	206

90	The Greatest Story Ever Told	208
91	The Holy Spirit the Director of Missions	210
92	Everywhere!	212
93	The Cost of Missions	214
94	Missionary Lessons from Elijah	216

SECTION 7: PRAYER AND SPIRITUAL WARFARE

95	Motivated for Mission	220
96	Prayer and the Mission of God	222
97	Overcoming the Enemy	224
98	Help Them with Our Prayers	226
99	Opening Prayers	228
100	Prayer and the Missionary Task	230

Scripture Text Index 233
Other Decade of Pentecost Books 237

Sermon Author Index

AC	Al Crane	Pastor, Crowley Assembly of God, Crowley, Texas. USA (71)
BD	Brett Deal	Assemblies of God World Missionary, Senegal (58, 72)
BVW	Barbara VanWyke	Assemblies of God World Missionary, Botswana (90)
CGS	Christopher Gornold-Smith	Assemblies of God World Missionary, International Media Ministries (20)
CK	Claver Kabandana	President, Pentecostal Assemblies of God, Rwanda (6)
DB	Darlene Banda	Principal, Assemblies of God Bible College, Lusaka, Zambia (70)
DC	Don Corbin	AGWM-Africa Regional Director (1985-2002) (30, 31, 95)
DG	Dean Galyen	Assemblies of God World Missionary, Africa (34)
DM	Daniel Mbiwan,	General Superintendent, Full Gospel Mission, Cameroon (77)
DMc	Daniel McGaffee	Chi Alpha Campus Pastor, Chico State University, Chico, California, USA (96)
DRM	Denzil R. Miller	Director, Acts in Africa Initiative, Springfield, Missouri, USA (1, 7, 8, 9, 10, 21, 24, 25, 26, 35, 36, 50, 52, 53, 65, 66, 78, 79, 80, 81, 82, 83, 84, 94, 97)
EC	Edward Chitsonga	President, Malawi Assemblies of God (3)

EG	Edwin Gbelly	President, Liberia Assemblies of God (37, 64)
EKA	Emmanuel Kwasi Amoafo	Attached Clergy, Anglican Church of Kenya Parish of Christ Church, Nairobi, Kenya (16)
EML	Enson Mbilikile Lwesya	AIA Team Member; Chairman, AAGA World Missions Commission; Lead Pastor, International Christian Assembly, Lilongwe, Malawi (49)
EYA	Emil Yaovi Adote	President, Benin Assemblies of God (69)
GB	Greg Beggs	Regional Director, AGWM-Africa (2, 27, 57)
GC	Gaylan Claunch	Assistant Superintendent/Missions Director, North Texas District, Assemblies of God (40, 42)
GM	Greg Mundis	Executive Director, Assemblies of God World Missions, Springfield, MO, USA (51)
JB	Jason Branson	Pastor, First Assembly of God, LaGrange, Georgia, USA (29)
JDE	Jimmy D. Easter	Assemblies of God minister (59, 73)
JF	Jerry Falley	Director, Link-Up Africa, Springfield, Missouri, USA (5, 61, 62)
JL	Jimmy Lemons	Pan Africa Theological Seminary, Francophone Coordinator, Togo (76)
JLE	John L. Easter	Director, Africa's Hope, Springfield, Missouri, USA (32, 74)

JM	Jim Mazurek	Assemblies of God World Missionary, Chile (63)
JN	Jeff Nelson	Missionary in Residence, Evangel University, Springfield, Missouri, USA (54)
JO	Jerry Orf	Pastor, First Assembly of God, Mansfield, Missouri, USA (85, 98)
JS	Jerry Spain	AGWM-East Africa Area Director (1992-2000) (44, 45)
JTG	Joegbéan Tokpah Gbanamou	President, Guinea Assemblies God (48)
LB	Lipenga Banda, General	General Secretary, Zambia Assemblies of God (46)
LC	Lazarus Chakwera	President, Malawi Congress Party; President, Malawi Assemblies of God (1989-2013) (47)
LE	Lavonna Ennis	Assemblies of God World Missionary, The Gambia (93)
LT	Loren Triplett	Director, Assemblies of God World Missions (1989-1997) (43, 67)
MO	Michel Ouedraogo	President, Burkina Faso, Assemblies of God (86)
MRT	Mark R. Turney	Associate Director, Acts in Africa Initiative; General Secretary, Africa AG Alliance (11, 26, 55, 68, 88)
NB	Nate Beggs	Assemblies of God World Missionary, Africa (17)
PFM	Paul Frimpong-Manso	General Superintendent, Ghana Assemblies of God (19, 33, 91)

PW	Peter Watt	General Superintendent, Assemblies of God, South Africa (99, 100)
PY	Paul York	Cross-cultural Missions Trainer, Chi Alpha, USA (56)
RSK	Reuben S. Kachala	Mobilization Base Leader, Frontier Missions International, Lilongwe, Malawi (23, 89)
SC	Sarah Cariens	Assemblies of God World Missionary, South Africa (18)
SE	Scott Ennis	Assemblies of God World Missionary, The Gambia (4, 60, 92)
SH	Scott Hanson	Strategic Leader for Unreached People, AGWM-Africa (22, 75)
SP	Steve Pennington	East Africa Area Director, Assemblies of God World Missions (38, 39, 87)
UA	Uche Ama	AIA Team Member; Director of Foreign Missions, Assemblies of God Nigeria (12, 13, 14, 15)
WS	Waly Sarr	President, Senegal Assemblies of God (41)

Introduction

The Africa Assemblies of God are mobilizing for missions. During their Decade of Pentecost emphasis from 2010 to 2020, the fifty national churches making up the Africa Assemblies of God Alliance (AAGA) have committed themselves to sending missionaries to many of the unreached peoples and places in their own and in neighboring countries. In this endeavor, national and local churches find themselves at various stages of development. Some have already established strong missions departments and are deploying missionaries to the field. Others are just beginning the process. Whatever their situation, all remain committed to do their part in sending the message of Christ to the unreached people and places of Africa and beyond.

God has richly blessed the Africa AG. The movement now reports 22 million adherents meeting in 81,000 local churches across the continent.[1] Jesus, however, taught that such blessing comes with great responsibility. He said, "To whom much is given, much will be required" (Luke 12:38). This certainly applies to the Africa AG. One of their great responsibilities (and challenges) is mobilizing and deploying a great army of missionaries to the field—and then supporting them with their prayers and finances. Imagine what could happen if a passion to reach the nations for Christ was implanted into the hearts all 22 million adherents of the Africa AG.

For this to occur, at least two things must happen. First, the Africa AG must continue to experience an outpouring of the Holy Spirit. We thank God for how He is showering His Spirit on the church of Africa. However, this Pentecostal revival must expand and accelerate. When Jesus was mobilizing His church in Jerusalem, He commanded them to go into all the world and preach the good news to every person. However, He directed them to first stay in Jerusalem until they had been clothed with the Spirit's power (Luke 24:49). Finally, just before He ascended into heaven, He left them with a final promise: "But you will receive power when the Holy Spirit has come upon you, and you will be my witnesses…to the ends of the earth" (Acts 1:8). To fulfill its missionary destiny, the Africa AG must intensify their prayers to the Lord of the Harvest. They must pray, "Lord, graciously pour out

---

[1] 2015 statistics.

your Spirit on us, and empower us to accomplish Your mission in the earth."

Another thing that must happen in the Africa AG is that our pastors must begin to preach frequently and effectively on missions. Only then will a passion for the unreached nations be implanted in the hearts of God's people.

Unfortunately, however, the African church has no centuries-long tradition of preaching on missions, as does the Western Church. This tradition in the Western Church dates back as far as William Carey and the late 18th century. While the African church has effectively pursued evangelism and church planting within their own national boarders, they have not historically sought to mobilize themselves for world missions. As result, they have not generally developed a long tradition of missions preaching.

This book is designed to address this issue. It was developed as a resource for African pastors wanting to mobilize their churches for missions outreach. Pastors and church leaders can use these sermon outlines to inspire and train their people in missions principles and practice. The book is a sequel to the first sermon outline book published by the Acts in Africa Initiative (AIA) in 2011. That first book was entitled, *Proclaiming Pentecost: 100 Sermon Outlines on the Power of the Holy Spirit.*[2]

The great success of the first book has been gratifying. To date, it has been translated from English into six other African languages, including in French, Portuguese, Spanish, Swahili, Mooré, and Amharic. It has, to date, been distributed to more than 35,000 pastors in 31 countries in Africa. It is further being used in Central and South America and the Philippines. The AIA office has received testimonies of how the book is being used, and how thousands of African Christians are being baptized in the Spirit as a result. One African pastor exulted, "The *Proclaiming Pentecost* book has brought revival to our national church." We pray that this book will experience similar success.

---

[2] These two books, and many others, can be downloaded for free in e-book format at www.DecadeofPentecost.org. They can be purchased in print form from my personal blogsite at www.DenzilRMiller.com.

Contributors

The 100 sermon outlines in this book have been contributed by forty-five Pentecostal preachers. These preachers include African missionaries and missions leaders, American missionaries, and missional pastors. I have personally contributed approximately one fourth of the outlines. You can identify who authored each sermon by the initials appearing at the bottom of each outline. You can then match these initials with the "Contributors List" on pages 9-12. Also, after each contributor's name and particulars you will find, in parentheses, a list of sermons he or she contributed.

I want to extend a heartfelt thank you to each of these men and women who allowed us to use their sermon outlines without cost.

How to Use This Book

Allow me to suggest how you may best use this book. The process begins with choosing a sermon. If, for instance, you want to preach from a certain text, you can begin your search by checking "Sermon Text Index" at the back of the book. This search will lead you to any sermon that may have been developed based on your chosen text.

Possibly, you want to preach a missions sermon, but you are unsure of exactly what you want to preach about. In such a case, you can browse the book for a sermon. You may want to begin your search in the "Table of Contents" at the beginning of the book. In doing this, you will note how the book is divided into seven sections, including the following:

- Proclaiming the Gospel
- The Great Commission
- Passion for the Lost
- The Holy Spirit and Missions
- The Call of God
- Mobilizing for Missions
- Prayer and Spiritual Warfare

One of these categories may appeal to you. You can then begin looking for a message in that section of the book, thus streamlining your search.

The "Sermon in a Sentence" feature can also be helpful. By reading this one-sentence summary of the message, you can get a quick idea of whether or not you want to investigate further. If the subject interests you, you can then look more closely at the outline.

Perhaps you want to achieve a particular goal with your sermon. For instance, you want to inspire your listeners to pray for missions, or you want them to open there hearts to God's call to missions. In this case, you may want to scan the "Sermon Purpose" feature at the beginning of each outline. In this way, you can choose a sermon that will help you to attain your goal.

Note further that each outline in this book has been formatted to fit onto two pages. In doing this, I have attempted to include enough content in each outline to give the user a clear indication of the substance and flow of the message. At the same time, I have sought to be brief enough to give preachers and teachers ample room to develop and customize the messages to the unique needs of their listeners. As you study, pray over, and preach these outlines, I trust that the Holy Spirit will inspire you with fresh ideas of how to develop your own missions messages.

There are number of ways you can use your chosen outline. The first and most obvious way is to preach the sermon exactly as it is written. It is more likely, however, that you will want to adapt the message to your own unique setting and the particular needs of your audience. You will also want to add your own insights to the message. In addition, as you pray over and meditate on the sermon, the Spirit will speak to you. You will certainly want to incorporate these insights into your message. And, of course, you will also want to add your own illustrations and anecdotes to the message. In other words, I encourage you to make the sermon your own.

How to Preach a Great Missions Message

I conclude with some recommendations on how you can take these sermon outlines and preach great missions messages.

Be filled with the Spirit. First, in order to preach an effective missions sermon—or for that matter, any sermon—you must be full of the Holy Spirit. Often in the Book of Acts the apostles began their sermons by being filled with the Spirit (Acts 2:4 and 14; 4:8; 4:31). There is no substitute for Spirit-anointed preaching. No amount of personal charm or showmanship can make up for a lack of the Spirit's presence upon the preacher. Let Jesus be your model. As He began His ministry, He announced, "The Spirit of the Lord is on me, because he has anointed me to preach good news…" (Luke 4:18).

Own the sermon. As suggested above, make the sermon your own. In other words, once you have chosen your sermon outline, begin to "internalize" it. Implant the message into your heart and mind by thoughtfully and prayerfully reading through it several times. Mentally preach the sermon to yourself. As you do, respond to its message. Heed what it says. If you need to stop and pray, then do so; if you need to repent, do that.

It is also important to memorize the sermon text and other key scriptures to be used in the sermon. This, too, will help to imbed the message in your heart. It will also help you as you preach. Because the texts are in your heart and mind, the message will flow better. Your listeners will sense your passion and your mastery of the subject, and they will respond better to what you are saying. It will also be helpful to memorize the main points of the sermon. By doing this will be liberated from your notes, and you will be able to speak more directly and more persuasively to the people.

Deliver your sermon. As you preach your missions message, keep two things in mind. First, *be concise.* That means that you should not load your message with unnecessary words and irrelevant thoughts. Stay on point. Remember your goal, and say nothing that will not help you to achieve that goal. Secondly, as you preach, *aim for the altar.* In other words, everything you say must be designed to bring people to a commitment. Then, as you conclude your message, "cast the net." As a fisherman casts his net into the water and pulls the fish into his boat, you should "cast the net" by inviting people to come to the altar. Call them to commit themselves to God's mission and to be empowered by the Spirit to accomplish that mission.

With these thoughts in mind, I commend this volume to you. It is my sincere prayer that you use it often as a tool to mobilize Christ's church to reach the nations in the power of the Holy Spirit.

I would love to hear from you concerning how these outlines have helped you. Please send your testimonies to and prayer requests to ActsinAfrica@agmd.org.

~ Dr. Denzil R. Miller
Editor

~ Section 1 ~

Proclaiming the Gospel

 1 Proclaiming Christ to the Nations

Sermon in a Sentence: We must proclaim Christ to the nations in the power of the Holy Spirit.

Sermon Purpose: That the people be filled with the Spirit and commit themselves to proclaiming Christ to the nations.

Text: Mark 16:15-18

Introduction
1. As God's missionary people, we have all been called to proclaim Christ to the nations.
2. Mark's Great Commission makes this clear: "Go into all the world and proclaim the good news to all creation."
3. This message will discuss four important issues concerning our responsibility of proclaiming Christ to the nations: Our mission, Our method, Our means, and Our required response.

I. OUR MISSION—THE WHOLE WORLD
A. Jesus said, "Go into *all the world...*" (Mk 16:15).
   1. On another occasion, He said, "This gospel of the kingdom will be preached in the whole world [*oikoumeme,* inhabited earth], as a testimony to all nations [*ethne,* people group]; and then the end will come" (Mt 24:14).
B. "All the world" includes...
   1. *Every place:* "You will be my witnesses in Jerusalem, and in all Judea... and to the ends of the earth" (Ac 1:8).
   2. *Every person:* "preach...to every creature" (v.15, KJV).
   3. *Every people:* "Go, therefore, and make disciples of all nations (Greek: *ethne* or people group)" (Mt 28:19).
B. What it will require: Some who will go; others who will send. (Read Ro 10:13-15a).
   1. Christ is calling some to go.
      a. To leave home and family and go to distant lands and unfamiliar cultures and proclaim the good news.
   2. He is calling the rest of us to send.
      a. To give financially to support those who go.
      b. To pray for the missionaries and for the lost.
   3. No one is exempt.

II. OUR MESSAGE—THE GOOD NEWS
A. Jesus said, "Go into all the world and *preach the gospel...*"

        1. The good news (gospel) is the message of Christ's death on the cross and of His glorious resurrection from the dead.
        2. It includes a call for people to repent of their sins and put their faith in Christ alone for salvation (Mk 1:15; Ac 20:21).
    B. Our action (or inaction) involves eternal consequences.
        1. Jesus said, "Whoever believes and is baptized will be saved, but whoever does not believe will be condemned" (v. 16).
        2. There are also consequences for not going and proclaiming:
            a. Read and discuss: Ezekiel 3:17-19
    C. We must not allow lesser messages to divert us.
        1. Paul's warning to Timothy (2Ti 4:3-5).
        2. Only the message of Christ can bring eternal life (Jn 17:3).

III. OUR MEANS—THE POWER OF THE HOLY SPIRIT
    A. Jesus promised, "And these signs will accompany…" (vv.17-18)
        1. These are all works of the Holy Spirit (Ac 4:30-33).
        2. In Acts: "Then the disciples went out and preached everywhere, and the Lord worked with them and confirmed his word by the signs that accompanied it" (Ac 16:20).
        3. Such Spirit-empowered ministry is seen throughout Acts.
    B. Jesus has promised this same power to us today.
        1. His final promise: (Ac 1:8) "You will receive power…"
        2. His final command: (Ac 1:4-5) "Do not leave Jerusalem, but wait for the gift my Father promised…"

IV. OUR REQUIRED RESPONSE—OBEDIENCE
    A. Our text says, "Then the disciples went out and preached everywhere…"
        1. In other words, they obeyed the Lord's command.
    B. God requires the same response from us today.
        1. Jesus: "If you love me you will obey what I command" (Jn 14:15).
        2. We must obey by going, giving, and praying.

Conclusion and Altar Call
    1. Come now and commit yourself to Christ's mission.
    2. Come and be empowered by the Holy Spirit.

[DRM]

2 Tears of the Harvest

Sermon in a Sentence: Even in times of hardship we must sow the seed of the gospel, trusting God for the harvest.

Sermon Purpose: To encourage people to preach the gospel even in the midst of great trials and difficulty.

Text: Psalm 126:4-6

Introduction
1. In this "Psalm of Ascension," those who were in captivity return Zion—only to find it in ruins.
    a. While they rejoice in their newfound freedom, they weep when they remember the city's former glory.
    b. As they rebuild their ruined city, and sow their precious seed in their barren fields, they weep.
    c. Yet, in faith they look to God for the promised harvest.
2. Today we weep over Africa.
    a. Across Africa, Satan has taken many captives.
    b. In many ways Africa, like Zion, lies in ruins.
        1) It is plagued with war, famine, disease, and corruption.
    c. And yet, while we weep for Africa, we must also sow.
3. In our text, we learn three important lessons about sowing and reaping a harvest:

I. APOSTOLIC AMBITION: THE LONGING TO SOW
Read v. 6 "He who goes out weeping…"
A. During times of drought, we are often tempted to do nothing.
    1. Because of the pain, we are tempted to hoard the seed.
B. However, apostolic ambition motivates us to go into the field to sow, no matter what the cost.
    1. Drought and hunger must not stop the farmer from sowing.
    2. African farmers understand what it means to sow in tears. In times famine they are tempted to eat the seed reserved for the next sowing season. They weep, yet they sow the seed in the field, trusting God to give them a harvest.
C. Apostolic ambitions drives us to sow even in times of hardship.
    1. We are moved by and faith in the Lord of the Harvest (Mt 9:38), by the promised harvest of souls (Ga. 6:9), and by the power of the Holy Spirit (Ac.11:12).
    2. Tears are often the Kingdom's price for progress.

II. APOSTOLIC RESOURCES: THE SOWER AND THE SEED
v. 6: "...carrying seed to sow..."
A. The gospel is like good seed (Lk 11:8; 1Pe 1:23).
   1. Never doubt its power to redeem people (Ro 1:16).
   2. It is good news for all people, no matter how hard, how lost, or how far they seem to be from the grace of God.
B The gospel continues to transform countless millions of people.
   1. It has turned societies who once cowered in fear of their ancestral spirits into people who live victorious lives.
   2. It has turned people groups who once abused, sold, and mutilated their women into a people who now ordain them as ministers of the gospel.
   3. It has transformed people filled with greed and self-interest into people who will give sacrificially to the cause of Christ.
C. Transformed lives are another good seed (Mt 12:23; Lk 8:15).
   1. God scatters His people into the world as seed.

III. APOSTOLIC CONFIDENCE: FAITH IN THE GOD OF THE HARVEST
v.6 "... will return with songs of joy, carrying sheaves with him."
A. Our confidence is in the God of the harvest.
   1. We know He will be faithful to the promises in His Word.
   2. He has the authority and power to cause harvest to happen.
   3. He will shape natural and spiritual conditions for harvest.
B. We are confident that God's harvest system works.
   1. We believe that sowing *will* produces a harvest.
   2. When the seed is sown and the rain comes, nothing can stop the seed from sprouting and producing.

Conclusion and Altar Call:
1. What then shall we do when we find Zion (Africa) lying in ruins? Shall we run away in fear? No! With tears we will sow the seed and trust God for the harvest.
2. Come now, and commit yourself to sowing the gospel seed.

[GB]

3 Proclaim Christ to All Creation

Sermon in a Sentence: We must proclaim Christ to all creation.
Sermon Purpose: That the people commit themselves to obeying Christ's command to preach the good news to all creation.
Text: Mark 16:15-20
Introduction
1. In our text, Jesus issues His Great Commission.
2. He commands us to "Go into all the world and preach the good news to all creation."
3. From this text, we learn three powerful principles about our duty of proclaiming Christ to all creation:

I. PROCLAIMING CHRIST TO ALL CREATION IS THE MASTER'S COMMAND
   A. Jesus has ordered us to "Go into all the world and preach the good news to all creation" (Mk 16:15).
   B. This command came from the throne room of heaven, that is, for the highest authority (Mt 28:18).
   C. Jesus has commanded, therefore, we must obey.
      1. Obedience is a necessity (Jn 14:15, 31).
      2. Obedience is a privilege for all sons and daughters of God.

II. PROCLAIMING CHRIST TO ALL CREATION IS THE BASIS FOR PEOPLE TO BELIEVE AND BE SAVED
   A. Jesus continued, "Whoever believes and is baptized will be saved, but whoever does not believe will be condemned" (v.16).
      1. Our job is not to condemn, but to call people to faith in Christ (Jn 3:16-17).
   B. We must tell all creation that Jesus saves.
      1. Jesus proclaimed the gospel (Mk 1:15).
      2. Paul proclaimed the gospel (Ac 16:31).
      3. We too must proclaim the gospel.
   C. If they will believe, they will be saved.
      1. "Whoever believes and is baptized will be saved" (v.16).
      2. Have you put your faith in Christ for salvation?
         a. If not, do it now!
         b. He is "mighty to save" all who call on His name (Is 63:1; Ro 10:13).

III. PROCLAIMING CHRIST TO ALL CREATION IS THE PURPOSE OF SIGNS AND WONDERS

A. Jesus further promised, "And these signs will accompany those who believe: In my name they will drive out demons; they will speak in new tongues; they will pick up snakes with their hands; and when they drink deadly poison, it will not hurt them at all; they will place their hands on sick people, and they will get well" (Mk 16:17-18).
B. We must go in the power of the Holy Spirit, expecting God to confirm the gospel with signs and wonders.
  1. Jesus ministered in the Spirit's power (Lk 4:18; Ac 10:38).
  2. If we will faithful proclaim the gospel, God will confirm our words with miraculous signs.
      a. He confirmed the disciples preaching (Mk 16:20).
      b. He confirmed Paul's preaching (Ro 15:18-19).
      c. He will confirm out preaching.
C. We must never forget, however, that the purpose of signs is to confirm the gospel and point people to Christ.
  1. Philip in Samaria (Ac 8:5).
  2. When God gives miracles, we must never forget their purpose—to point people to Christ.

Conclusion and Altar Call
  1. Come now, and commit yourself to proclaiming Christ to all creation.
  2. Come and be empowered by the Holy Spirit.

[EC]

4 Declare to the Nations

Sermon in a Sentence: We must declare to the nations that Jesus Christ is Savior and King.

Sermon Purpose: To call the people to commit themselves to declare the message of God's salvation to the nations.

Text: Psalm 96:1-13

Introduction
1. David wrote Psalm 96 when he brought the Ark back to Jerusalem (Compare 1Chr 16:7, 23-33 with Ps 96:1-13).
2. It is a missionary hymn celebrating Yahweh's kingship over all the earth.
3. In this Psalm, God is calling on us to make three declarations to the nations:

I. WE ARE TO DECLARE TO THE NATIONS THAT GOD IS THE SAVIOR

A. David calls on all the earth to worship Yahweh (vv.1-2).
   1. This is right because the nations rightly belong to God.
   2. In response to His greatness, all nations and peoples are to "sing a new song" to God (v.1).
   3. This will one day come to pass (Re 5:9-10).
B. As God's missionary people, our worship must turn into witness:
   1. Not only are we to worship God's glory, we are to "declare his glory among the nations…" (Ps 96:3).
   2. We are to "proclaim the good news of His salvation from day to day" (v.2).
C. Jesus is the message we declare to the nations.
   1. We are to proclaim that Jesus is the Savior of all mankind.
   2. He is the one who has given us salvation and has defeated the enemies of our souls (Ep 1:19-23; Col 2:13-15).
   3. Like the apostles, we must never stop proclaiming that Jesus is Savior ("We cannot stop speaking!"—Ac 4:20).

II. WE ARE TO DECLARE TO THE NATIONS THAT GOD IS GREAT

A. We serve a great God.
   1. In Psalm 95 David spoke of God's greatness (vv.4-6).
   2. He is "greatly to be praised" (v 4). (See also Ex 15:11.)

3. We serve a Great Savior:
   a. Jesus is "King of kings and Lord of lords" (1Ti 6:15).
   b. He is the Savior or the world! (Jn 4:44; 1Jn 4:14).
B. We must declare His greatness to the nations.
   1. David tells us *what* we are to do: *declare Him!* (v.3).
   3. He also tell us *why* we are to do this: *He is great!* (v.4).
   2. Jesus is not only "greatly to be praised," He is also to be greatly proclaimed (Mk.15:15-16).

III. WE ARE TO DECLARE TO THE NATIONS THAT GOD IS HOLY

A. David calls on the nations to "worship the Lord in the beauty of holiness" (v.9).
   1. This is the second time he calls us to worship.
   2. This reveals the missionary heartbeat of this Psalm—all ethnic groups will one day worship the King (v.10).
B. What "offering" does the Lord require of us?
   1. He requires that we give our all to Him (Mk 8:34-38).
   2. We must live before Him in the "beauty of holiness" (v. 9).
   3. He is coming for "a glorious church, not having spot or wrinkle or any such thing," a church that is "holy and without blemish" (Ep 5:27).
C. We must declare His holiness among the nations.
   1. We must "say among the nations that the Lord reigns."
   2. Once again, worship turns to witness (v.10).
      a. The "families of the peoples" are now called on to proclaim Him among the nations (v.7).
      b. This confession challenges all other gods, all other rulers and authorities—there is only one King.

Conclusion and Altar Call

1. Christ has commissioned us to join Him in declaring God's reign to the nations (Mt 23:14; 28:19-20).
2. Come, commit yourself to go, give, and pray so that the nations can hear of God's salvation in Jesus Christ.

[SE]

5 Preach the Gospel

Sermon in a Sentence: We must faithfully preach the gospel in the power of the Holy Spirit.

Sermon Purpose: That believers will commit themselves to preach the gospel with signs following.

Text: Mark 16:15–20

Introduction
1. We have just read Jesus' Great Commission in Mark 16.
2. Here, Jesus tells us to "preach the good news," that is, we must insistently and persuasively declare the message of Christ.
3. From this passage we can learn three important lessons:

I. JESUS HAS COMMANDED US TO PREACH
   A. Jesus has commanded us to "Go…and preach."
      1. Reread Mark 16:15
      2. We are to go *everywhere*—and to *every person.*
      3. We are to deliver the message of the gospel…
         a. …that Jesus paid the price for our sins and now offers eternal life to all who will put their trust in Him.
         b. They must repent and believe the good news (Mk 1:15).
   B. We must preach the gospel because people's eternal destiny is at stake.
      1. Jesus said, "Whoever believes and is baptized will be saved, but whoever does not believe will be condemned" (v.16).
      2. We must not neglect this all-important task.
   C. Consequently, every believer must preach the gospel.
      1. Will you obey Christ's command to preach the gospel?
      2. But not only has Jesus commanded us to preach…

II. JESUS HAS COMMISSIONED US WITH POWER
   A. Along with Jesus' command to preach is a promise of power.
      1. Read vv.17-18: "And these signs will follow…"
      2. This promise is to "whoever believes."
      3. It includes pastors, missionaries, Sunday school teachers, church members and every believing youth.
   B. If we will go and believe, Christ will confirm the word with supernatural signs following.
      1. But remember, we must go "in His Name," that is, under His authority and for His glory.
      2. These miraculous signs will include…

a. Divine deliverances ("they will drive out demons")
  b. Divine utterances ("they will speak with new tongues")
  c. Divine healings ("sick people...will get well")
  d. Divine protection ("snakes...poison...will not hurt them").
C. This supernatural power to preach the gospel comes when we are baptized in the Holy Spirit.
  1. Jesus' final command and promise (Read Ac 1:4-5, 8)
  2. The disciples received the promise at Pentecost (2:4).
  3. They then began to preach the gospel with signs following.

III. JESUS EXPECTS US TO ACCEPT GOD'S WORD

A. After receiving the command the, disciples accepted Christ's word and obeyed His command.
  1. After giving the command, Jesus was taken into heaven.
  2. Immediately the disciples obeyed. They "went and preached everywhere" (v.20).
B. They soon discovered they were not alone.
  1. "The Lord worked with them and confirmed his word by the signs that accompanied it" (v.20).
  2. Jesus, by His Spirit, was there beside them.
  3. As a result, they saw amazing results.
C. Today, Jesus wants to do the same through each of us.
  1. Jesus makes this clear in John 14:12: "Anyone who has faith in me will do what I have been doing. He will do even greater things than these, because I am going to the Father."
  2. Not greater in quality, but greater in quantity.
D. What do we need today to minister in this way?
  1. We must *believe the message.*
  2. We must be *empowered by the Spirit.*
  3. We must *go in Jesus' name.*
  4. We must boldly *preach the good news,*
  5. We must *expect God to confirm the word* with miraculous signs following.

Conclusion and Altar Call

1. Come now and commit yourself to preaching the gospel.
2. Come and be empowered by the Holy Spirit.

[JF]

6 Jesus, the Model Soul Winner

Sermon in a Sentence: Jesus has given us an example of soul winning that we can follow.

Sermon Purpose: To encourage the people to be soul winners like Jesus.

Text: John 4:4-42

Introduction
1. Jesus was the first and greatest soul winner.
2. In the story of the Woman at the Well, Jesus has given us an example we can follow.
3. Note three things about how Jesus won this woman to Himself:

I. NOTE HOW JESUS PRESENTED THE GOSPEL TO THE WOMAN
  A. Jesus began by making a simple request of the woman.
  1. He asked her, "Will you give me a drink?" (v.7).
  2. This was a hook, opening the conversation.
  3. The woman was surprised, for Jesus was a Jewish man and she was Samaritan woman (v.9).
  4. We must deliberately begin conversations with lost people.
  B. Jesus shared the good news with the woman.
  1. He revealed to her that He was the Messiah (vv.25-26).
  2. He offered her living water (vv.13-14).
  3. Like Jesus, we must share the gospel with lost people.

II. NOTE HOW THE WOMAN RESPONDED TO JESUS
  A. The Samaritan woman was thirsty, but not for natural water only.
  1. Jesus told her about spiritual water (vv.13-14).
  2. She asked Jesus to give her living water (v.15).
  B. She was willing to acknowledge that she was living a sinful life.
  1. Jesus revealed her sinful lifestyle (vv.16-18).
  2. She acknowledged her sin and repented (vv.17, 19).
  C. The woman repented and put her faith in Jesus (vv.25-29).
  1. She admitted her sin.
  2. She put her faith in Christ.

    D. The woman took the message of Jesus to others (vv.28-30).
        1. The Samaritans from the town believed in Jesus because of the woman's testimony (v.30).
        2. We must do as the Samaritan woman.

III. NOTE HOW JESUS TAUGHT HIS DISCIPLES
    A. Jesus taught them about the importance of soul winning.
        1. Doing the will of the Father and winning souls was His "food"—the thing that gave Him life (vv.31-34).
        2. It should be the same with us today.
        3. Jesus has commanded that we go and make disciples of all nations (Mt 28:18-20).
        4. Lost people cannot be saved unless someone goes and tells them about Jesus (Ro 10:13-15).
    B. Jesus taught them about the urgency of winning souls.
        1. The harvest is now—not four months from now (v.35).
        2. We must reap souls now, before it is eternally too late (Jn 9:4).
    C. Jesus taught them about the reward of winning souls.
        1. The soul winner draws "eternal wages" (v.36).
        2. The sower and reaper rejoice together (vv.36-37).
        3. And heaven rejoices with them (Lk 15:10).

Conclusion and Altar Call:
    1. Jesus is our model soul winner; we must follow in His footsteps.
    2. Come now and commit yourself to being a soul winner.

[CK]

7 Four Necessities for the Harvest

Sermon in a Sentence: If we are to complete the harvest, we must boldly embrace Christ's "four necessities for the harvest."
Sermon Purpose: That the people commit themselves to proclaiming Christ to the nations in the power of the Holy Spirit.
Text: Luke 24:33-49 (NKJV)

Introduction
1. Some things are *important*... some things are *really important*... and some things are *absolute necessities!*
2. Jesus speaks of four absolute necessities for the harvest.
3. Notice the phrase in v.46 (NKJV) *"thus it was necessary"*
4. The Greek word translated "necessary *(edei)* means "a logical necessity" or a "binding necessity" (Vine).
5. Thus Jesus reveals four binding necessities for the harvest— that is, four things that are necessary for the salvation of man:

I. IT WAS ABSOLUTELY NECESSARY FOR JESUS TO DIE ON THE CROSS *"It was necessary for the Christ to suffer..."* (v.46).
   A. An eternal principle: "Without the shedding of blood...there is no remission [of sins]" (He 9:22).
   B. On the cross Christ paid the price for all people.
      1. "The Lord has laid upon him the iniquity of us all" (Is 53:6).
   C. No cross = No redemption = No harvest.

II. IT WAS ABSOLUTELY NECESSARY FOR JESUS TO RISE FROM THE DEAD *"It was necessary for the Christ...to rise from the dead..."* (v.46)
   A. Christ staked His entire ministry on the resurrection event.
      1. Illustration: When His critics asked, "Show us a sign," He told them about His resurrection (Mt 9:38-40).
      2. He staked all of His claims on His resurrection.
   B. Look what Paul says about Christ's resurrection:
      1. "If Christ has not been raised....our preaching is in useless; our faith is in vain; we are false witnesses; and we are still in our sins" (1Co 15:14-17).
      2. One must believe in the resurrection to be saved (Ro 10:9-10).
   C. Without the resurrection: No redemption, no harvest.

III. IT IS ABSOLUTELY NECESSARY THAT THE GOSPEL BE PREACHED TO ALL NATIONS. *"It was necessary…that repentance and remission of sins should be preached in His name to all nations…"* (vv.46-47).

A. The effect of the first two necessities rises or falls on the third.
 1. Eliminate any one and God's redemptive plan is aborted.
 2. It was absolutely necessary for Jesus to suffer, but that was not enough… He had to rise from the dead. But surprisingly, even that is not enough…
 3. It is also necessary that people hear about and believe in His death and resurrection (Ro 10:9-10).
 4. Read and explain Romans 10:13-14.

B. We are privileged to have a part in God's redemptive plan:
 1. Only He could suffer on the cross, and only God could raise Him for the dead; however, the task of proclaiming Him to the nations has been given to us, His church.
 2. Christ has therefore given us a Commission: Mk16:15-6.

IV. IT IS ABSOLUTELY NECESSARY THAT THE CHURCH BE EMPOWERED BY THE HOLY SPIRIT TO ACCOMPLISH THE TASK *"…you are witnesses… but stay in the city until you have been clothed with power from on high"* (vv.48-49).

A. For the church to accomplish the task of preaching the gospel to the nations, it must be empowered by the Spirit.
 1. This is the fourth necessity for the harvest.

B. Before Jesus ascended into heaven, He left the church with a mandate, a command, and a promise. (Ac 1:4-8)
 1. The mandate: "You will be my witnesses…" (v.8b)
 2. The command: "Wait for the…Holy Spirit" (v.4-5)
 3. The promise: "You will receive power…" (v.8a)

C. We must be empowered by the Spirit.

Conclusion
1. We must embrace all four "harvest necessities."
2. Come now to be empowered by the Spirit and to recommit yourself to the harvest

[DRM]

8 This Gospel Shall Be Preached

Sermon in a Sentence: The church's primary task is to preach the gospel to all nations before Jesus comes again.
Sermon Purpose: That people might commit themselves to advancing the gospel to all nations.
Text: Matthew 24:3-14 (emphasizing v.14)
Introduction
1. Note carefully the disciple's question to Jesus:
   a. "What will be *the sign* [singular] of your coming and the end of the age?" (Mt 24:3).
   b. Jesus begins His answer by describing events characterizing the course of this age.
      1) Things that are *not* necessarily the signs of the end.
      2) Commenting on Jesus' answer in verse 3, Stanley Horton wrote, "Jesus, therefore, took time to warn His disciples of distractions which might draw their attention away from the one great task of spreading the gospel." (*The Promise of His Coming,* p.33)
2. Finally, in v.14 Jesus answers their question: "This gospel of the kingdom will be preached in all the world…"
   a. George Eldon Ladd calls this verse "perhaps the most important single verse in the Word of God."
   b. It is the key to understanding history.
   c. In Mt 24:14 Jesus addresses three important concepts concerning the kingdom of God:

I. THE MESSAGE OF THE KINGDOM
A. Jesus begins the promise, "This gospel of the kingdom…"
   1. Note the phrase, *"This gospel…"*
   2. That is, the same gospel He and the apostles preached.
   3. There is no other gospel. (Read Ga 1:6-9.)
B. What is *this gospel* that Jesus was referring to?
   1. The *gospel of the kingdom* is the message that Jesus has come to establish God's kingdom in the earth.
   2. It is the message of Jesus death and resurrection.
      a. Read 1Co 15:1-4; 1Co 2:1-2: "Jesus Christ…crucified"
   3. The *gospel of the kingdom* involves a demonstration of kingdom power and authority.
      a. Mt 12:28: "If I by the Spirit of God cast out..."
      b. Lk 9:1-2 "He gave them power…he sent them out…"
      c. 1Co 2:4: In words and in demonstration.

       4. The *gospel of the kingdom* calls on people to "repent and believe the good news" (Mk 1:5).
   C. We should imitate this pattern in all of our missions endeavors.

II. THE MISSION OF THE KINGDOM
   A. In Mt 24:14 Jesus continues, "...will be preached in all the world as a witness to all the nations..."
      1. The mission of the church is world evangelization.
      2. Compare Mt 24:14 with Mt 28:18-20.
   B. In Mt 24:14 Jesus reveals *the extent* of the mission:
      1. We are to go into *"all the world."*
         a. "World" = Greek: *oikoumeme* = the inhabited earth.
         b. Acts 1:8 speaks of "the ends of the earth."
      2. We are to *"witness to all the nations."*
         a. "Nations" = Greek *ethne* = tribes, people groups
         b. From *ethne* we get the English word *ethnic.*
   C. Jesus assures us of *certain success.*
      1. "This gospel...*will* be preached. It will happen!
      2. The question, then, is not, "Will it be accomplished?" but "Will we have a part in in?"
      3. The Bible gives us a glimpse into the future, into heaven:
         a. There we see people from "every tribe and language and people and nation" (Re 5:9, ref. Re 7:9).
      4. We can have a part in assembling this great harvest of souls.

III. THE CULMINATION OF THE KINGDOM
   A. Jesus ends Mt 24:14 by saying "...then the end will come."
      1. When will the end come?
      2. Once this gospel of the kingdom has been preached in all the world as a witness of every nation.
      3. QUOTE: Stanley Horton, "God will have a people redeemed by the blood of Jesus 'out of every...nation...' Until He gets them, the end will not come. We need, then, not more concern about what is going to happen next, but over concern over the spread of the gospel." (*Promise,* p.33)
   B. We can help to "speed" the coming of the Lord by preaching the gospel in all the world. (Read 2Pe 3:12.)

Conclusion and Altar Call
   1. Come now and commit yourself to Christ and His mission.

[DRM]

9 We Will Not Stop Proclaiming

Sermon in a Sentence: We must resolve to faithfully proclaim the message of Christ in the power of the Holy Spirit.

Sermon Purpose: That the people commit themselves to Christ and the proclamation of His gospel.

Texts: Acts 4:1-20 (note verses 8 and 20)

Introduction
1. Sometimes pastors are tempted to preach popular, yet shallow, messages.
    a. As a result, they forsake the true message of the gospel.
    b. Today we learn an important lesson from Peter and John.
2. Tell the story of the arrest and confession of Peter and John in Acts 4. (When they were commanded to stop preaching in Jesus' name, they were filled with the Holy Spirit and replied, "We cannot not stop speaking about Christ!")
3. We would do well to make four similar commitments:

I. *Commitment 1:* **"WE WILL NOT STOP PROCLAIMING CHRIST TO THE LOST"**
   A. Sadly, many so-called "Pentecostal" churches have forsaken the message of Christ for "other gospels" (see Ga 1:6-9).
   B. However, when commanded to stop preaching Christ, the apostles answered, "We cannot stop speaking about Christ!"
   C. Christ was the one message of the church in the book of Acts.
      1. Philip went to Samaria and preached Christ (Ac 8:5).
      2. Paul preached Christ to the Philippian jailer (Ac 16:30-31).
      3. Peter: "Neither is there salvation in any other…" (Ac 4:12).
   D. We must never stop proclaiming the message of Christ.

II. *Commitment 2:* **"WE WILL NOT STOP PREACHING IN THE POWER OF THE SPIRIT"**
   A. The apostles and preachers in the Book of Acts proclaimed Christ in the power of the Spirit.
      1. Peter on the Day of Pentecost (Ac 2:4, 14, 22-24).
      2. Peter again (Ac 4:8-12).
   B. We too must proclaim Christ in the Spirit's power.
      1. Jesus' final command: Ac 1:4-5: "Do not leave Jerusalem, but wait for the gift my Father promised…"

    2. Jesus' final promise: Ac 1:8: "You will receive power…"
    3. Ask the Spirit to come upon you and fill you right now.

III. *Commitment 3:* **"WE WILL NOT STOP PLANTING SPIRIT-EMPOWERED MISSIONARY CHURCHES"**
  A. In the book of Acts, the apostles planted Spirit-empowered missionary churches.
    1. That is, churches that would quickly plant other Spirit-empowered missionary churches.
    2. Like the church in Antioch (Ac 11:19-21).
    3. As a result, churches multiplied through the Roman Empire.
  B. We too must plant Spirit-empowered missionary churches.
    1. That is, churches that are empowered by the Holy Spirit…
      a. …and will soon plant other churches of the same type.
      b. …and will get involved in sending missionaries.
    2 Such churches will not result without an intentional, well thought out plan to plant them.

IV. Commitment 4: **"WE WILL NOT STOP MOBILIZING OUR CHURCHES FOR MISSIONS"**
  A. When the apostles mobilized Spirit-empowered missionary churches, they did so with the intent of spreading the gospel "in Jerusalem, Judea, and to the ends of the earth" (Ac 1:8).
    1. Every local church must be mobilized to participate in the work of missions.
    2. Every believer must be taught about his or her responsibility to participate in missions.
  B. We must all participate in missions in three ways:
    1. We must all *go* to the lost and share the gospel.
    2. We must all *pray* for the harvest at home and abroad.
    3. We must all *give* to the work of missions.

Conclusion and Altar Call
    1. Come and commit yourself to Christ and the proclamation of His gospel to the lost.
    2. Come and be empowered by the Spirit to proclaim the gospel.

[DRM]

10 Fully Proclaiming the Gospel of Christ

Sermon in a Sentence: We are obligated the "fully proclaim the gospel of Christ" to all.

Sermon Purpose: That Christians will commit themselves to fully proclaiming the gospel at home and around the world.

Text: Romans 15:15-21

Introduction
1. In verse 19 Paul states, "I have fully proclaimed the gospel of Christ."
2. What then does it mean to "fully proclaim" the gospel?
3. From our text, we learn that we have fully proclaimed the gospel *only* when we have done three things:

First, we have fully proclaimed the gospel only…

I. WHEN WE HAVE CLEARLY AND ACCURATELY DECLARED THE MESSAGE OF JESUS CHRIST

A. As God's missionary people, our primary responsibility is to proclaim the message of Christ's death on the cross and His victorious resurrection from the grave.
   1. Paul understood this awesome responsibility.
      a. He told the Romans (v.19): "I have fully preached…"
      b. He continued (v.20): "It has always been my ambition to preach the gospel…"
   2. He defined the gospel as the message of Christ's death, burial, and resurrection. (Read 1Co 15:1-4.)
   3. It is "the power of God unto salvation." (Read Ro 1:16-17.)
B. Fully proclaiming the gospel further involves calling people to faith and repentance (Mk 1:15; Ac 20:21).
C. We must boldly proclaim the "full gospel"…
   1. Jesus saves! Jesus heals! Jesus baptizes in the Holy Spirit! Jesus is coming again!

Next, we have fully proclaimed the gospel only…

II. WHEN WE HAVE DEMONSTRATED THE POWER OF THE GOSPEL BY "SIGNS AND MIRACLES THROUGH THE POWER OF THE HOLY SPIRIT"

A. Fully proclaiming the gospel involves more than just talking; it involves demonstrations of kingdom power. (Read 1Co 4:20.)

1. Paul told the Romans that he won the Gentiles "by the power of signs and miracles, through the power of the Spirit" (vv.18-19).
2. In another place, he reminded the Thessalonians how the gospel had come to them in power. (Read 1Th 1:5.)
3. He further reminded the Corinthians… (Read 1Co 2:4.)
4. We too can expect God to confirm the proclamation of the gospel with "signs following" (Mk 16:15-20).

B. The NT model includes both proclamation and demonstration:
  1. Jesus set the pattern (Mt 4:23).
  2. Philip followed Jesus' example (Ac 8:5-7).
  3. Paul used the same method in Lystra (Ac 14:7-10).

C. If we are to follow this NT pattern, we must do two things:
  1. We must be empowered by the Spirit (Lk 24:49; Ac 1:8).
  2. We must act in bold faith like Paul in Lystra (Ac 14:9-10).

Finally, we have fully proclaimed the gospel only…

III. WHEN WE HAVE TAKEN THE GOSPEL TO PLACES WHERE CHRIST IS NOT KNOWN

A. Note how Paul connects "fully proclaiming the gospel" with preaching the gospel "where Christ was not known":
  1. "So from Jerusalem all the way around to Illyricum, I have fully proclaimed the gospel of Christ. It has always been my ambition to preach the gospel where Christ was not known…" (vv.19-20).
  2. He then quotes the prophet Isaiah: "Those who were not told about him will see, and those who have not heard will understand" (v.21; ref. Is 52:15).

B. Jesus expects us to "Go into all the world and preach the good news to all creation" (Mk 16:15).
  1. We all share the responsibility of proclaiming Christ to the nations.
  2. Some must go, others must send, but all must participate (Ro 10:13-15).
  3. We have not "fully proclaimed the gospel of Christ" until we have shared Christ with those who have never heard.

Conclusion and Altar Call
1. Come, commit yourself to fully preaching the gospel.
2. Come, and be empowered by the Holy Spirit

[DRM]

11. One Hope for the World

Sermon in a Sentence: We must proclaim the message of hope in Christ to the world in the power of the Holy Spirit.

Sermon Purpose: That the hearers be filled with the Spirit and committed to proclaiming the message of the cross to all people.

Texts: 1 Corinthians 1:17-25 (Keep your Bibles open to 1Co 1-2.)

Introduction
1. The powerful message of Christ's death and resurrection is the one hope for the world.
2. The only way that the world will know Him is through a Holy Spirit empowered church proclaiming the gospel of Christ.
3. In 1Co 1-2 Paul powerfully argues and illustrates this truth.

I. PAUL ARGUES THAT THE MESSAGE OF THE CROSS IS THE ONE HOPE FOR THE WORLD (1Co 1:17-25)
  A. Preaching the message of the cross seems foolish to the world.
     1. It is "foolish," and a "stumbling block" (1Co 1:23).
  B. Carnal people vainly look to themselves and their own resources to find answers to their deepest problems.
     1. From the beginning of time, people have tried to find the right leaders, economic, social and educational programs.
     2. All of these schemes (even the best of them) ultimately fail.
        a. Unspiritual people try to treat symptoms while ignoring the root cause of their problems.
        b. The real sickness is sin, and sin's only cure is Christ.
        c. Man will never find the answer on his own (1Co 1:20).
  C. What looks to the world like the foolishness and weakness is really God's wisdom and power to save (vv. 24-25).
     1. We are reconciled to God through repentance and faith in Christ.
     2. Christ is truly the One Hope for the World.

II. PAUL FURTHER ARGUES THAT WE MUST FAITHFULLY PROCLAIM THE MESSAGE OF HOPE IN CHRIST
  A. In Corinth, Paul intentionally focused on proclaiming of the message of Jesus Christ crucified. (Read 1Co 2:1-2.)
     1. He chose to proclaim no other message.
     2. He wrote 1Corinthians because the church was losing its focus on gospel message.

      3. The church was divided and was becoming spiritually weak and inwardly focused.
      4. It was losing its ability to be a powerful witness for Christ.
  B. The church in Corinth—like every church—was called to advance God's mission through Spirit-empowered witness.
      1. Every local congregation is called to be a missionary force.
      2. Paul wrote Corinthians from Ephesus during his 3rd journey.
      3. In Ephesus, he had established a powerful missionary church that had reached all of Asia Minor in just 2 years (Ac 19:10).
      4. Paul wanted the Corinthian church to become such a church.
      5. He was concerned both for the church itself, and for its ability to fulfill the mission of God.
  C. Paul therefore pleaded with them to put aside petty differences and unite around the message of the gospel (1Co 1:10).

III. PAUL FINALLY ARGUES THAT, TO EFFECTIVELY PROCLAIM THE MESSAGE OF HOPE, WE MUST RELY ON THE POWER OF THE HOLY SPIRIT (1Co 2:3-5, 10-14)
  A. The power of the Holy Spirit enabled Paul to powerfully present the message of Christ to the Corinthians. (Read 1Co 2:3-5.)
  B. We, like Paul, need the Spirit's power to be able to proclaim the message of Christ in our context.
      1. We need the Spirit to understand the message (1Co 2:10, 12).
      2. We need the Spirit to teach the message (v.13).
      3. We need the Spirit to demonstrate the message (vv.4-5).
      4. We need the Spirit to convict and open hearts to receive it.
  C. Corinth started out in a mighty revival with demonstrations of the Spirit's power.
      1. But then, they began to falter and turn inward.
      2. Paul deals with some of these distractions later in 1Co.
  D. In Acts 1:8 Jesus described the power needed to proclaim Christ.
      1. Sadly, many churches have abandoned this message.
      2. We must rededicate ourselves to this biblical strategy.

Conclusion and Altar Call
1. Come now, rededicate yourself to God's mission.
2. Come, be empowered by His Spirit to help fulfill that mission.

[MRT]

~ Section 2 ~
The Great Commission

12 Great Commission Mandate 1: "Pray!"
~ Mandates of the Great Commission ~

Sermon in a Sentence: To effectively participate in the Great Commission, we must fulfill the mandate of prayer.
Sermon Purpose: That the people will commit themselves to prayer for the harvest.
Text: Matthew 9:35-38
Introduction
1. Jesus left His church with a "Great Commission."
    a. He said, "Go…make disciples of all nations" (Mt 28:18-20).
2. In our text, Jesus observed the harvest field. (Read vv.35-37.)
    a. The people were "harassed and helpless."
    b. Jesus therefore commands His disciples to "Pray!" (v.38).
3. This message: Five ways we are to pray for the harvest:

I. PRAY FOR THE HARVEST FORCE (Mt 9:35-38)
A. Jesus gave His disciples specific instructions on prayer:
1. They were to pray *to* the "Lord of the Harvest."
2. They were to pray *for* "workers to go into His harvest field."
3. In other words, they were to pray for the *Harvest Force.*
B. Reaping the harvest requires resources.
1. It requires human resources—Therefore, we must pray.
2. It requires financial resources—Therefore, we must pray.
C. The Harvest Force also needs strategic placement.
1. We must cooperate with the Holy Spirit to deploy harvest workers to where He wants them to go.
2. We must therefore pray for wisdom and guidance.

II. PRAY FOR THE HARVEST FIELD (Read Jn 4:35-36.)
A. Jesus told His disciples to "Look at the fields."
1. He informed them that the harvest was both "plentiful" (Mt 9:37) and "ripe" (Jn 4:35)
2. *Plentiful* speaks of its magnitude—*ripe* of its "readiness."
B. Because the harvest is ripe, the time is urgent.
1. We must reap the harvest before it is too late.
C. We must therefore pray for the harvest field.

III. PRAY FOR THE HARVEST YIELD (Read Re 5:9.)
A. John saw into the future and saw the ultimate yield of God's great end-time harvest.

1. He saw great multitude of people "from every tribe and language and people and nation" (Re 5:9).
2. God promised Abraham that his seed would number as the "stars in the sky and as the sand on the seashore" (Ge 22:17).
   B. Researchers estimate 16,000+ people groups in the world.
   1. Each one of these must be represented among the redeemed.
   2. Presently about 6,600+ groups have not been reached.
   3. We must move to engage these yet-to-be-reached peoples.
   C. We must pray that the church will mobilize itself to reach these unreached people groups.

IV. PRAY AGAINST THE ENEMY OF THE HARVEST
(Read Mt 13:19; 28; 2Co 4:4)
   A. The enemy of the harvest is the devil. (Read Mt 13:19, 28.)
   1. We are in a spiritual battle (Eph 6:12).
   B. The enemy opposes the harvest in three ways:
   1. He "snatches away" the effects of the gospel seed (v.19).
   2. He sows weeds (evil doers) among the wheat (Mt 13:25).
   3. He blinds the minds of unbelievers (2Co 4:4).
   C. We must fight spiritual battles with spiritual weapons (2Co 10:4).
   1. One of those weapons is prayer (Ep 6:18).
   2. We must use this weapon against the enemy of the harvest.

V. PRAY FOR POWER TO REAP THE HARVEST (Read Ac 1:8.)
   A. We must have God's power to accomplish God's work.
   1. Jesus promised power to witness (Ac 1:8).
   2. We receive the Spirit's power when we are baptized in the Holy Spirit (Ac 2:4).
   3. The New Testament harvest began at Pentecost (Ac 2:41).
   B. If the missionary enterprise of the church is to be effective, it must be empowered by the Holy Spirit.
   C. The power of the Spirit is received through prayer.
   1. Jesus said, "Ask and I will be given you" (Lk 11:9).
   2. The power of the Spirit is also maintained through prayer.

Conclusion and Altar Call
1. Praying for missions is not an option. It is a mandate!
2. Come now and commit yourself to prayer for missions.

[UA]

13 Great Commission Mandate 2: "Go!"
~ Mandates of the Great Commission ~

Sermon in a Sentence: We must go and proclaim Christ to the nations in the power of the Holy Spirit.
Sermon Purpose: That the people will commit themselves to Christ's command to go to the nation.
Texts: Matthew 28:18-19; Matthew 21:28-31
Introduction
1. Both of our texts speak to our responsibility as Christ's disciples to go to the nations
2. The first text is known as the "Great Commission."
    a. Jesus gives us a direct, authoritative command to *"Go!"*
3. The second is the parable of the two sons. (Tell the story)
    a. The first son said he would not go, repented, and went.
    b. The second son said he would go—but did not.
    c. The first son was the one who did the will of his father.
    d. The lesson: Obedience is more than confession—it is action.
4. The extent to which we obey is the extent to which we do the will of God.
5. This message is about our obeying the Great Commission.
    a. Five statements concerning why and how we must go:

I. WHY WE MUST GO (Mt 28:19)
A. We must go because Jesus has *commanded* us to go.
  1. He is the Lord of the Harvest with "all authority in heaven and earth" (v.18).
  2. …because going is a mark of our *loyalty and love* for Him.
     a. Jesus: "If you love me, you will obey… (Jn 14:15).
     b. It is an honor to obey Christ.
  3. …because we must have *compassion* for the lost (2Co 5:14).
     a. Just as Jesus had compassion on the people (Mt 9:36).
B. Our response cannot be to say, "We will go," then not go. It must rather be, "Yes, we will go," and then to truly go.

II. WHERE WE MUST GO (Ac 1:8)
A. Jesus first sent His disciples only to the "lost sheep of Israel" (Matt. 10:5; 15:24).
  1. Yet, when "His own" rejected Him, the gospel went to everyone who would "believe on His name" (Jn 1:11-12).

B. Jesus ultimately commanded that the gospel be taken to every people, person, and place on earth (Mt 28:19; Mk 16:15; Ac 1:8).
      1. To "all the world...to every nation" (Mt 24:14).
      2. To both the "wise and the foolish" (Ro 1:14).
      3. To the "ends of the earth" (Ac 1:8).
      4. To everywhere "Christ is not named" (Ro 15:20).
   C. Let us therefore go everywhere and proclaim the good news!

III. WHEN WE MUST GO (Jn 4:35)
   A. We must go *now!*
      1. Jesus: "Look on the fields, they are ripe for harvest" (v.35)
      2. He was speaking of the *urgency* of the harvest.
      3. Jesus: "As long as it is day, we must do the work of him who sent me. Night is coming, when no one can work" (Jn 9:4).
   B. Are you ready now to go, pray, and send?

IV. HOW WE MUST GO (Ac 26:16)
   A. We must go as "servants and witnesses" (Ac 26:16)
   B We must have the mindset of a *servant* (not a master).
      1. We are to minister "as sheep among wolves" (Mt 10:16).
      2. We must go as servants, totally dependent on the presence of Christ and the power of the Spirit (Mt 28:20; Ac 1:8).
   C. Our purpose in going is to *witness* for Christ (Lk 24:46-48).

V. WHAT WE MUST GO WITH (Mk 3:14; Ac 1:8)
   A. First, we must go with a *message.*
      1. Jesus said, "...you will be *my* witnesses..." (Ac 1:8).
      2. We both witness *for* Christ and *about* Christ.
   B. Secondly, we must go with the *power of the Holy Spirit.*
      1. Jesus: "You will receive power when the Holy Spirit comes on you..." (Ac 1:8).
      2. Without the Spirit's power, we will surely to fail.
      3. But in the Spirit's power we will surely succeed.

Conclusion and Altar Call
   1. Come now, and commit yourself to Christ's mission.
   2. Come and be empowered by the Holy Spirit.

[UA]

14 Great Commission Mandate 3: "Preach!"
~ Mandates of the Great Commission ~

Sermon in a Sentence: We must faithfully preach the gospel in every place and to everyone.
Sermon Purpose: That God's people will commit themselves to preaching the gospel to the lost.
Texts: 1 Corinthians 1:21; Matthew 24:14
Introduction
1. What distinguishes preaching the gospel from the speeches of politicians and performers?
    a. The content of the message and the motive of the speaker.
    b. The message politicians and performers is empty promises—and their motive is self-promotion.
    c. The message of the preacher is Christ—and his motive is the salvation of the lost.
2. This message will focus on our responsibility to preach the gospel to all people everywhere before Jesus returns.
    a. Paul said, "God was pleased through the foolishness of what was preached to save those who believe" (1Co 1:21).
    b. Jesus declared, "This gospel of the kingdom will be preached in the whole world as a testimony to all nations, and then the end will come" (Mt 24:14).
3. Let's look at five critical issues relating to our responsibility to preach the gospel:

I. THE COMMAND TO PREACH (Read Mark 16:15-16.)
A. Spirit-empowered proclamation of the gospel is the God-ordained means of fulfilling the Great Commission.
   1. Jesus himself preached the gospel (Mk 1:14; Mt 9:35).
   2. Peter preached the gospel (Ac 2:31-32, 36; 10:42).
   3. Paul preached the gospel (1Co 2:2-4; Ro 15:19).
B. It is now our time to preach the gospel.
   1. Jesus commanded His disciples to preach... (Read Mt 10:7).
   2. Paul commanded Timothy to preach... (Read 2Ti 4:2).
   3. Now Christ commands us to preach (Mk 16:15).

II. THE MESSAGE WE MUST PREACH (Read Acts 8:5)
A. Our message to the nations is Christ.
   1. He is the only One who can save (Ac 4:12).

   B. Philip the "deacon" understood this powerful truth:
   1. He preached Christ to the Samaritans (Ac 8:5).
   2. Then he preached Christ to the Ethiopian (v. 35).
   C. We must never be guilty of replacing the message of Christ and His saving gospel with other false "gospels" (Ga 1:7-9).

III. THE TIME WE ARE TO PREACH (Read John 4:35)
   A. The time to preach the gospel is *now.*
   1. Jesus tells us, "Look at the fields! They are ripe for harvest."
   2. He cautioned, "Work… while it is day, for the night is coming when no one can work" (Jn 9:4).
   B. We must go quickly to the harvest to reap the grain (Mk 4:29).

IV. THE PEOPLE WE ARE TO PREACH TO (Read Acts 1:8)
   A. We are to preach the gospel to people everywhere.
   1. Jesus went everywhere preaching the gospel (Mt 9:35).
   2. We are to Christ's witnesses "to the ends of the earth."
   B. We are to preach the gospel to "every creature" (Mk 16:15 KJV).
   1. Paul felt obligated to preach to all people (Ro 1:14).
   2. We must not concentrate on one people and neglect the rest.
   3. We must go to "the regions beyond" (2Co 10:16, KJV).

V. THE POWER OF THE MESSAGE WE PREACH (Ro 1:16)
   A. The gospel has power within itself to produce a harvest.
   1. It is the "the power of God unto salvation to everyone who believes…" (Ro 1:16).
   B. The gospel must be preached in the power of the Spirit (Ac 1:8).
   1. The apostles preached in the Spirit's power (Ac 4:8, 31, 33).
   2. The gospel is confirmed by "the power of signs and miracles, through the…Holy Spirit" (Ro 15:19; Mk 16:20).
   C. Let's go everywhere proclaiming the good news about Christ, knowing that it is truly "the power of God unto salvation."

Conclusion and Altar Call
1. You must strike a match to produce a flame, and you must proclaim the gospel to produce a harvest.
2. Come now, commit yourself to proclaiming Christ to all.

[UA]

15 Great Commission Mandate 4: "Witness!"
~ Mandates of the Great Commission ~

Sermon in a Sentence: We must commit ourselves to being Christ's Spirit-empowered witnesses.
Sermon Purpose: That Christians will understand what it means to be Christ's witnesses, and will then commit themselves to the same.
Bible Texts: Luke 24:46-48; Acts 1:8
Introduction
1. Spirit-empowered witness is at the very heart of Jesus' Great Commission.
    a. Immediately before returning to heaven Jesus told His disciples, "You are *witnesses* of these things,"—meaning His death and resurrection (Lk 24:46-48).
    b. On the same occasion, He told them, "You will be *my witnesses*...to the ends of the earth" (Ac 1:8).
2. In this message, we will examine our Great Commission mandate to be Christ's witnesses.
3. We will discuss four issues concerning our responsibility to be Christ's witnesses at home and to the ends of the earth:

I. WE ARE CALLED TO BE WITNESSES (Acts 1:8)
A. Jesus' final words to His disciples were, "You will be my witnesses...to the ends of the earth" (Ac 1:8-9).
   1. Twice Paul testified that God had called him to be "a servant and a witness..." (Ac 22:15; 26:16).
   2. The words "witness" and "testify" appear 25 times in Acts.
B. A witness is someone who has seen or heard something.
   1. For instance, a witness in court.
   2. "We proclaim...what we have seen and heard" (1Jn 1:3).
   3. To be Christ's witnesses, we must have experienced His saving grace and His empowering Spirit.
C. We witness for Christ in three ways:
   1. We witness with our words (proclamational witness).
   2. We witness with our lives (incarnational witness).
   3. We witness with signs and miracles (evidential witness).

II. WE MUST COMMITTED TO WITNESS (Ac 21:13)
A. Paul testified that he was ready to die for the gospel (Ac 21:13).

B. We too have been called to witness for Christ in all circumstances.
       1. Jesus came to testify to the truth (Jn 3:11; 7:7)—And then He was crucified for what He said and did.
       2. Stephen boldly testified about Christ—And then he was brutally stoned for his testimony (Ac 7:54-60).
       3. Throughout history, thousands have given themselves as martyrs in order to witness for Christ.
   B. Like Jesus, the apostles, and the great Christian martyrs, we must be fully committed to Christ and His gospel.
       1. Christ has committed to us "the message of reconciliation" (2Co 5:19)—Now we must commit to sharing the message.
       2. The Spirit will give us boldness (Ac 4:31-33).

III. THE SPIRIT COMPELS US TO WITNESS (Ac 2:14-36)
   A. The Spirit compelled Peter preach at Pentecost.
       1. The apostles could not stop witnessing (Ac 4:17-20)
       2. The Spirit compelled Peter to go to Caesarea (Ac 11:12).
   B. We must allow the Spirit to work in our hearts compelling us to witness for Christ.

IV. THE SPIRIT WILL GUIDE US TO WITNESS (Ac 8:29)
   A. Throughout Acts, the Spirit guided Christians to witness.
       1. He guided Philip to Ethiopian nobleman (Ac 8:27-30).
       2. He directed Peter to Cornelius' home (Ac 10).
       3. He directed Paul and his team into Europe (Ac 16:6-10).
   B. If we will be filled with the Spirit and pray, He will guide us too.
   C. To be filled with the Spirit…
       1. Ask in faith (Lk 11:9, 13).
       2. Receive by faith (Lk 11:10; Mk 11:24).
       3. Speak in faith (Ac 2:4)

Conclusion and Altar Call
   1. Christ has called us all to be His witnesses at home and to the ends of the earth.
   2. Come now, and commit yourself to be His witness.
   3. Come and be filled with the Spirit.

[UA]

16 The Great Commission Never Ends

Sermon in a Sentence: Our commitment to fulfilling Christ's Great Commission must never end.

Sermon Purpose: That believers be filled with the Spirit and commit themselves to fulfilling the Great Commission.

Text: Acts 1:8; 28:17-31.

Introduction
1. Before Jesus returned to heaven, He made a final statement to His disciples. (It included both a promise and a commission:)
   a. *The promise:* "You will receive power when… (Ac 1:8a).
   b. *The commission:* "…you will be my witnesses in Jerusalem, Judea, and Samaria and to the ends of the earth" (Ac 1:8b).
   c. This was Jesus' final giving of the Great Commission.
   d. The book of Acts tells the story of how the early church fulfilled that commission in the power of the Holy Spirit.
2. In Acts 9 we learn of Saul's (Paul's) conversion (9:1-18).
   a. Jesus tells Paul what his part will be in fulfilling the Great Commission. (Read: vv.15-16) "This man…[will] carry my name before the Gentiles…and before the people of Israel."
   b. Acts 13-28 tells of how Paul obeyed that commission.
3. Now in our text we come to the closing passage of Acts.
   a. It has been 25 years since Paul received his commission.
   b. Paul remains committed to the Great Commission.
   c. Because, for Paul, the Great Commission never ended.
4. From Paul's ministry in Rome we can learn two great lessons concerning an unending commitment to the Great Commission:

I. PAUL'S UNENDING COMMITMENT TO THE GREAT COMMISSION CAN BE SEEN IN HIS RESPONSE TO HIS SITUATION IN ROME (vv.11-29)

A. Paul's arrival in Rome was the fulfillment of a dream of his.
   1. He had long wanted to preach the gospel in Rome.
      a. Ten years earlier he wrote… (Read Ro 1:11-12).
      b. In the same letter he wrote, "I have been longing for many years to see you" (Ro 15:23).
   2. Now, with Paul's arrival in Rome, this time had come.

B. Yet, Paul did not come to Rome as he had intended.
   1. He arrived in Rome a prisoner in chains.
   2. En route to Rome, he had suffered many things.
   3. Paul was willing to endure any hardship to fulfill his calling.
   4. We must make the same commitment.
C. In spite of past grievances, Paul continued to reach out to the very people who were persecuting him.
   1. Throughout His ministry the Jews had opposed Him.
   2. Yet, Paul never forgot his commission (Read Ac 9:15).
   3. Now, in our text, Paul is still reaching out to the Jews.
      a. For him, the Great Commission never ended.
      b. He remained true to his commission to proclaim the good news to Jews and Gentiles alike.
   4. Like Paul, our commitment to the GC must never end.

II. PAUL'S UNENDING COMMITMENT TO THE GREAT COMMISSION CAN BE SEEN IN HIS MINISTRY IN ROME AND AFTER (vv.30-31)
A. Paul remained in Rome for two years under armed guard.
   1. He was unable to move freely to preach as he desired.
   2. Yet he did what he could—because he knew that whether he was free or in chains, the Great Commission never ends.
   3. So he received visitors and preached to them (Phm 1:12-13).
B. While in chains in Rome Paul wrote his "Prison Letters."
   1. Including Ephesians, Colossians, Philippians, Philemon.
   2. During a later imprisonment he wrote 1-2Tim and Titus.
   3 Through the centuries, these letters have impacted millions.
C. After two years, Paul was released.
   1. He then continued his missionary travels.
   1. He even went Spain as he had planned (Ro 15:28).
   2. About four years later he was martyred in Rome.
D We can learn from Paul's example.
   1. Like him, we must be filled with the Spirit and continue to fulfill the Great Commission in all circumstances.
   2. For us, as with Paul, the Great Commission must never end.

Conclusion and Altar Call
1. Come now and be filled with the Spirit.
2. Come and commit yourself to doing your part to fulfill the Great Commission.

[EKA]

17 Finding Your Place in the Great Commission

Sermon in a Sentence: As members of Christ's body, we each have an important role to play in fulfilling the Great Commission.
Sermon Purpose: That believers will understand the significance of the Great Commission and will commit themselves to do their part in fulfilling it.
Texts: Matthew 28:18-20; 1 Corinthians 12:12-14, 27-31
Introduction
1. In our first text, Jesus issues His Great Commission.
2. It is a clear mandate to the church—both then and now.
3. Since Christ mandates that His body, the Church, fulfill the Great Commission, it follows that every member of His body should do their part in fulfilling this divine mandate.
4. Let's look more closely at how this thought develops:

I. JESUS ISSUED THE GREAT COMMISSION TO HIS CHURCH
A. Right before Jesus ascended to heaven He issued His Great Commission to His disciples (Mt 28:19).
   1. He told them to "go and make disciples of all nations" (v.19).
   2. He promised that He would be with then "even to the end of the age" (v.20).
   3. This Commission is possibly the most significant command Jesus gave to His church.
      a. It is about taking the good news to "all nations."
B. Note, however, that this Commission was not only directed to the eleven apostles, but to all disciples of Christ.
   1. Jesus told the eleven that they were to teach their disciples "to obey everything I have commanded you…" (v.20).
   2. And Jesus had just commanded them "go and make disciples of all nations" (v.19).
   3. In other words, the Great Commission applies to all disciples until "the end of the age," that is, until the Commission has been completed. (See Mt 24:14.)
C. Therefore, the Great Commission is directed to every believer.
   1. Every believer (that is, every disciple) includes you and me.

II. BECAUSE WE ARE ALL MEMBERS OF CHRIST'S BODY, WE MUST EACH DO HIS OR HER PART IN FULFILLING THE GREAT COMMISSION

A. We have all been baptized into one body. (Read 1Co 12:12-14.)
   1. When we were saved, the Holy Spirit put us into the body of Christ—the Church.
   2. As members of Christ's body, we must live accordingly.
B. As head of the body, Christ tells it what to do (Col 1:18).
   1. Illustration: Just as our head tells our body what to do.
   2. In the same way, the body—that is, the Church—must do what its head, Christ, tells it to do.
C. Each member of the body has a unique role to play in fulfilling the Great Commission.
   1. We do not all have the same role to play
   2. However, we function as a part of the body (1Co 12:27-31).
   3. Ask yourself, "As a member of Christ's body, am I doing my part?"

III. WE MUST EACH FIND AND PERFORM OUR ROLE IN FULFILLING THE GREAT COMMISSION

A. In order to fulfill the Great Commission, the church needs different people fulfilling different roles.
   1. Everyone must do his or her part.
   2. If one member fails, the entire work suffers.
B. The work of missions requires healthy churches who will send and faithfully support missionaries.
   1. It further needs faithful people who are willing to be sent out as missionaries as directed by the Spirit. (See Ac 13:1-4.)
   2. It needs faithful members who will go, give, and pray.
   3. Truly, in some way, we can each do all three of the above.
   4. It's just a matter of looking and finding someone who is lost.
C. What is your role the church in fulfilling the Great Commission?
   1. Are you faithfully fulfilling that role?

Conclusion and Altar Call
   1. Come forward and ask the Holy Spirit to show you your place in the church in fulfilling the Great Commission.
   2. Come and be empowered by the Holy Spirit to fulfill that role.

[NB]

18 Living the Great Commission

Sermon in a Sentence: Jesus has called us to live the Great Commission and teach others to do the same.

Sermon Purpose: To call the people to apply the Great Commission to their own lives and to the lives of others.

Text: Matthew 28:18-20

Introduction
1. When one thinks of missions, this is the verse that usually comes to mind. We call it the Great Commission.
2. These were among the last words that Jesus spoke to His disciples.
3. Jesus did not say that we are to go and make believers—or even Christians. No, He said that we are to make disciples.
4. Today, we will talk about living the Great Commission.
5. Three essential ways we must *live the Great Commission:*

I. WE ARE TO LIVE AS DISCIPLE MAKERS
A. Jesus has sent us to "make disciples" (v.19).
   1. In NT, the word *Christian* occurs 3 times—*Believers* 7 times—and *Disciple* 294 times.
B. A disciple is a learner, one who accepts the teaching of Christ—not only in belief, but also in lifestyle.
C. Jesus not only wants to be our Savior; He demands to be our Lord.
   1. Jesus desires for us to live our lives as disciple makers.
   2. That is, disciples who will make other disciples (2Ti 2:2).
D. Commit yourself today to be a disciple maker.

II. WE ARE TO TEACH THEM TO LIVE IN OBEDIENCE
A. We are to "teach them to obey all that He commanded" (v.19)
   1. To show them that God has the best plan for their lives.
   2. That obedience becomes easy when they love and trust Him.
B. We must teach them to be "doers of the word..." (Ja 1:22).
   1. Knowing the word is not enough.
      a. The Pharisees knew the word, but they did not live it.
   2. Believing the word is not enough.
      a. Even the demons believe (Ja 2:19).

3. Disciples are required to "do the word."
   a. Faith without works is dead (Ja 2:20, 26).
   b. The nations are to "believe *and obey"* Christ (Ro 16:26)
   c. To bear fruit we must "remain in Christ" (Jn 15:3-7).

III. WE ARE TO SHOW THEM HOW TO LIVE IN RELATIONSHIP

A. For true disciples, even obedience itself is not enough.
   1. The Great Commission requires loving Jesus more than anything else (Mk 8:34).
   2. We obey Him because we love Him (Jn 14:15).
   3. The Rich Young Ruler obeyed but he did not love.
      a. He wasn't willing to give all (Mk 10:17-27).
      b. We must be willing to give up everything to serve Jesus (Lk 14:33).
B. All of this requires the power and presence of the Spirit in our lives.
   1. In the Great Commission Jesus promised, "I am with you always" (Mt 28:20).
      a. This is a promise of the Holy Spirit.
   2. Jesus knew that the disciples could not live out the Great Commission without the power of the Spirit.
      a. Jesus said, "Apart me you can do nothing" (Jn 15:5).
      b. This is why Jesus told the disciples to wait for the Holy Spirit (Ac 1:4-5, 8).
   3. The disciples we make will need the power of the Spirit to…
      a. … overcome temptation and live in obedience (Ga 5:16)
      b. … be effective witnesses and make disciples (Ac 1:8).

Conclusion and Altar Call

1. Jesus has called us to go and make disciples, disciples who will live the Great Commission.
2. Come now to be filled with the Spirit and to commit yourself to be a disciple who makes other disciples.

[SC]

19 Go and Make Disciples

Sermon in a Sentence: We must all obey Christ's commission to go and make disciples of all nations.

Sermon Purpose: That believers will commit themselves to participating in Christ's commission to "make disciples of all nations."

Text: Matthew 28:16-20

Introduction
1. In our text Jesus is issuing His "Great Commission."
   a. This is His last great challenge to His disciples.
   b. Fulfilling this commission is the Church's greatest responsibility.
   c. This will require the full commitment of every member.
2. Our text answers three critical questions about the Great Commission:

I. WHY DO WE GO AND MAKE DISCIPLES?
A. We go because we are disciples of Christ, and as His disciples, we must follow our Teacher.
   1. Jesus gave His commission to His disciples (that is, to us).
   2. He was a fisher of men (Lk 19:19), and as His disciples, we are to continue His work (Mk 1:17).
   3. If we fail, nobody will go in our place.
B. We go because the One who sends us holds all authority in heaven and earth.
   1. Read Mt 28:18 (Ref. Mt 11:27; Jn 3:35, 13:3, 17:2).
   2. Christ's authority is "galactic," in other words, He rules the whole universe.
   3. Therefore, He has the right to command us to go.
C. However, we must *know* before we *go.*
   1. We must know our Lord before we can know His mission.
   2. We must know Him before we can make Him known.
   3. We must know about Him before we explain Him to others.
   4. We must know His message before we can proclaim it to the nations.

II. HOW DO WE GO AND MAKE DISCIPLES?
(According to our text, we are to go three ways:)
A. We are to *go and preach* the good news (Mk 16:15, Lk 2:10).

1. The gospel is good news because it saves people from the wrath to come (Jn 3:36, 1Jn 5:11-12).
2. ...because it makes us new creatures in Christ (2Co 5:17).
3. ...because it gives hope to the hopeless (Col 1:5).
B. We are to *go and baptize* them in water (v.19).
1. Baptism is a sign that we died to sin and now live a new life in Christ (Ro 6:4-5).
2. It is further a sign that we are united with Christ in fulfilling His mission (Mt 3:15).
C. We are to *go and teach* them to obey God's word (v.20).
1. Jesus intended for His church to be a teaching church.
2. He intended for us to nurture disciples in "everything He has commanded" (v. 20).
3. Further, we are to empower them to teach others (2Ti 2:2).

II. WHERE DO WE GO TO MAKE DISCIPLES?
A. We are to "make disciples of *all nations*" (v.19).
1. The Greek words translated "all nations" are *ta ethne.*
2. The words mean every tribe or ethnic group (Lk 24:47).
3. According to the Joshua Project, there are more than 6,500 unreached people groups in the world today.
   a. They make up more than 3 billion lost people.
   b. 850+ unreached people groups in Sub-Saharan Africa.
4. We must make disciples of all of these peoples.
B. We must take the gospel to the *ends of the earth.*
1. Jesus said that we were to be His witnesses in Jerusalem, Judea, Samaria "and to the ends of the earth" (Ac 1:8).
2. This means that we must go to every place that does not have a Spirit-empowered witness of the gospel.
3. But before we go, we must "receive power when the Holy Spirit comes on [us]" (Ac 1:8).

Conclusion and Altar Call
1. We must go, pray, and give in the Spirit's power.
2. Come and commit yourself to obey Christ Great Commission.

[PFM]

20 Fulfilling the Great Commission

Sermon in a Sentence: God calls us all to fulfill our role in completing the Great Commission

Sermon Purpose: That the hearers may better understand the Great Commission and their role in fulfilling it.

Text: Matthew 28:18-20

`Introduction
1. When one wants to say something important, they must choose the right words *and* the right moment to say them.
    a. In our text, Jesus did both.
    b. His words were well crafted, and the moment was significant—shortly after His resurrection from the grave.
2. This message: three things we must understand about Jesus' Great Commission to the church:

I. HE SPOKE OF CONTROL (v.18)
A. Jesus began His Great Commission by saying, *"All authority* in heaven and on earth has been given to me."
   1. This declaration speaks of control.
   2. The Greek word translated "authority" is *exousia,* meaning to be in control, to be in charge, to have authority over.
   3. The resurrected Lord has control over heaven and earth.
B. This control will not begin at His second coming.
   1. Jesus is already in control—right now! (Jn 5:27; 17:2).
   2. We as Christ's followers must submit ourselves to His supreme authority.
C. This same control forms the basis for what Jesus says next.
   1. "All authority…has been given to me…*therefore, go*…"
   2. *Because* Jesus has all control in heaven and on earth, He legitimately gives us this command.
   3. Someone has said, "If you see the word *therefore* in the Bible, always see what it is *there for.*"

II. HE ISSUED A COMMISSION (vv.19-20)
A Jesus then told us what we must do. (Read vv.19-20.)
   1. We must *"make disciples* of all nations…"
   2. We must *"baptize* them in the name of the Father and of the Son and of the Holy Spirit."
   3. We must *"teach* them to obey everything…"

B. We call this statement of Jesus the "Great Commission."
 1. This is not the "Great Suggestion"—It is a command from the risen Christ—a direct order from the one who has "all authority in heaven and in earth."
 2. If we are true followers of Christ, we must obey without hesitation (Jn 14:15, 21-24).

III. OBEDIENCE REQUIRES COMMUNITY
A. An important question we must ask is, "How did the disciples go about fulfilling the Great Commission?"
 1. They did it in community.
 2. In other words, they did it together.
B. Not one disciple among those standing there listening to Jesus' words would be able to do the work alone.
 1. The job was (and still is) too great to be carried out alone.
 2. Each of the Twelve had his unique role to fill.
 3. According to church history...
    a. John went northwest and died near Ephesus (Turkey).
    b. Peter went further west and eventually was crucified upside down at Rome.
    c. Andrew went north to the Scythians (now the Ukraine).
    d. Thomas went to Persia (Iran) and India.
    e. Others went other places—each one doing his part.
    f. Together they did what none of them could have done alone.
 4. Eventually, they left succeeding generations to continue the work.
C. Now, the Commission has come to us.
 1. Each of us, as a member of Christ's body, has his or her unique role to fill.
 2. We cannot individually go to all nations—but together we can accomplish the mission (Mt 24:14).
 3. Some go, some give, some pray, but everyone participates.
 4. And together, we will get the job done.

Conclusion and Altar Call
1. Come now, and submit yourself to the lordship of Christ.
2. Come, and commit yourself to doing your part to fulfill the Great Commission.

[CGS]

21 Don't Leave Home Without It
~The Great Commission and the Final Command~

Sermon in a Sentence: To fulfill Jesus' Great Commission, we must first obey His Final Command.
Sermon Purpose: That believers might be empowered with the Spirit with the view of becoming Christ's witnesses at home and abroad.
Texts: Matthew 28:18-20; Acts 1:4-9
Introduction
1. An advertising campaign for the Visa credit card once used the slogan, "Don't leave home without it!"
2. The same thing can be said about the relationship between the empowering of the Spirit and the proclamation of the gospel.

I. IN OUR TWO TEXTS CHRIST GAVE HIS CHURCH A GREAT COMMISSION AND A FINAL COMMAND
A. In the first passage He issues His *Great Commission.*
   1. Re-read Matthew 28:18-20.
   2. This Commission is also found in the other three gospels:
      a. Read Mk 16:15-16, Lk 24:46-48, and Jn 20:21.
   3. These four mandates were delivered during the 40 days between Jesus' resurrection and His ascension.
      a. The Master was driving home the all-important message.
      b. Illustration: Like repeatedly hitting a nail with a hammer.
   4. Fulfilling the GC is the church's primary responsibility.
B. In the second text, Jesus' issues His *Final Command.*
   1. Read Acts 1:4-6 (emphasizing the word "commanded").
   2. This Final Command was immediately followed by a *Final Promise.* (Read v.8.)
   3. Look what happens next! Jesus ascends into heaven (v. 9).

II. NOTE HOW CHRIST'S GREAT COMMISSION AND HIS FINAL COMMAND ARE INDIVISIBLY LINKED
A. Jesus indivisibly wedded the empowering of the Holy Spirit to the fulfillment of the Great Commission.
B. Every time Jesus issued His Great Commission, He also promised the Spirit's power or presence:
   1. Matthew version: "Go, make disciples of all nations…" (Mt 28:19). *Then*… "Surely, I am with you always… "(v.20).
   2. Mark version: "Go into all the world and preach…" (Mk 16:15). *Then*… "These signs will accompany…" (vv.17-18).

3. Luke version: "Repentance and forgiveness of sins will be preached…to all nations…" (Lk 24:47-48). *Then…* "I'm going to send what my Father promised…" (v.49).
   4. John's version: "As the Father has sent me, I am sending you" (Jn 20:21). *Then…* "He breathed on them and said, 'Receive the Holy Spirit" (v.22).
 B. This connection between the empowering of the Holy Spirit and the fulfillment of the Great Commission is most clearly seen in Ac 1:8:
   1. The Commission: "You will be my witnesses in Jerusalem..."
   2. The Empowering: "You will receive power when the Holy Spirit comes upon you."

III. THE TWO MANDATES CANNOT BE SEPARATED WITHOUT CAUSING IRREPARABLE DAMAGE TO BOTH
 A. To separate them does severe damage to our understanding and experience of the baptism in the Holy Spirit.
   1. The experience becomes a self-centered event.
   2. It is sought merely as a means of personal blessing.
 B. To separate them also does severe damage to our ability to fulfill the Great Commission.
   1. Without the Spirit's empowering, we are left to attempt the work in our own strength. We are sure to fail.
 C. But look what happens when we keep them together:
   1. A powerful spiritual transformation occurs.
   2. We are supernaturally enabled to fulfill the Gt. Commission.
   3. This is the story of the book of Acts.

IV. HOW THEN SHOULD WE RESPOND TO THESE POWERFUL TRUTHS? (Four responses:)
 A. We must clarify our understanding of the relationship between the baptism in the Holy Spirit and missions.
 B. We must refocus our preaching and teaching on the subject.
 C. We must reevaluate our evangelism, church planting, and missions strategies in light of this new understanding.
 D. We must move out in the power of the Spirit.

Conclusion
 1. Come now and commit yourself to the Great Commission.
 2. Come, and be empowered by the Holy Spirit.

[DRM]

22 Understanding the Great Commission

Sermon in a Sentence: We must all understand and participate in fulfilling the Great Commission.

Sermon Purpose: That the hearers fully commit themselves to Christ and to fulfilling His Great Commission.

Texts: Matthew 28:18-20; Mark 16:15-16; Luke 24:46-49; John 20:21; Acts 1:8

Introduction
1. With a magnifying glass we can focus light into on concentrated place—and even start a fire.
2. This is what Jesus is doing in the Great Commission.
   a. For three years He had been teaching His disciples about His mission and their role in it.
   b. He was now ready to send them out into the world.
3. By giving them the Great Commission, Jesus was focusing all of their preparation into a single defining point.
4. In this message we will discuss six important truths concerning this final mandate of Jesus to His church:

I. THE IMPORTANCE OF THE GREAT COMMISSION
A. It was Jesus last message to the Church.
   1. Jesus had come to His last few days on earth. He therefore carefully considered His final message to His disciples.
B. As if to emphasize its importance, He repeated it five times!
   1. Mt 28:18b-20; Mk 16:15-16; Lk 24:46-49; Jn 20:21; Ac 1:8
   2. We repeat the things we want to emphasize, the things we think are important.
C. Together, these verses make up the Great Commission.

II. THE BASIS FOR THE GREAT COMMISSION
A. The basis for the Great Commission is Christ's authority.
   1. Read and discuss Mt 28:18
   2. Christ has been given all authority (Jn 5:27; 17:2).
   3. It is out of that authority that He commands us to "Go!"
B. We have no choice but to obey.

III. THE MESSAGE OF THE GREAT COMMISSION

A. The message of the Great Commission is the gospel of Christ (Mt 16:15; Lk 24:46-48; Ac 1:8).
B. The gospel is the good news that Jesus saves, Jesus heals, Jesus died for you (1Co 15:1-5).
C. It is the message we must proclaim to the nations (Mt 24:14).

IV. THE TASK OF THE GREAT COMMISSION
A. The continuing task of the Great Commission is discipleship (Mt 28:19-20).
B. Two ways we make disciples is through baptism and teaching.
 1. *We must baptize all who have been saved.*
   a. Baptism represents new life in Christ.
   b. It testifies to one's genuine conversion.
   c. It identifies one with the body and mission of Christ.
 2. *We must teach all who have been baptized.*
   a. We are to make disciples, not just converts.
   b. We are to lead them into full obedience to Christ (Ro 1:5).

V. THE SCOPE OF THE GREAT COMMISSION
A. Each version of the Commission makes it clear that we are to evangelize and make disciples in the whole world.
 1. Review each Great Commission emphasizing this fact.
 2. God's heart is for whole world, and so must ours be.
B. Wherever there are groups of people where the good news is not being preached, where people are not being baptized, where they are not being discipled, that is where we must go.

VI. POWER FOR THE GREAT COMMISSION
A. God has promised us His power to accomplish His mission (Mk 16:17-18; Lk 24:49; Ac 1:8).
B. We must each be empowered by the Spirit to effectively participate in fulfilling the Great Commission (Ac.1:4-5; Ac 1:8; Ep.5:18).

Conclusion
1. We have all been commissioned by Christ to take the gospel to lost people in the whole world.
2. Will you come now to be filled with the Spirit and to commit yourself to this greatest of all tasks?

[SH]

23 Obeying the Great Commission

Sermon in a Sentence: We must repent of our neglect and commit ourselves to fulfilling the Great Commission of Christ.
Sermon Purpose: That believers will repent and commit themselves to fulfilling the Great Commission
Text: Matthew 28:18-20
Introduction
1. Today, I remind the church about the Great Commission.
2. It is the command of Christ to cover the whole earth with His glorious gospel.
3. This message will deal with four Great Commission issues:

I. THE GREAT COMMISSION STATED
A. Jesus stated His Great Commission at least five times:
   1. Mathew 28:18-20
   2. Mark 16:15-16
   3. Luke 24:47
   4. John 20:21
   5. Acts 1:8
B. The Great Commission is Christ's primary command to His church.

II. THE GREAT COMMISSION DELAYED
A. Tragically, 2000 years after Jesus issued it, the Great Commission remains His *unfulfilled* command to the church.
B. It is tragic because we have all the resources we need:
   1. We have technology, mega-churches, great preachers, money, and the power of the Spirit.
   2. We have over 600 million "Spirit-filled" Pentecostals in the world today.
C. And yet, the fulfillment of the Great Commission is progressing as a slow speed.
   1. This is because too few are trying to reach the unreached.
      a. 90% of all missionaries go to "Christianized" places.
      b. There is only 1 missionary for every 3 million Muslims.
      c. 80% of the world's people have never owned a Bible.
      d. Little money is invested in reaching the unreached.
   3. Transition: Why are these things so? Why is the Great Commission being delayed? It is because…

III. THE GREAT COMMISSION DISOBEYED

(The fulfilment of the Great Commission has been delayed because of four harmful viruses in the church:)
  A. The virus of *spiritual compromise.*
     1. We love things of the world more than we love Christ.
     2. We must repent of our spiritual compromise.
  B. The virus of *selfishness.*
     1. We think only of ourselves.
     2. We focus on our church members more than on the lost.
     3. May God send us revival and move us from our selfishness.
  C. The virus of *marginalization.*
     1. We have marginalized God's mission to a department in the church—and then, to add insult to injury, we have marginalized that department.
     2. However, missions is the very reason the church exists.
     3. We must put missions at the center of the church.
  D. The virus of *materialism.*
     1. We love riches more than we love unreached souls.
     2. Our preachers talk about material prosperity rather than souls and the reality of heaven and hell.
     3. The accumulation of things has made us dull to the urgency of the harvest.

IV. THE GREAT COMMISSION OBEYED

(What then must we do about these things?)
  A. We must *repent* of our neglect of the Great Commission (Re 2:2-5).
  B. We must *obey* the Great Commission and "Go!"
     1. Like Isaiah we must cry out, "Lord, send us" (Is 6: 8).
  C. We must send those who are ready to go (Ac 13:2-3).
     1. By giving.
     2. By praying.

Conclusion and Altar Call
  1. Come now and commit yourself to Christ and His Great Commission.

[RSK]

24 Four Superlatives for the Harvest

Sermon in a Sentence: In His Great Commission, Jesus gave us some comprehensive orders and a powerful promise.

Sermon Purpose: That the hearers be filled with the Spirit and commit themselves to fulfilling Christ's Great Commission.

Text: Matthew 28:18-20

Introduction
1. We have just read Jesus' "Great Commission."
2. Note how Jesus uses the word "all" four times.
3. This message: "Four Superlatives for the Harvest."

I. JESUS CLAIMED "ALL AUTHORITY"
— v.18 *"All authority has been given to me in heaven and on earth."*
- A. The Father has given to Jesus supreme authority.
    1. Greek for authority = *exousia* = the right to exercise power
    2. Read: Jn 5:27; 10:18
    3. Jesus is "Lord of the Harvest" (Mt 9:38).
- B. Jesus' authority gives Him the power and right to command.
    1. Note the "Therefore" in verse 19.
    2. The Great Commission is the Great Command.
- C. Our only proper response to absolute authority is unquestioning obedience.

II. JESUS SENDS US TO "ALL THE NATIONS"
— v.19 "Go...make disciples of *all nations...*"
- A. The goal of the Great Commission is world evangelization.
    1. "Go into all the world and preach the gospel..." (Mk 16:15).
    2. "You will be my witnesses to the ends of the earth" (Ac 1:8).
- B. Jesus said that the task will be accomplished:
    1. "This gospel of the kingdom *will* be preached in the whole world as a testimony to all nations, and then the end will come" (Mt 24:14).
    2. When with the end come? When the gospel has been preached in all the world (Greek: *oikoumeme,* inhabited earth) as a witness to every (Greek; *ethne,* people group).
- C. Every other task must become secondary to the supreme task of declaring the good news to all nations.

III. WE ARE TO TEACH "ALL THAT HE HAS COMMANDED"
— v.20 *"teaching them to obey all* I have commanded you."
A. We are to "make disciples" of them and teach them to obey *all* that Christ has commanded.
   1. We are not just to evangelize but to "make disciples."
   2. In other words, Jesus is saying that we should do with them what Jesus did with His twelve disciples.
B. We have not fulfilled the Great Commission until we teach them to obey the Great Commission.
   1. Jesus had just commanded them to "Go make disciples of all nations…"
   2. This is one of the commands we must teach.

IV. JESUS PROMISES TO BE WITH US "ALL THE DAYS"
— v.20b "I am with you *always* (literally *"all the days"*), to the very end of the age."
A. When we go out to disciple the nations, we do not go alone.
   1. Jesus promises to go with us. (But how?)
   2. He goes with us in the power and presence of the Spirit.
   3. Jesus (Jn 14:16): "I will ask the Father, and he will give you another Counselor to be with you forever…"
B. Every Great Commission contains a promise of the Spirit.
   1. Matt.28:18-20: "Go… I am with you always…"
   2. Mark16:15-16: "Go…and these signs shall accompany…"
   3. Luke 24:47-49: "My witnesses…stay in the city until…"
   4. John 20:21-22 "I send you…receive the Holy Spirit…"
   5. Acts 1:8: "You will be my witnesses…receive power…"
C. This promise extends to the end of the age.
   1. It is for us today (Read Ac 2:38-39).
   2. It is ours for the asking (See Lk 11:9-13).

Conclusion and Altar Call
   1. Come, commit yourself to fulfilling the Great Commission.
   2. Come and be filled with the Spirit today.

[DRM]

25 "Great Comissioners"
~ Revisiting Missions in Light of the Great Commission ~

Sermon in a Sentence: The time has come for us to recommit ourselves to the message and mandate of the Great Commission.
Sermon Purpose: That Christians recommit themselves to fulfilling the Great Commission of Christ.
Texts: Six Recorded Great Commissions: Matthew 24:14; Matthew 28:18-20; Mark 16:15-16; Luke 24:46-49; John 20:21-22; Acts 1:4-8

Introduction
1. In recent years missions scholars have emphasized the *missio Dei* (mission of God)—and this is good.
2. However, we must be careful that this new understanding of missions does not lead us away from Jesus' basic teaching on missions as revealed in His Great Commission.
3. In His Great Commission, Jesus stresses at seven important insights about His mission and how it is to be carried out:

I. OUR AUTHORITY TO CARRY OUT THE MISSION COMES FROM CHRIST
A. Jesus: Mt 28:18-19: "All authority in heaven and on earth…"
B. A clear chain of command (Jn 20:21):
   1. Christ received His authority from the Father.
   2. We receive our authority from Christ.
C. We have both the right and the obligation to go to the nations.

II. THE CONTEXT IN WHICH THE MISSION IS CARRIED OUT IS THE SPREAD OF GOD'S KINGDOM
A. Jesus: Mt 24:14: "And this gospel of the kingdom shall…"
   1. The message of John and Jesus (Mt 3:1-2; 4:17; Ac 1:3)
   2. The message of the early church in Acts (8:12; 19:8; 28:31).
B. We too must announce that Jesus has come to inaugurate His kingdom in the earth.

III. THE SCOPE OF THE MISSION IS GLOBAL
A. Jesus: "Go into all the world and preach…" (Mk 16:15-16).
B. We must proclaim the gospel…
   1. …in *every place* (Mt 24:14; Ac 1:8)
   2. …to *every person* (Mk 16:15 [KJV], Jn 3:16)
   3. …to *all peoples* (Mt 24:14; 28:19; Lk 24:47).

IV. THE MESSAGE OF THE MISSION IS THE GOSPEL
  A. Jesus: "Go…and proclaim the gospel" (Mk 16:15).
  B. The gospel is the good news about of Christ.
   1. About His death and resurrection (1Co 15:1-4).
   2. Includes a call to faith and repentance (Mk 1:5; Ac 20:21).
  C. We must go everywhere and boldly announce the good news.
   1. We must be like Paul: "Woe is me if preach not the gospel…" (1Co 9:16).

V. THE METHODS TO BE USED IN EXECUTING THE MISSION ARE REVEALED (Including the following:)
  A. We must *go and proclaim* the good news (Mk 16:15-16).
  B. We must *make disciples* of those who believe (Mt 28:19-20).
  C. We must present Christ's claims in the *power of the Holy Spirit* (Lk 24:48-49; Ac 1:8; Ac 2:4).

VI. CHRIST HAS GIVEN SUPERNATURAL PROVISION TO ACCOMPLISH THE MISSION
  A. Christ promised both His presence and His power to enable us to accomplish the mission (Mt 28:20; Mk 16:17-18).
  B. This power comes when we are baptized in the Holy Spirit (Ac 1:4-5, 8).

VII. THE MISSION WILL CONTINUE UNTIL JESUS RETURNS
  A. It will continue until the end of the age (Mt 24:14a).
  B. It will further continue until we reach the last people group (Mt 24:14b)
  C. It will continue until we reach the "remotest parts of the earth" (Acts 1:8).
  D. In other words we must continue to advance the gospel until Jesus comes again (Ac 1:9-11).

Conclusion and Altar Call
   1. We must dedicate all to fulfilling Christ's mandate.
   2. Come now a commit yourself to fulfilling the Great Commission in the power of the Spirit.

[DRM]

26 Perspectives on the Great Commission

Sermon in a Sentence: We must all understand and obey Jesus' Great Commission to go to the nations.
Sermon Purpose: That God's people will commit themselves to obeying the Great Commission.
Text: Matthew 28:18-20
Introduction
1. We have just read Jesus' "Great Commission" as recorded in the gospel of Matthew.
2. These are the "marching orders of the church."
3. It is recorded five more times in the gospels and Acts:
   a. Read the following passages: Mt 24:14; Mk 16:15-16; Lk 24:46-49; Jn 20:21-22; Ac 1:8.
4. This message: "Perspectives on the Great Commission."

I. FIVE PERSPECTIVES ON THE GREAT COMMISSION
A. It is an *authoritative* command.
   1. It comes from the highest authority. (Read Mt 28:18.)
   2. We have but one option—to wholeheartedly obey (Jn 14:16)
B. It is a *clear* command. (Read Mk 16:15.)
   1. Loren Triplett: "Which part of *'Go'* do you not understand?"
   1. It is too clear to misunderstand.
   2. We must "Go preach," "Go witness," "Go make disciples."
C. It is a *prophetic* command.
   It is "prophetic" in two senses:
   1. In the sense that it was divinely inspired (2Pe 1:20-21).
   2. In the sense that it reveals how the gospel will prosper in the future (Mt 24:14).
D. It is a *repeated* command.
   1. Jesus spoke it 6 times, as we read above.
   2. It was Jesus' primary message during the 40 days between His resurrection and His ascension.
E. It is an *empowered* command.
   1. *As we go*...Jesus promised His presence (Mt 28:20).
   2. *As we go*...Jesus promised the Spirit's power (Ac 1:8; Mk 16:16; Lk 24:49; Jn 20:21).

II. HOW WE MUST RESPOND TO THE GREAT COMMISSION

A. We must *hear* it.
   1. That is, we must "pay attention" and "give heed" to Jesus words (Mk 4:9).
   2. Sadly, many are ignoring Jesus' clear command.
   3. They are "sleeping during the harvest" (Pr 10:5).
   4. This must stop—now (Jn 4:35).
B. We must *understand* it.
   1. We must take time to know what it really says.
   2. Must come to understand its awesome implications.
C. We must *"internalize"* it.
   1. That is, we must take it to heart.
   2. We must let it shape our life values and opinions.
D. We must *give all* to fulfill it.
   1. Ultimately, the Great Commission is not meant to be discussed, or even understood; it is meant to be obeyed.
   2. Three ways we must all obey the Great Commission:
      a. We must all *go* (some to the nations; some next door; but all must go).
      b. We must all *pray* (Mt 9:35-38).
      c. We must all *give* (Mk 12:17; Lk 14:33).

Conclusion and Altar Call
   1. We must each make the Great Commission our own personal passion.
   2. Come now, and commit yourself to helping to fulfill this primary command of Jesus.
   3. Come and be empowered by the Holy Spirit.

[DRM]

~ SECTION 3 ~
PASSION FOR THE LOST

27 Mastered by the Cross

Sermon in a Sentence: We must allow the cross of Christ to master our lives.

Sermon Purpose: That the hearers submit themselves totally to the cross of Christ and to His mission.

Text: 1 Corinthians 1:18

Introduction
1. Paul's entire life was dominated by the cross of Christ.
   a. Including his ministry and his theology.
2. This "mastery of the cross" manifested itself in three ways:

I. **PAUL WAS MASTERED BY THE CROSS**
   A. He said of the cross: "May I never boast except in the cross of our Lord Jesus Christ, through which the world has been crucified to me, and I to the world" (Ga 6:14).
   B. Unlike Paul, many of us are mastered by the quest for power, money, drugs, alcohol, sexual pleasure, and intellectual pride.
   C. If we are to be useful in advancing God's kingdom in the earth, we must allow the cross to master our lives (Ro 6:6).
      1. We must be crucified to self-will and ambition.
      2. We must be crucified to the flesh and its sinful passions.
      3. We must die daily with Christ (1 Co 15:31, KJV).
   D. The gospel has the power to change our lives (Ro 1:16).

II. **PAUL WAS MARKED BY THE CROSS**
   A. Paul said, "I bear on my body the marks of Jesus" (Ga 6:17).
      1. He was saying that he had been branded by Jesus.
         a. The Greek word for "mark" is *stigmata*.
         b. It can mean "burned in" or "tattooed."
      2. Paul was first "branded" on the Road to Damascus.
         a. The persecutor became the bond slave (Ac 9:6; 26:19).
      3 Paul's life and character took on the likeness of Jesus.
         a. He surrendered his rebellious will to Christ.
         b. He became a "servant of the gospel" (Ep 3:7; Col 1:23).
         c. He surrendered his ambitions to the gospel (Ro.15:20).
   B. These same "marks of the cross" should be visible in our lives.
      1. "If anyone is in Christ, he is a new creation…" (2Co 5:17)
      2. Jesus should shine through in all we do.
   C. The cross of Christ has the power to change us (1Co 6:9-11).

1. What we were ("sexually immoral, idolaters, etc. [vv.9-10]), we are no longer.
2. Now we have been "washed…sanctified…justified…in the name of the Lord Jesus Christ and by the Spirit of our God" (v.11).
3. No sin is so bad that God cannot forgive and cleanse by the power of the cross (Is 1:18).

III. PAUL WAS MOTIVATED BY THE CROSS
A. In Ephesus Paul spoke of this motivation: "I consider my life worth nothing to me, if only I may finish the race and complete the task the Lord Jesus has given me—the task of testifying to the gospel of God's grace" (Ac 20:24).
B. The cross dominated Paul's entire life and ministry.
 1. It drove him to the "regions beyond" to preach the gospel to those who had never heard (2Co 10:16, KJV).
 2. It caused him to keep preaching, even in prison (Ac 28:30-31).
 3. He committed his life to preaching the cross.
 4. Illustration: Early Pentecostal missionaries went to Africa with their goods packed in coffins expecting to die for Christ.
C. Like Paul, we have all been given the task of reaching the lost.
 1. And like Paul, we must be motivated by the cross to fulfill that task.

Conclusion and Altar Call
1. What masters your life today?
2. Come now, and submit yourself to the cross of Christ and to His mission.

[GB]

28 God's Mission—Our Mission

Sermon in a Sentence: As God's missionary people, we must be empowered by God's missionary Spirit to fulfill His mission.
Sermon Purpose: To call God's people to Spirit-empowered mission.
Texts: Matthew 1:1; 28:18-20

Introduction
1. Matthew 28:18-20 is often called the "Great Commission."
2. However, we must not forget that the whole book of Matthew (and indeed the whole Bible) is about God's mission.
    a. This is indicated in Mt 1:1, as we will discuss later.
3. This message: God's mission must become our mission.

I. **GOD IS A MISSIONARY GOD** (vv.18-19)
    A. Two key phrases in Mt 28:18-19 point to God's mission:
        1. First Jesus spoke of *"all authority* in heaven and earth."
            a. He is referencing God's kingdom and himself as King.
        2. Second said, "Go…and make disciples of *all nations…"*
            a. Greek for "nations" is *ethne* (tribes or people groups).
            b. We must work to bring people from every people group into the kingdom as followers of Christ the King.
        3. Jesus is not introducing a new idea—He is simply underscoring a *highpoint point* in the mission of God, a mission that has been revealed throughout the Bible.
    B. God's missions is revealed in 2 foundational promises of the OT:
        1. *God promised Abraham,* "Through your offspring (or seed, NKJV) all nations on earth will be blessed" (Ge 22:18).
            a. This is a prophecy concerning Jesus. (Read Ga 3:8, 16)
        2. *God promised David,* "I will raise up your offspring to succeed you…and I will establish the throne of his kingdom forever."
            a. This too was a prophecy concerning Jesus (Lk 1:32).
    C. Matthew understood these 2 promises concerning God's mission.
        1. So he began his gospel by saying, "A record of the genealogy of Jesus Christ the *son of David,* the *son of Abraham"* (Mt 1:1)
        2. Thus, Matthew wrote about God's mission to bless all nations by establishing His kingdom with Jesus as the king.
        3. The kingdom of heaven (or God) in a major theme in Matthew. (For example: Mt 4:17, 23; 24:14)
    D. What is true of Matthew is true of all of the Bible.

1. God is a missionary God & the Bible is a missionary book.
2. If we miss this powerful truth, we miss really knowing and understanding God.
   a. And neither can we understand the Bible,
   b. Nor can we understand what the Christian life is about.
3. You may ask, "What does all of this have to do with me?"

II. WE ARE TO BE GOD'S MISSIONARY PEOPLE (vv. 19-20a)
A. In His Great Commission, Jesus commissioned us as God's missionary people. (He said *"Therefore, go…"*)
   1. *Therefore* is a significant word.
      a. Someone has said, "When you see the word *therefore*, you should look and see what it is *there for."*
   2. *Therefore...* since Jesus is king, and He has all authority in heaven and earth, we must obey His command to "Go!"
   3. *Therefore...* since God a missionary God, we as God's missionary people, must be about His mission.
B. Two things we must understand about our role in God's mission:
   1 First, we must understand that every believer and every church has been called to participate in God's mission.
      a. Everywhere the gospel goes *to,* it must also go *from.*
      b. Being a disciple of Christ means we commit ourselves to Christ and His mission. (See Mt 28:20a; Mk 8:34-35.)
   2. Next, Jesus promised power to fulfill the mission:
      a. He promised, "Surely I am with you always…" (v.20).
      b. This is a promise of the Holy Spirit. (See Jn 14:16-18.)
C. The missionary God sends His missionary Spirit to empower His missionary people to fulfill His missionary mandate.
   1. We are Pentecostal for the purpose of fulfilling God's mission in God's power (Ac 1:8).
   2. We receive this power when we are baptized in the Holy Spirit as were the disciples at Pentecost (Ac 2:1-4).
   3. You can receive the Spirit today—if you will…
      a. Ask in faith (Lk 11:9, 13).
      b. Receive by faith (Lk 11:10; Mk 11:24).
      c. Speak in faith (Ac 2:4).

Conclusion and Altar Call
1. Come now and commit yourself to God's mission.
2. Come and receive God's missionary Spirit.

[MRT]

29 What Time Is It?

Sermon in a Sentence: It is time to be filled with the Spirit and get busy in God's harvest of lost souls.
Sermon Purpose: To see believers filled with the Spirit and committed to winning souls.
Text: Romans 13:11-14
Introduction
1. Does anyone know what time it is? It's harvest time!
2. In our text, Paul wrote the Roman Christians reminding them that "it is high time to awake out of sleep; for now our salvation is nearer than when we first believed" (v.11, NKJV).
3. Just as in Paul's day, time is short today; Jesus is coming; we must reap the harvest while it is yet day.
4. In light of this truth, there are three things that we must know about the timing of the harvest:

I. IT IS TIME WE REPENT OF OUR CALLOUSNESS CONCERNING GOD'S HARVEST
   A. The writer of Proverbs describes the sad state of many Christians today:
      1. They are lazy in the time of harvest (Pr.24:30-34).
      2. They sleep when they should be working (Pr 6:9-11; Pr 10:4-5).
      3. If this describes any of us, we must repent.
   B. If we refuse to repent, then…
      1. …much grain will remain in the fields unharvested (Jer 8:20).
      2. …our prayers go unanswered (Ps 66:18).
      3. …we thus become part of the problem, rather than part of the solution.
   C. Jesus declared judgment on the unrepentant religious leaders of His day (Mt 23:13-39).
      1. In the same way, He will judge us if we do not change our ways and follow His ways.
      2. God's way is the way of harvest (Lk 19:10).
      3. He now commands all people everywhere to repent (Ac 17:30).

II. IT IS TIME WE STOP THINKING THAT SOMEONE ELSE WILL DO OUR JOB FOR US

A. Our responsibility is to be active in the Master's harvest.
   1. Jesus' only prayer request is for the harvest (Lk.10:2).
   2. Time is short, and many are in danger of going to hell (Ro 13:11-12; Jn 4:35).
B. We have all been given a role in the harvest, a task that we must each faithfully fulfill (1Co 4:2).

III. IT IS TIME WE GET EMPOWERED FOR THE HARVEST

A. Jesus insisted that His disciples not go to the harvest until they were properly equipped (Lk 24:49; Ac 1:4).
B. This empowering comes from the Holy Spirit (Ac 1:8).
   1. Every believer must be empowered by the Holy Spirit (Ac 1:4-5).
   2. And we must remain full of the Spirit (Ep 5:18).
C. The book of Acts records how God empowered ordinary people with the Holy Spirit, and how they went on and reached others.
   1. Peter was an ordinary fisherman, but once he was empowered, he became a powerful preacher (Ac 2).
   2. Ananias was an ordinary disciple; however, because he was full of the Spirit, God used him to pray with Paul to receive the Spirit (Ac 9:10-18).
D. How can we be filled with the Spirit today?
   1. We must ask in faith (Lk 11:9, 13).
   2. We must receive by faith (Lk 11:10; Mk.11:24).
   3. We must speak in faith (Ac 2:4).

Conclusion and Altar Call
1. What time is it?
   a. It is time to wake up and look on the fields.
   b. It is time to commit ourselves to the Lord of the Harvest.
   c. It is time to be empowered by the Holy Spirit.
2. Come now and commit yourself to God's harvest.

[JB]

30 Buying Fields When It Seems to Make No Sense

Sermon in a Sentence: God is calling us to "buy fields," that is, to move forward in His mission—even when it does not seem rational.
Sermon Purpose: That God's people will obey God's voice and move forward in mission, even if it does not seem to make sense.
Text: Jeremiah 32:1-9; 17-21
Introduction
1. God asked Jeremiah to do something that seemed irrational—to buy a field near Jerusalem.
2. It was irrational because Jerusalem was about to be destroyed.
   a. Jeremiah himself had prophesied its downfall (Read v.3).
   b. The army of Babylon was besieging the city, and it was about to be destroyed and its people carried into captivity (vv.2, 4-5).
   d. Yet, God's directive to Jeremiah is, "Buy a field!" (vv.6-7).
3. How could God give Jeremiah such an irrational order?
   a. Because God had plans that went beyond human understanding.
   b. Thus, from God's perspective, buying a field in a city facing destruction was a wise and strategic move.
   c. Jeremiah heard from God—so he could move with confidence.
4. Today the Lord of the Harvest still sends his servants to "buy harvest fields" in seeming illogical circumstances.
   a. He directs to go places that we've never gone before.
   b. He wants us to attempt things we've never attempted before.
   c. He sends us to engage peoples we have historically shunned.
5. After obeying God and buying the field, Jeremiah reflects on his response (vv.17–24). He concluded that he had made a wise decision—based on three things He understood about God:
   a. *God's great power:* (v.17): "Ah, Sovereign Lord, you have made the heavens…by your great *power*…"
   b. *God's great purpose:* (v.19): "Great are your *purposes* and mighty are your deeds."
   c. *God's great performance:* (v.20): "You *performed* miraculous signs and wonders…to this day…"

6. As we think about "buying new fields," let's consider how these three attributes of God give us confidence that we will succeed:

We can confidently "by new fields" because...
I. WE SERVE A GOD OF GREAT POWER (Read verse 17)
   A. Jeremiah could by the field with confidence because he knew God had the power to accomplish His will.
      1. "Sovereign Lord… Nothing is too hard for you…" (v.17).
   B. Like, Jeremiah, we can trust in God's great power…
      1. …as we reach out to the lost.
      2. …as we plant new churches.
      3. …as we send out missionaries.
   C. We must further seek the power of the Holy Spirit to enable and guide us to accomplish God's mission (Ac 1:8).

We can confidently "by new fields" when...
II. WE ARE LINKED TO GOD'S GREAT PURPOSES
   A. Jeremiah was guided by the Holy Spirit; therefore, he understood God's purposes for Israel. (Read v.19.)
      1. v.19: "Great are your purposes…)
   B. We too must understand God's purpose for the nations.
      1. We discover God's purpose in God's word.
      2. His purpose is to redeem and call unto himself a people out of every tongue, tribe and nation on earth (Re 5:9).
   C. Like Jeremiah, we must zealously pursue God's purposes—even when they seem illogical.

We can confidently "by fields" when...
III. WE HAVE FAITH IN OF GOD'S GREAT PERFORMANCE
   A. Jeremiah acted in faith knowing that what God had promised, He would perform. (Read vv.20-21.)
      1. Note v.20: "You performed signs and wonders…"
   B. As we move forward to "by new fields," we must trust God, believing that what He has promised, He will perform.
   C. We must move out in faith—even when it seems irrational.
      1. God's powerful works "have continued to this day… among all nations" (v.21).

Conclusion and Altar Call
   1. God is calling us to "by new fields."
   2. Come and commit yourself today [DC]

31 Motivated for Mission

Sermon in a Sentence: Like Paul, we must be motived for mission through intercession, impartation, and proclamation.

Sermon Purpose: That the hearers understand the true motivators for mission, and that they commit themselves to doing God's work.

Text: Romans 1:9-17 (NIV)

Introduction
1. What kind of compelling motivation must one have to be an effective servant of the Lord today?
2. In our text Paul spoke of his motivation (or inner drive) for mission: (v.9): "I serve *with my whole heart* in preaching the gospel of his Son."
3. Our text further reveals what motivated Paul—and how that same motivation will help us to effectively carry out God's mission today.
4. Consider with me the importance of Intercession, Impartation, and Proclamation in motivating us for mission today.

I. PAUL WAS MOTIVATED BY INTERCESSION
A. Intercession was the underlying source of Paul's service to God.
  1. Note vv.9-10: "I constantly I remember you in *my prayers.*"
  2. Paul literally lived in prayer (1Th 5:17).
  3. Prayer was the thing that urged him to go to the Romans.
B. Authentic passion for *going* is a product of *prayer*.
  1. Passion born of anything but prayer is little more than a profession or job.
  2. However, when one's heart is linked by prayer to God and people, their going will be divinely motived.
  3. Paul testified: "I pray that now at last *by God's will* the way may be opened for me to come to you" (v.10).
  4. Authentic desire for going starts with impassioned prayer.
C. We must commit ourselves to passionate intercession for the lost.

II. PAUL WAS MOTIVATED BY IMPARTATION
A. This was a primary reason for Paul's missionary journeys.
  1. Paul told the Roman Christians, "I long to see you *so that I may impart* to you some spiritual gift…" (v.11).
  2. Paul wanted to share what he had received from God.

B. Paul's desire to be an agent of impartation drove him to go.
1. Hear his impassioned words: "I long to see you…" (v.11).
2. Understand his reason: "…that I may impart to you…"

C. Paul wanted to impart what was most needed:
1. "I long to see you so that I may impart to you *some spiritual gift* to make you strong" (v. 11).
2. Paul's chief desire was not to give the buildings, or goods, or programs, or methods but something spiritual.
3. Christians are engaged in spiritual ministry and warfare, and they need to be strong.
4. Only *some spiritual gift* will do!

D. Paul's ultimate desire "that I might have a harvest among you" (v.13).
1. Only spiritual impartation will result in a spiritual harvest.
2. We cannot give what we do not possess.

III. PAUL WAS MOTIVATED BY PROCLAMATION (vv.14-16)
A. Proclamation of the gospel of Christ was the overarching purpose of Paul's life. (See Ac 9:15; 1Co 9:16-17.)
B. This noble purpose is summed in Paul's three "I am's":
1. *"I am obligated* to both Greeks and non-Greeks…" (Ro 1:14).
   a. Paul was not motivated primarily by need or opportunity, but rather by God's love (see 2Co 5:14.).
2. *"I am eager* to preach the gospel…" (v.15).
   a. The harvest needs technicians and specialists…
   b. …but more than anything else, it needs anointed preachers of the gospel.
3. *"I am not ashamed* of the gospel…" (v.16).
   a. Paul had ultimate faith that the message of Christ was "the power of God unto salvation to everyone who believes."

C. We must share in Paul's confidence in the gospel—and His passion and commitment to share the good news about Christ with all people.

Conclusion and Altar Call
1. Come now and commit yourself to God's mission.
2. Ask God to fill you with His Spirit and give you the right motivations for doing His work.

[DC]

32 Three Foundation Stones for Missions

Sermon in a Sentence: Because all people are created in the image of God, all people have value, capacity, and significance.

Sermon Purpose: That the people commit themselves to reaching all people with the message of the gospel.

Text: Genesis 1:26-27

Introduction
1. Our text speaks of the creation of man.
   a. Adam and Eve were created in the image of God.
   b. This is sometimes called the *imagio Dei*.
2. The same is true for every human who has ever lived.
   a. Every person is created in God's image.
   b. Even though people are fallen, they still retain God's image.
3. This belief shapes how we view the people around us.
   a. And how we view God's mission in the world.
4. *This message:* Three foundation stones of missions based on the fact that all people are created in the image of God:

Foundation Stone #1:
I. ALL PEOPLE HAVE VALUE
   A. Because all people are created in God's image, all people have immeasurable value.
      1. Every person is the object of God's infinite love.
      2. No one is excluded.
      3. This truth applies to people of every tribe and race; rich or poor; male or female; young or old.
   B. We must see people as God sees them.
      1. We must value them as God values them.
      2. We must love them as God loves them.
      3. We must be willing to sacrifice for them as Christ sacrificed for them (Jn 3:16).

Foundations Stone #2:
II. ALL PEOPLE HAVE CAPACITY
   A. Not only do all people have *value*, they also have *capacity*.
      1. That is, they have the capacity to say "yes" to the gospel.

2. This is because they have been created in the image of God.
   3. This capacity to say "yes" includes…
      a. … people in the slum and in the government office.
      b. … people in the city or in the village.
      c. … people in this place and around the world.
   B. Our belief that every human can receive the gospel and be saved drives us in mission.
      1 Because we believe in capacity, we are moved to share the gospel with them.
      2. We are thus motivated to go, give, and pray.
      3. And when things get hard, it causes us to stay.

Foundations Stone #3:
III. ALL PEOPLE HAVE SIGNIFICANCE
   A. Not only do all people have *value* and *capacity,* all people have want *significance.*
      1. Because we are created in God's image, we all want our lives to matter.
      2. We want our lives to count for something.
   B. Our significance is not found in self-esteem but in our esteem for Christ and His mission.
      1. It is found in the *imagio Dei.*
      2. It is found in our participation in God's mission.
   C. Not only can we can have significance in Christ, we can offer significance to others.
      1. They too can find their significance in Christ.
      2. This truth makes us want to engage our world.

Conclusion and Altar Call
   1. Every person has value, capacity, and significance.
   2. Because of this we should share the gospel with all.
   3. Come and commit yourself to God's mission

[JLE]

33 It's Harvest Time: Let's Get Involved

Sermon in a Sentence: It is time to get involved in God's worldwide harvest of souls.
Sermon Purpose: That Christians will commit themselves to reaching the lost for Christ.
Texts: Matthew 9:35-38; John 4:34-38
Introduction
1. God is in the business of reaping souls into His kingdom.
2. He is looking for workers to join Him in the harvest.
3. To effectively participate in His harvest we need three things:

I. **WE NEED A VISION FOR THE HARVEST**
   (Three reasons from Jn 4:34-38:)
   A. We need vision because God has given us a work to finish.
      1. Jesus testified to a Samaritan woman.
      2. He told her, "My food is to do the will of him who sent me *and to finish his work* (v 34).
      3. We, too, must finish the work of proclaiming the gospel to the ends of the earth.
   B. We need vision for it will help us see the urgency of the harvest.
      1. Jesus said that the fields are "ripe for harvest" (v 35).
      2. People are ready to respond to the gospel—if only we will tell them.
      3. The harvest is urgent; we must go now.
   C. We need vision because it will drive us into the harvest fields.
      1. Jesus told his disciples, "I send you to reap" (v 38).
      2. It is not enough to see the need, we must respond to the need and go to the harvest fields.

II. **WE NEED COMPASSION IN THE HARVEST**
   (Three reasons from Mt 9:35-38:)
   A. We need compassion because people are lost.
      1. Jesus saw them as "harassed and helpless" before the attacks of the devil (v 36).
      2. They needed to know Jesus, the Good Shepherd (Jn 10: 14-15).

B. We need compassion because "the harvest is plentiful but the labors are few" (v 37).
   1. Millions worldwide need to hear the good news.
   2. God is looking for laborers to take the gospel to them.
C. We need compassion because it will move us to do something (v 38).
   1. When Jesus saw the needs of people, He was moved with compassion for them.
   2. He then told his disciples to pray for harvesters (v.38).
   3. We must let the Spirit move us to compassion (Ro 5:5).

III. WE NEED THE WORKERS FOR THE HARVEST
(Read: Mt 9:37-38)
A. We need workers because the work is greater than the workforce.
   1. "The harvest is plentiful but the workers are few" (v 37).
   2. Jesus calls every believer to become a worker in the fields.
   3. The early Christians got involved in the soul harvest (Ac 5:42).
   4. Paul preached "publicly and from house to house" (Ac 20:20).
B. How can we as workers get involved in the in the harvest? *(Four practical ways:)*
   1. We can *be empowered* for the harvest (Ac 1:8).
   2. We can *pray* for the harvest (Mt 9:38).
   3. We can *go* to the harvest field (Mk 16:15).
   4. We can *give* to the harvest.
   5. We can practice *personal witnessing.*
      a. John pointed Andrew to Jesus (Jn 1:35-37), then Andrew brought his brother Peter to Jesus (vv.40-42).
      b. Christ invited Philip, then Philip won Nathaniel (vv.45-49)

Conclusion and Altar Call
1. God has called us to join Him in the harvest of souls.
2. Come now and commit yourself to His harvest.

[PFM]

34 Ripe for Harvest

Sermon in a Sentence: The time is now; we must each do our part to reap and preserve the harvest.

Sermon Purpose: That believers fully surrender themselves to the work of missions.

Text: John 4:27-42

Introduction
1. Many only think of the harvest in terms of the future.
2. That attitude will cripple the church.
3. Today, we must be gripped by a sense of urgency concerning the harvest.
4. We cannot say "four months."
5. The time for harvest is now!
6. This message will deal with three critical harvest issues:

I. THE SIGNS OF THE HARVEST
A. Christ preached at the well in Sychar—and one woman was saved.
   1. She then went out and told others about Jesus (vv.28-29).
   2. They came to hear Jesus for themselves (v.30; Ac 8:39).
B. But there was a problem, those who were coming to hear Jesus, were despised Samaritans.
   1. They were the least likely to people to listen Jesus.
   2. However, they were stirred by the woman's testimony.
   3. Many believed on Christ.
C. We too must be willing to preach the gospel to those who are outcast.
   1. If we will do this, they too will believe.

II. THE NEEDS OF THE HARVEST
(Five things are needed to complete the harvest:)
A. First, the harvest needs more *laborers* (Mt 9:37-38; Lk 10:2).
B. Second, the harvest needs more *sharp tools,* including...
   1. The Word of God
   2. Prayer
C. Third, the harvest needs more *sheaf binders*.
   1. Sheaf binders are those who will talk to people.
   2. They are people who will "bind" them into fellowship with the people of God.

- D. Fourth, the harvest needs more *sheaf gatherers*.
    1. Sheaf gatherers are those who will disciple converts.
    2. Converts must be brought into the storehouse.
- E. Fifth, the harvest needs more *refreshment bringers*.
    1. Refreshment bringers are encouragers.
    2. Everyone needs encouragement.

III. THE DANGERS OF THE HARVEST
(Three great dangers of the harvest:)
- A. Danger 1: Some of the harvest may be *damaged.*
    1. The enemy is doing everything he can to spoil the harvest.
- B. Danger 2: Some of the harvest may be *lost.*
    1. The harvest may rot in the very place it grows.
- C. Danger 3: *Someone else* may gather in the harvest.
    1. False religions, the messengers of Satan, are busy doing their work—gathering their harvest.
    2. Death, the "grim reaper," is silently gathering in his harvest every day. Every day, part of the harvest s taken to the graveyard.
    3. We must gather the harvest ahead of them.

Conclusion and Altar Call:
1. The only thing that stands between us and the harvest, is our response to the call of the Lord of the Harvest.
2. We must each do our part in reaping the harvest before it is eternally too late.
3. Come now and commit yourself to the harvest.

[DG]

35 God's Desire for the Nations

Sermon in a Sentence: God desires that people from all nations come to know and serve Him.

Sermon Purpose: That believers commit themselves to working with God to fulfill His desire to reconcile the nations to Himself.

Text: Acts 17:22-27

Introduction

1. Does God really have a plan for the nations?
   a. Is He working to bring that plan to completion?
   b. Do we, as His people, have a part in fulfilling that plan?
   c. Our text today holds the answer to these questions.
2. Paul is in Athens during his 2nd missionary journey.
   a. He is distressed by the city's idolatry.
   b. Finally, he gets a chance to speak.
3. Paul's audience, the Athenians, can be seen as representative of many people around the world today (vv.22-23).
   a. They were *"very religious."*
   b. They were *ignorant* of the true and living God.
   c. They *needed someone* to tell them the truth about God.
4. In verses 24-28 Paul declares God to be the God of the nations who is at work seeking to redeem the nations.
5. In this text we learn three things about God's desire for the nations and about how we should respond to that desire:

I. GOD'S HAS ONE GREAT COMPASSIONATE DESIRE FOR THE NATIONS

A. God's desire for the nations is that all people everywhere on earth come to know and serve Him (vv.26-27).
   1. "God did this so men would seek Him..." (v.26).
   2. He is already near to us all: "He is not far..." (v.27).
B. This desire of God is based on His relationship with mankind.
   1. He is Creator and Sustainer of all people.
      a. God "made the world and everything in it" (v.24).
      b. "He himself gives all men life and breath..." (v.25).
      c. "In him we live and move and have..." (v.25).
   2. He created all people to love them and be loved by them.
   3. Transition: The second thing we learn from this text is...

II. IN HIS GREAT WISDOM AND LOVE FOR ALL PEOPLE, GOD DEALS PROVIDENTIALLY WITH THE NATIONS

- A. God sovereignly guides and directs the affairs of mankind.
    1. "From one man He made every nation of men…and He determined the times set for them and the exact places where they should live" (v.26).
    2. From this statement, we learn two important truths about God's dealing with the nations:
- B. First, in His great wisdom God created only *one race of men*.
    1. "From one man (KJV "blood") he made every nation" (v.26).
    2. There is only one race of people—the human race.
- C. Second, in fulfilling His redemptive plan, God has put all the peoples of the world in *the right place at the right time* in order that they might be best reached with the truth.
    1. "He determined the times set for them and the exact places where they should live. God did this so that men would seek him and perhaps reach out for him and find him…" (vv.26-27).
    2. The immigration patterns in the world today are by God's design. He is preparing the nations to receive the gospel. (Mt 24:14).
    3. Finally, from what we have learned…

III. WE CAN IDENTIFY THREE WAYS WE SHOULD RESPOND TO THESE POWERFUL TRUTHS

- A. We must not despise nor disregard any person or people on the face of the earth.
    1. Because we are all of the same race—the human race.
    2. Because all people bear the image of God—the *imagio Dei*.
    3. Because we must love them and value them as does God.
- B. We must share in God's desire to see all nations come to know and serve Him.
- C. We must actively cooperate with God in His plan to redeem all people.

Conclusion
  1. Come and commit yourself to God's mission to the nations.

[DRM]

36 Rekindling Our Passion for the Lost

Sermon in a Sentence: We must each rekindle our passion for the lost and then reach out to them with the message of Christ.

Sermon Purpose: To inspire God's people to reach out to the lost and win them to Christ.

Text: Romans 9:1-4a

Introduction
1. In Romans 12:2 the Bible gives us a warning: "Do not be conformed to this world." And yet, it happens to all of us!
2. One way we conform to the world is in our attitude toward the people around us.
    a. We lose our awareness of their lostness.
    b. As a result, we lose our evangelistic zeal.
    c. Today, we will address this critical issue.
3. In our text we read of Paul's passion for the lost:
    a. "I am telling you the truth in Christ...I am not lying!"
    b. "My conscience bears me witness in the Holy Spirit."
    c. "I have great sorrow and continual grief in my heart."
    d. "I could wish myself accursed from Christ..."
4. How can we rekindle our passion for the lost?

I. WE MUST UNDERSTAND THREE THINGS
A. We must understand the *utter lostness* of people without Christ.
   1. Popular culture scoffs at this belief.
   2. Yet Paul understood the utter lostness of mankind
       a. Read and Explain: Ro 1:18-20
       b. We too must understand that, apart from a saving relationship with Jesus Christ, every person on earth is hopelessly and eternally lost.
   3. Jesus referred to people as being "lost" (Mt 18:11-14).
   4. To be lost means…
       a. …to be without purpose in life (Mt 9:36-38).
       b. …to be without God and without hope in this world and in the world to come (Ep 2:12).
       c. …to face a future of eternal separation from God in hell (Mk 9:48).
   5. As with Paul, this understanding must compel us to preach the gospel to the lost wherever they are.

B. We must understand and believe that Christ is the *only Savior*.
   1. Culture would have us believe that there are many ways to God.
   2. However, the Bible teaches that Christ is the only way:
      a. Peter: "There is no other name…" (Ac 4:12).
      b. Paul: "There is…one mediator…" (1Ti 2:5).
      c. Jesus: "No one comes to the Father but…" (Jn 14:6).
C. We must understand the *absolute necessity* of a personal life-changing encounter with Christ.
   1. To be saved, people must hear and believe the gospel.
   2. Paul understood this: "I am not ashamed…" (Ro1:15-16)
   3. We must proclaim the gospel to the lost (Ro. 10:13-15).
   4. Transition: Not only must we believe these things, we must also do something about it.

II. WE MUST DO THREE THINGS
A. We must repent of our callousness toward God, His mission, and those He created in His own image (Ac 3:19).
B. We must allow the Spirit to seize out hearts and place within us a sense of personal responsibility toward the lost.
   1. Paul felt that way: "I am obligated..." (Ro.1:14); "Woe to me if I do not preach the gospel" (1Co 9:16).
   2. Do you feel the same way?
C. We must be powerfully filled and refilled with the Holy Spirit.
   1. Only the Spirit can do the works we have discussed.
   2. However, we must be filled with a clear understanding of why God is filling us with His Spirit (Ac 1:8).
   3. Then, we must respond to the Spirit's inner promptings to go out and share Christ with the lost.

Conclusion and Altar Call
1. Come now, be filled with the Spirit.
2. And commit yourself to reaching the lost.

[DRM]

37. Partnering with God in His Mission

Sermon in a Sentence: We can partner with Christ in fulfilling God's mission in the earth.

Sermon Purpose: That Christians might understand their part and Christ's part in fulfilling God's mission, and that they might commit themselves to doing their part.

Text: Luke 5:17-25

Introduction
1. Every follower of Christ has an important part to play in carrying out God's mission.
2. God's mission is that people be brought into His kingdom "from every tribe and language and people and nation" (Re 5:9).
3. Christ calls us to partner with Him in fulfilling God's mission.
4. From our story, we learn something about Christ's part and our part in advancing God's mission.

I. OUR STORY ILLUSTRATES CHRIST'S PART IN FULFILLING GOD'S MISSION
A. In our text story, Jesus both healed the crippled man and forgave his sins (Lk 5:20, 24-25).
   1. Christ provided the way for all people to be saved.
   2. He died on the cross for the sins of all people (Jn 3:15-16).
   3. He is truly the Savoir of the world (Jn 4:42).
B. In our story Jesus gave the cripple man "complete salvation."
   1. He forgave him of his sins (v.20)—Salvation.
   2. He healed his body (v.24)—Healing.
   3. He brought joy to his life (v.25)—Blessing.
C. To receive Christ's complete salvation today, do this:
   1. Come to Jesus, the Savior (Jn 7:37).
   2. Repent of your sins and ask His forgiveness (Ac 17:30).
   3. Put your faith in Him alone for salvation (Ac 16:31).
   4. Follow him (Mt 16:24).

II. OUR STORY ALSO ILLUSTRATES OUR PART IN FULFILLING GOD'S MISSION
(Our story teaches us two thing about our part in God's mission:)
A. First, *our part* is to bring lost ones to Jesus.
   1. The disciples knew that if they could get the cripple man to Jesus, He had the power to make him walk again (vv.18-19).

2. Our job is to get people to Jesus.
      a. We cannot save them—only God can do that.
      b. But we can bring them to the Savior.
   3. We must help people to Jesus because…
      a. …they are sick and feeble and cannot help themselves.
      b. …they are lost and blind and cannot find the way alone.
   4. Only Jesus can meet their deepest needs (Ps 103:3).
B. Second, our part is to overcome every obstacle that keeps people from getting to Jesus.
   1. The crowd blocked the way for the disciples to get the crippled man to Jesus.
      a. However, the men would not be deterred.
      b. They went on the house, made a hole in the roof, and lowered the man to where Jesus was.
   2. We must do the same.
      a. We must remove any obstacle that keeps people from getting to Jesus.
      b. This includes religious obstacles, tribal obstacles, and the obstacles of wrong thinking.
   3. The greatest obstacle between people and Christ: Many in the world have never even heard of Jesus.
      a. We must go and tell them about Jesus (Mk 16:15).
      b. We must do this "in Jerusalem, and in all Judea and Samaria, and to the ends of the earth" (Ac 1:8).
C. Christ has promised us power to do our part in God's mission.
   1. Jesus ministered in the power of the Spirit (Lk 5:17).
   2. He has promised us that same power. (Read Ac 1:8.)
   3. We receive this power when we are baptized in the Holy Spirit like the disciples at Pentecost. (Read Ac 2:1-4.)

Conclusion and Altar Call
1. Come and receive Christ as Savior.
2. Come and commit yourself to bring others to Jesus.
3. Come and be filled with the Spirit.

[EG]

38   The "Insignificant" Woman

Sermon in a Sentence: No one is insignificant in Jesus' eyes; we must take the gospel to all.
Sermon Purpose: That God's people will commit themselves to loving and reaching those others deem as "insignificant."
Text: John 4:4-10
Introduction
1. In today's story, Jesus approaches and talks with an "insignificant" Samaritan woman. (Briefly tell the story).
    a. John doesn't even give her name.
    b. In the minds of most, she was an insignificant person.
2. The world is full of such "insignificant," despised people.
3. However, in our story we learn from Jesus that we should never view anyone as insignificant.

I. LOOK FIRST AT THE "INSIGNIFICANT" WOMAN
A. The woman at the well was a woman with issues.
   1. She had *racial issues:* She was a Samaritan, an ethnic nobody, belonging to a despised group of people.
   2. She had *social issues:* She was a divorcee and was probably childless. She was thus of no social value, unacceptable.
   3. She had *moral issues:* She had been married 5 times and was now living with a man who was not her husband.
B. However, she was also a woman who was searching.
   1. She was searching for meaning, for security, for love.
      a. She had been discarded by 5 men, and the last one did not care enough to call her his wife.
      b. She was his mere cook, his water carrier, his toy.
   2. Yet, deep in her heart she was searching for a relationship with God.
C. Then along comes Jesus.

II. LOOK AT HOW JESUS TREATED THE "INSIGNIFICANT" WOMAN
A. Note how Jesus' every action was *redemptive*.
   1. He relentlessly pursued this "insignificant" woman.
   2. We know this because John stated that he "had to go through Samaria" (Jn 4:4).

       a. This was not the normal route from Jerusalem to Galilee. It was out of the way, off the beaten path.
       b. No good Jew would ever defile himself by going through Samaria.
       c. This was no geographic necessity; it was rather a missiological necessity—a kingdom necessity.
  B. His actions were also *risky*.
    1. To associate with this woman in any form was a social risk —to approach a fallen woman was even more risky.
    2. Then, to drink from her cup was defilement!
    3. Jesus chose to risk it all to reach out to her.
  C. Finally, His actions were *compassionate*.
    1. He "looked beyond her faults and saw her need."
    2. He offered her forgiveness, eternal life, living water.
    3. The journey, the risks, and the conversation lay bare the pulsating heart of the Savior—in Jesus' eyes no one is insignificant.

III. WE, LIKE JESUS, SHOULD SEE NO ONE AS INSIGNIFICANT
  A. Jesus goes out of His way to reach those the world despises.
    1. He relentlessly purses the lost (Lk 3:10).
    2. That's what the gospel means—God pursues sinful humanity.
    3. Jesus pursues us because in His eyes, everyone is of eternal value—no one is insignificant (Jn 3:16).
  B. We must have the heart of Jesus.
    1. Jesus has called us to love those the world deems as insignificant (Phi 2:5-8).
    2. He has called each of us to pray, to give, and to go to them with the good news.

Conclusion and Altar Call
    1. Will you allow the Spirit to work in your heart until you see all people as significant?
    2. Will you commit yourself to reaching them with the love of Christ? Come now!

[SP]

39 The Seeking God

Sermon in a Sentence: We must join God in His mission of seeking the lost and blessing the nations.
Sermon Purpose: That the people of God commit themselves to God and His mission.
Text: Genesis 3:6-9, 15
Introduction
1. In our text God calls out to Adam and Eve, asking them, "Where are you?"
2. God asks them this question, not for His sake, but for theirs.
3. He wanted them to consider their fallen condition and their broken relationship with Him.
4. Even today, God is pursuing lost humanity, seeking to repair the broken relationship between Him and the ones He loves.

I. **GOD'S QUESTION TO ADAM AND EVE**
   A. God asks the fallen couple, "Where are you?"
   B. He had created them good and perfect…
   C. …however, with the entrance of sin, problems began (Ge 3:1-7).
      1. Adam and Eve were ashamed and hid from God (v.8).
      2. Yet, God pursued them, calling out, "Where are you?" (v.9).

II. **THE MISSIONAL SIGNIFICANCE OF GOD'S QUESTION**
   A. The story of Adam and Eve exposes the human predicament.
      1. Mankind is fallen, filled with shame, and hiding from God.
      2. It also shows the compassionate, seeking nature of God.
      3. We run and hide; He *loves* us, *searches* for us, *brings* us back to Himself, *clothes* us, and *restores* us.
   B. One reason God loves us is because He created us.
      1. We are created in the image of God (the *imago Dei*).
      2. And because all people are created in His image…
         a. …all people have *value*.
         b. …all people are *accountable* to Him.
         c. …all people are *capable* of responding to the gospel.
         d. …all people are *competent* to declare the gospel.
   C. However, because all of humanity is in a fallen state, we all desperately need a Redeemer—a Savior.

D. God's question also sets the stage for the rest of the Bible.
   1. It introduces a concept known as the *missio Dei*.
   2. The *mission Dei* (or mission of God) is the central concept that binds the entire biblical text together.

III. UNDERSTANDING THE MISSION OF GOD
A. What then is the *mission of God?*
   1. The *mission of God* is the unrelenting action of the Creator to call His creation back to Himself and to bless all nations.
   2. It is God pursuing His lost creation.
   3. In missions, we wrongly tend to focus on ourselves, but ultimately mission is not about us, it is about God.
B. It is helpful for us to distinguish between *mission* and *missions*.
   1. *Mission* primarily refers, not to our actions, but to God's.
   2. *Missions* is our obedient response to—and passionate participation in—the *mission of God.*
C. Genesis 3:15 shows how God responds to our sin and rebellion.
   1. It demonstrates the *missio Dei* in action.
   2. It is often called the *protoevangelium*, or "first gospel."
   3. Notice what God did in this verse:
      a. He promises redemption through a coming "offspring"
      b. It is a promise of Jesus, the "seed of woman" (Ge 3:15), the "seed of Abraham" (Ge 26:4).
      c. It is a promise of Christ's coming, His death, His resurrection, and His ultimate victory over sin and Satan.
D. This helps us to understand that the gospel is not primarily about our finding God; it is about God pursuing us.
   1. God is relentlessly on a mission to redeem every man, woman, boy, and girl on earth to Himself.
   2. God now calls us to join Him in His mission of pursuing the lost and blessing the nations.
   3. We must join Him in his cry to the lost, "Where are you?"

Conclusion and Altar Call
1. Come now and commit yourself to God's mission.
2. Come and be empowered by the Spirit.

[SP]

40 The Heartbeat of God for Lost People

Sermon in a Sentence: We must share God's heartbeat for the lost, and we must act on that belief.
Sermon Purpose: That the people will commit themselves to joining God in His mission to reach the lost.
Text: Matthew 9:35-38
Introduction
1. How important is missions to God? How important is it to you?
   a. Missions was so important to God that He sent His Son to die on the cross for all people (Jn 3:16).
   b. Missions is the reason Jesus founded the church—to advance His mission in the earth.
   c. Missions is the tangible expression of God's love and heartbeat for all people to be saved.
2. Now, through missions, God calls on us to join Him in His mission to redeem the lost.
   a. Jesus was doing His part to fulfill God's mission when He came to earth, died on the cross and rose again.
   b. He told the Father, "I have brought you glory on earth by completing the work you gave me to do" (Jn 17:4).
   c. Now he has called us to participate in that mission.
3. From our text we learn three important lessons about missions:

I. WE LEARN ABOUT THE COMPASSION OF THE SHEPHERD
A. In our text, Jesus saw the people as being "harassed and helpless, like sheep without a shepherd" (v.36).
   1. He does not see people as statistics—He rather sees each person with eyes of compassion, like a faithful shepherd.
   2. He is "the good shepherd...[who] lays down his life for the sheep" (Jn 10:11).
B. Jesus told a story illustrating his heartbeat for the lost...
   1. Tell the story of the lost sheep (Lk 15:3-7).
   2. The shepherd was more concerned with the one who was lost than the 99 who were safely in the fold.
C. We must be like the Good Shepherd.
   1. It is easy to care for those we know, who are like us—It is more difficult to care for those who are unlike us, far away from us, and of a different culture or race.

2. However, we must be like Jesus and care for all people—even those we do not understand.

II. WE LEARN ABOUT HIS CONCERN FOR THE HARVEST
   A. In our text, the metaphor shifts from sheep without a shepherd to an un-reaped and undermanned harvest (v.37).
      1. The harvest was *un-reaped:* "The harvest is plentiful…"
      2. It was un-reaped because it was *undermanned:* "The laborers are few."
   B. Jesus wanted to His disciples to join Him in the ministry He was already doing. (Read Mt 4:23.)
      1. His mission was to become their mission.
      2. He told them, "Come, follow me…and I will make you fishers of men" (Mt 4:19).
      3. He later commissioned them, "Go…" (Read Mk 16:15).
      4. They were to go *any place,* at *any price,* to reach *any person.*
   C. That mission is now our mission too!
      1. Read Mt 24:14: "This gospel of the kingdom…"
      2. He has promised us power to complete the mission (Ac 1:8).

III. WE LEARN ABOUT HIS CALL FOR MORE WORKERS
   A. Now (in our text) Jesus pleads for more workers.
      1. He says, "Ask (pray) the Lord of the harvest, therefore, to send out workers into his harvest field" (v.38).
      2. Literally, "Ask *the Lord who is harvesting* to send out more workers so that the harvest is not lost."
      3. Again, He calls us join Him in His mission.
      4. This is why we are to send missionaries to the unreached people and places of Africa and beyond.
   B. We do this for at least three reasons:
      1. Because Jesus commanded us to "preach the gospel" and "make disciples" of all nations (Mk 16:15; Mt 28:19).
      2. Because someone must go and others must send before people can hear and be saved (Ro 10:13-15).
      3. Because He has promised to empower us to get the job done (Luke 24:49; Ac 1:8).

Conclusion and Altar Call
   1. Now is God's time for us to work together to gather the world's unreached harvest of lost people.
   2. Come now and commit yourself to God's mission. [GC]

41 Missions, the Heart of God

Sermon in a Sentence: Missions is at the center of God's heart.
Sermon Purpose: That the people will come to share God's heart for missions.
Texts: Matthew 28:18-20; Acts 1:8
Introduction
1. Missions is no human enterprise; it is not a modern idea or invention. It did not begin in the heart of a man, or even in the heart of one of the Lord's greatest apostles. The source of missions was God Himself.
2. The missionary heart of God is the supreme revelation of His nature and the ultimate expression of His love.
    a. Missions comes from the Latin word *missio,* "to send"
    b. God sent His Son to save the world (Jn 3:16-17).
3. God has now transferred His mission to us—we must fulfill it.
    a. Jesus: "You will be my witnesses…" (Ac 1:8)
    b. Jesus: "Go and make disciples of all nations…" (Mt 28:19).
4. God's great heart for missions can be seen in four ways:

God's great heart for missions can be seen in…
I. THE "COMMISSIONS" HE GAVE TO HIS PEOPLE
  A. He "commissioned" the Old Testament patriarchs:
   1. He called *Abraham* so that through his seed "all peoples on earth will be blessed." (Read Ge 12:3; 26:4; ref. Ga 3:16.)
   2. He called *Israel* to become a "kingdom of priests" (Ex 19:6).
      a. Israel was to reveal Jehovah God to the Gentile nations.
  B. He revealed His plan to kings and prophets:
   1. He made a covenant with King David (2Sa 7:11-13).
      a. That He would establish David's throne forever.
      b. Fulfilled in Jesus, the Son of David (Mt 1:1; Lk 1:32)
   2. He inspired the prophets to speak to the Gentile nations.

God's great heart for missions can be seen in…
II. HIS LOVING CONCERN FOR THE GENTILE NATIONS
  1. In the OT, God reached out to pagans—and they served Him.
      a. Jethro, the father-in-law of Moses, a Midianite (Ex 18:8-12).
      b. Ruth, the Moabitess woman (Ru 1:16-17).
      c. Rahab, the harlot of Jericho (Josh 6:25; He 11:31).
      d. Naaman, the Syrian army commander (2Ki 5:15).
  2. Old Testament kings and prophets testified to the Gentiles.

      a. Joseph told the Egyptians about Jehovah God.
      b. David testified to the Philistines.
      c. Jonah preached to the Assyrians (Jonah 3:4-5).

God's great heart for missions can be seen in...
III. THE LIFE AND MINISTRY OF JESUS
  A. He was the Messiah for all peoples.
    1. There are four Gentile women in His genealogy (Mt 1:3-6):
      (a) Tamar a Canaanite woman, (b) Rahab another Canaanite, (c) Ruth a Moabitess, and (d) Bathsheba a Hittite
  B. The gospel is the good news that Jesus came, died on the cross for the sins of all people, and made the way that everyone can be restored to fellowship with God (1Co.15:1-4).
    1. Jesus is the "Savior of the world" (Jn 4:42; 1Jn 4:14).
    2. Through faith in Him any person, of any tribe, in any place can be reconciled to God (Ro 3:21-26).

God's great heart for missions can be seen in...
IV. THE MISSION OF THE NEW TESTAMENT CHURCH
  A. Jesus has commissions His Church to be His witness "to all nations" and "to the ends of the earth."
    1. Read Mt 28:18-20.
    2. Explain Acts 1:8.
  B. The mission will be accomplished:
    1. The gospel "will be preached in the whole world as a testimony to all nations, and then the end will come" (Mt 24:14).
    2. This will happen in spite of tribulations, wars, persecutions, natural disasters, or any other thing (Mt 24:4-12).
  C. Jesus has promised His Church power to accomplish the mission
    1. "But you will receive power when the Holy Spirit comes on you; and you will be my witnesses in Jerusalem, and in all Judea and Samaria, and to the ends of the earth" (Ac 1:8).

Conclusion and Altar Call
    1. Come and join your heart with God's great missionary heart.
    2. Come and be cmpowered by the Holy Spirit.

                                                                                    [WS]

42 Four Great Facts about the Harvest

Sermon in a Sentence: As God's missionary people, we must commit ourselves fully to God's last-days harvest.

Sermon Purpose: That Christians will commit themselves to reaching the lost at home and around the world.

Text: Matthew 28:18-20

Introduction
1. We have just read Jesus' "Great Commission."
   a. Fulfilling this commission must remain the number one priority of the church.
2. Christ never intended for evangelism (the harvest of souls) to take place inside the church building.
   a. Just as a farmer's harvest does not take place inside the barn.
   b. Such a flawed strategy is surely a recipe for failure.
   c. Authentic NT evangelism occurs out where the people are.
3. This message: Four Great Facts about the Harvest:

I. WE HAVE THE GREATEST STORY EVER TOLD
A. Without doubt, the story of Jesus is the greatest story ever told.
   1. The writer of Hebrews refers to the gospel story as a message of God's "great salvation" (He 2:3).
   2. Advertisers often push inferior products with fantastic claims.
   3. But, the message of Christ is the greatest story ever told.
   4. It is the story of God's great love for humanity (Jn 3:16).
B. We must declare this great message to the nations.

II. WE HAVE A GREAT COMMISSION FROM CHRIST
A. Jesus left His church with a "Great Commission."
   1. Read and comment on Mt 28:18-20.
   2. A truly "Great Church" is a "Great Commission Church."
      a. That is, a church whose members are committed to sharing the story of Jesus with everyone everywhere.
B. Jesus has promised the Spirit's power to aid us in fulfilling the Great Commission. (Read Ac 1:8.)
   1. The early church experienced that great power.
   2. They then went everywhere preaching with great success
      a. It happened first at Pentecost (Ac 2:1-4; then 40-41, 47).
      b. It happened again in Jerusalem (Ac 4:31-33).
      c. It happened in Philip's ministry (Ac 8:5-8).
   3. We must receive that same power today.

III. WE HAVE A GREAT AUDIENCE WAITING TO HEAR THE MESSAGE

A. John spoke this great audience in Revelation 7:9.
 1. He looked into the future and saw a "great multitude" in heaven—the redeemed from all nations.
 2. We are now focused on harvesting this great audience.
    a. Our task is to reap the unreached nations before Jesus comes again (Mt 24:14).
    b. They live next door and to "the ends of the earth."
B. When Jesus saw the multitudes, He urged His disciples to pray for the harvest.
 1. Read and comment on Mt 9:35-36 and Jn 4:35.
 2. We must go into the "highways and the hedges" and compel them to come in (Lk 14:23).
 3. We must send missionaries to the nations (Ro 10:13-15).

IV. THERE IS A GREAT NEED FOR WORKERS IN THE HARVEST

A. Jesus spoke of this great need. (Read again Mt 9:37-38.)
 1. He took note of the harvest: "The harvest is plentiful…"
 2. He recognized the need: "…but the workers are few."
 3. He issued an order: *Pray for workers!*
B. God is calling for workers in the harvest.
 1. His priority must become our priority.
 2. We must see what Jeremiah saw (Je 8:20)—And we must weep for the people as he wept for them (Je 9:1).
 3. And, we must be like the Good Samaritan who stopped what he was doing to care for a dying man (Lk 10:33).
 4. "As the Father has sent me, I am sending you" (Jn 20:21.)
C. We must all pray, give, and go
 1. We must all *pray*—for the lost, for missionaries.
 2. We must all *give*—for evangelism and missions.
 3. We must all *go*—some next door, other to the nations.

Conclusion and altar call
 1. We must not fail in this crucial hour of need.
 2. Come now and commit yourself to God's great last-days harvest.

[GC]

43 Committed to the World

Sermon in a Sentence: Christ is calling us to preach the gospel to "other towns," that is, to the world's unreached places.
Sermon Purpose: That the people will commit to going to the world's unreached peoples and places.
Text: Luke 4:40-44
Introduction
1. Jesus said, "I must preach the good news of the kingdom to *other towns* also, because that is why I was sent" (v.43).
   a. He was sharing His attitude toward His ministry.
   b. He was telling *why* He was sent and *what* He was sent to do.
2. Jesus' disciples adopted this same attitude toward ministry.
   a. They obeyed His command: "As the Father has sent me, I am sending you" (Jn 20:21).
3. They lived out Jesus' model—They packed their bags and went everywhere preaching the gospel. (For example…)
   a. Philip went to Samaria and preached Christ (Ac 8:2).
   b. Peter went to western Judea (Ac 9:32-43).
   c. Paul went to Cyprus, Asia Minor, Europe, Rome, and to "the regions beyond" (Ac 13-28; 2Co 10:16, KJV).
4. This message: Three reasons why we, like Jesus and the early disciples, must go to "other towns" and places:

We must go to "other towns"…
I. BECAUSE THOSE WHO HAVE NEVER HEARD ARE LOST
A. We must get back to the basics of the gospel. (Including…)
   1. Those without Christ are eternally lost (Jn 3:18, 36).
   2. Christ is the only way to eternal life (Jn 14:6; Ac 4:12).
   3. People must be born again to be saved (Jn 3:3).
   4. If we don't tell them, they will remain lost (Ro 10:14).
B. We must beware of the subtle universalism that has crept into our churches. (Note: universalism it the unbiblical belief that in the end everyone will be saved.)
C. Our knowledge of the truth must drive us to respond.
   1. It should drive us to *pray*.
      a. If we don't pray, the work of God will suffer.
      b. If we do pray, demonic forces will be defeated—nations will hear—people will be saved.
   2. It should drive us to *give* and *go*.

We must go to "other towns"...
II. BECAUSE IT IS THE MANDATE OF THE MASTER
  A. Our Commander-in Chief has commanded, "Go into all the world and preach the gospel to all creation" (Mt 16:15).
   1. Our Master's mandate in nonnegotiable.
   2. The command is too plain to be misunderstood.
  B. We must go, no matter what the cost—or the sacrifice.
   1. Throughout the world, Christian martyrs are dying.
   2. Are we, like Paul, willing to die for the gospel? (Ac 20:24).
  C. The command of Jesus remains—as does His power.
   1. He has "all authority in heaven and earth" (Mt 28:18).
   2. As we go in His name, we go with His authority:
      a. Mk 16:16: "In my name they shall cast out demons…"
      b. Jn 14:14: "If you asking anything in my name…"
   3. Let's boldly go to "other towns"—to the ends of the earth.

We must go to other "towns"...
III. BECAUSE, LIKE JESUS, WE EXIST FOR THIS REASON
  A. Note Jesus' words: "That is why I was sent" (Lk 4:43).
   1. In other words, Jesus was sent to "seek and to save" the lost in every place in all the world (Lk 19:10).
   2. We have been sent to do the same (Mk 16:15; Ac 1:8).
  B. We must go to the nations because we have been "called into the kingdom for such a time as this" (Est 4:14, KJV)
   1. Africa has a great missionary destiny.
   2. Now is Africa's time (Ps. 68:31).
   3. God is pouring out His Spirit on the Assemblies of God in Africa for a great missionary purpose (Ac 1:8; 2:17-18, 21).
  C. We must receive the Spirit and move out in Pentecostal power.
   1. The revival is here—and it is increasing.
   2. It is a revival of Pentecostal missions!
   3. Let's not miss the hour of our visitation! (Lk 19:45).

Conclusion and Altar Call
  1. Come and commit yourself to going to "other towns."
  2. Come and be filled with the Spirit.

[LT]

44 Kingdom Treasures

Sermon in a Sentence: We have a great kingdom treasure in Christ, and we must gladly share Him with all people.
Sermon Person: That the people commit themselves to sharing the gospel with the lost at home and around the world.
Text: Matthew 13:44
Introduction
1. Imagine an African man crossing a field. Something catches his eye. He discovers a small box of very valuable coins. He knows, however, that whoever owns the field also owns what is in it. So, he thinks to himself, "I must buy this field, but how can I afford it?" He decides to sell everything he has to buy the field. "Then," he says, "The treasure in the field will also be mine."
2. Discovering great treasure changes everything.
   a. In this parable, Jesus is teaching that finding the Treasure, that is, salvation in Christ, will change how we live and what we do with our lives.
   b. The treasure becomes our passion in life.
3. From this story, we learn about two amazing "kingdom treasures":

I. THE JOY OF DISCOVERING THE TREASURE
A. The greatest happiness in this life is the joy of discovering Jesus.
   1. He is the greatest treasure of all.
   2. Upon finding Him, all else fades into insignificance.
   3. Paul described salvation in Christ as "God's indescribable gift!" (2Co 9:15).
B. Once we discover Him, we are ready to sell all to obtain Him.
   1. We are like Peter who testified, "[Lord] we have left all we had to follow you!" (Lk 18:28).
   2. Will you sell all and follow Christ today?
C. Yet an even greater truth is that *Christ has found us.*
   1. Illustration: Jesus is like the Shepherd who sought for and found the lost sheep (Lk 15:4-6).
   2. When this happens, heaven rejoices! (v.7).
   3. You can find Christ today if you will come to Him, repent of your sins, and follow Him.

II. THE JOY OF SHARING THE TREASURE
  A. Along with the joy of discovering the treasure is the joy of sharing it with others.
   1. Jesus taught, "It is more blessed to give than to receive" (Ac 20:35).
   2. This applies to the indescribable treasure of salvation.
  B. We must not miss the great missionary principle here…
   1. …Out of a deep gratitude for having found the treasure, we want to share it with others.
   2. Jesus told His disciples, "Freely you have received, freely give" (Mt 10: 8).
   3. Illustration: Tell the story of the four lepers (2Ki 7:3-9). From this story we learn three great lessons:
      a. In Christ, we have been provided a great feast.
      b. And yet, others are starving without spiritual food.
      c. We are under obligation to share what we have found.
   4. The joy of giving must be taken a step beyond verbally sharing the good news:
      a. We are owners of nothing but stewards of everything
      b. We must therefore be willing to share our *time,* our *talent,* and our *treasures* with those in need.
  C. Our sharing includes our finances.
   1. The Bible teaches that there is a fundamental connection between our faith and our finances.
   2. God sees the two as inseparable.
      a. Read Matthew 6:19-21 noting the phrase "where your treasure is, there your heart will be also."
      b. Paul also taught this same principle. (Read 2Co 9:6-7.)
   3. We must be willing to give all so others can have the treasure of Christ's salvation too.

Conclusion and Altar Call
   1. Jim Elliott, who died trying to reach the Auca Indians in Ecuador wrote in his journal "He is no fool who gives what he cannot keep to gain what he cannot lose."
   2. Come commit your life and finances to reaching the lost.

[JS]

45 The Priority of the Harvest

Sermon in a Sentence: Like Jesus, we must place a priority on the harvest of lost souls.
Sermon Purpose: That people will commit themselves to the harvest.
Text: John 4:27-35
Introduction
1. The story of the Woman at the Well teaches us much about Jesus and His mission. (Tell the story: Jn 4:3-35.)
2. The disciples were concerned about earthly matters (food for their stomachs); Jesus was concerned about eternal matters (doing the will of His Father).
   a. They urged Him to eat (verse 31).
   b. Jesus refused, saying "My food is to do the will of him who sent me and to finish his work" (v.34).
   c. Jesus was teaching His disciples about the harvest.
3. From this passage we learn three important "harvest principles":

I. THE PRIORITY OF THE HARVEST (Read v.34)
A. Jesus' priority was higher than His disciples':
   1. The disciples were focused on present, physical needs—how to fill their empty stomachs. Jesus was focused on eternal needs—how to fill empty hearts.
   2. Jesus: "My food is to do the will of him who sent me" (v.34)
   3. Food is important, but what is most important is the eternal souls of people.
B. Like Jesus, we must focus on what is eternally important.
   1. We must prioritize our time, talent, and treasure, focusing our lives on the harvest of souls.
   2. Jim Elliott died as a missionary martyr. He prayed "Lord release me from the tension of the grasping hand."
   3. Will you join me in praying that prayer?

II. THE PRESSURE OF THE HARVEST (Read v.35)
A. Jesus reminded His disciples of the harvest.
   1. Jesus wanted the disciples to see clearly: "I tell you, open your eyes and look at the fields! They are ripe for harvest."
   2. Harvest time is a time of pressure.
B. This "pressure of the harvest" is related to three things:

1. *Time:* Jesus told His disciples, "You have a saying, 'Four months until the harvest.'"
    a. The disciples lived as though the harvest was delayed.
    b. So Jesus used this proverb to reveal their laxity in reaping the harvest.
    c. Jesus was saying, "The time is now!" (v.36).
2. *Truth:* Jesus shared truth with the woman (vv.21-24).
    a. People must hear the truth (Jn 8:32).
    b. Jesus: "Salvation is found in no one else, for there is no other name…by which we must be saved" (Ac 4:11).
    c. We must declare the truth about Jesus to all (Jn 4:16).
3 *Travail:* Jesus spoke of the work (or travail) of the harvest (vv.34, 38).
    a. We are to strive to reach out to the suffering people of Africa (and other places) with the compassion of Christ.
    b. The lostness of man should lead us to travail in intercession and loving action for them.

C. Jesus is our example of how we must respond to the pressure of the harvest: He said,
    1. "As long as it is day, we must do the works of him who sent me. Night is coming, when no one can work" (Jn 9:4).
    2. Jesus lived, loved, and labored as no other.
    3. Like Him, we must work tirelessly in the harvest field.

III. THE PLEASURE OF THE HARVEST (vv.36)

A. Jesus took pleasure in the harvest (v.34).
    1. "My food (pleasure) is to do the will" of the Father (v.34).
B. And He promised reward to those who work in the harvest (v.36).
    1. Notice that the sower and reaper "may be glad together."
    2. Great satisfaction comes from doing God's will.
C. When we work in the harvest, we join the early pioneers who sowed the seeds of the gospel to Africa and the nations.
    1. They sowed the seed, we are now reaping the harvest.
    2. Someday we will rejoice together in heaven (Ps 126:6 KJV).

Conclusion and Altar Call

1. The cry of the harvest is "Now is the time to reap!"
2. Come, and commit yourself to working in God's last-days harvest of souls.

[JS]

~ Section 4 ~
The Holy Spirit and Missions

46 The Pentecost Question

Sermon in a Sentence: To fully participate in God's mission, we must all be able to answer "Yes!" to the "Pentecost Question."

Sermon Purpose: That believers may be empowered by God's Spirit to effectively participate in God's mission.

Text: Acts 19:1-10

Introduction
1. In our text, Paul asks a thought provoking question: "Did you receive the Holy Spirit when you believed?" (v.2).
2. This is a question every disciple needs to ask himself today.
3. It is essential, however, that we understand why Paul asked the twelve Ephesian disciples this question.
4. We must each ask ourselves this "Pentecost Question" for four important reasons:

I. BECAUSE THE HOLY SPIRIT GIVES US POWER TO DO THE WORK OF GOD EFFECTIVELY

A. When Paul entered Ephesus, he must have remembered Jesus' promise of power. (Read Ac 1:8.)
  1. Jesus promised power to witness in Jerusalem, Judea, Samaria, and "to the ends of the earth."
  2. In Acts, Ephesus was part of "the ends of the earth."
B. Paul thus entered Ephesus with an objective—to reach that great city—and all of Asia Minor—with the gospel. (Read v.10).
  1. He asked the question because he wanted to know if the 12 disciples were ready to help him fulfill this objective.
  2. To do this, they needed to be empowered by the Spirit.
C. Today, the power of Pentecost will help us do the work of God more effectively:
  1. It will cause us to *witness* with power (Ac 1:8; 4:31, 33).
  2. It will help us to *pray* with power (Ro 8:26-27).
  3. It will enable us to *live* in holiness (Ro 8:1-5).

II. BECAUSE THE PROMISE OF THE SPIRIT'S POWER IS FOR EVERY PERSON OF EVERY AGE UNTIL JESUS RETURNS

A. Peter made this clear in his Pentecost declaration.
  1. Read Ac 2:38-39.
  2. The promise is for "all who are far off—for all whom the Lord our God will call." (v.39).

B. This means that the promise is for each of us today,
   1. If you are saved, you need the promised power of God.
   2. Paul's question to the 12 disciples applies to you too: "Did you receive the Holy Spirit when you believed?"

III. BECAUSE THE QUESTION APPLIES TO THE CHURCH TODAY
A. Just as did the church in Acts, the church today needs the Spirit's power to be effective witnesses to those around us.
   1. Jesus needed the Spirit's power (Lk 4:18; Ac 10:38).
   2. The apostles needed the Spirit's power (Ac 2:33).
   3. We need the Spirit's power (Ac 1:8).
B. We must therefore emphasize Spirit's empowering today.
   1. This is what Paul was doing in Ephesus.
   2. If we fail to do this, our churches will become weak and powerless, "having a form of godliness, but denying the power thereof" (2Ti 3:5 KJV).

IV. BECAUSE THE GIFT OF THE HOLY SPIRIT HAS THE POWER TO CHANGE A PERSON'S LIFE FOREVER
A. It will change your life's priorities.
   1. God's agenda (missions) will become your agenda.
   2. Your priority will be to speak about the kingdom of God.
B. You will begin to do things that you never did before:
   1. You will share your faith with others (Ac 4:20).
   2. You will begin to do the works of Jesus (Jn 14:12-18).
   3. You will participate in the missions program of the church.
C. To receive the Holy Spirit today, do this:
   1. Ask in faith (Lk 11:9, 13).
   2. Receive by faith (Lk 11:10; Mk 11:24).
   3. Speak in faith (Ac 2:4).

Conclusion and Altar Call
1. So, I ask you again, "Did you receive the Holy Spirit when you believed? Would you like to receive Him today?"
2. Come now and be empowered as Christ's witness.

[LB]

47 Spirit-Directed Missions

Sermon in a Sentence: We must to join together and allow God to empower and direct us into His mission.

Sermon Purpose: That people will commit themselves to God and to one another to advance God's mission in the power of the Spirit.

Text: Acts 10:9-48; 11:1-18

Introduction
1. A new reality in the 21st century is that sending churches are becoming receiving churches and receiving churches are becoming sending churches.
2. Missions is now "from all nations to all nations."
3. Based on Peter's ministry to the household of Cornelius, we would do well to make 5 strong missionary commitments:

I. LET THE SPIRIT ADDRESS ISSUES THAT ARE PREJUDICIAL TO THE MISSION OF GOD (Ac 10:9-16).
   A. At Pentecost God used Peter to define the church as a last-days, Spirit-empowered missionary movement (Acts 2:17-18).
   B. Yet in our story, Peter still held prejudices God had to address.
      1. These prejudices could impede the progress of missions.
      2. God showed Peter that he should look down on no one.
   C. Today, God is dealing with the church worldwide to reexamine its "missional prejudices."
      1. "Powerful" national and local churches must not think that their role in the mission is more important than their smaller, "less powerful," brothers and sisters in Christ.
      2. Rather, we must join hands as equal partners, knowing that each stakeholder has something valuable to contribute.

II. LET THE CHURCH NOT CEASE TO GO AS THE SPIRIT BIDS (Ac 10:17-23; 11:1-14)
   A. In Joppa, the Spirit of God challenged Peter not to doubt but to go with certain men from Caesarea because God had sent them.
      1. We too must continue to follow the Spirit's superintendence.
      2. We should never allow our institutional structures to have preeminence over the voice of the Spirit.
   B. We must remain ever open to the Spirit's direction.
      1. The Spirit is calling us, not so much to ecclesiastical debate or theological reflection, but to missional obedience.

2. Illustration: When Peter was quizzed about his actions, his defense was "the Sprit bade me go" (Ac 11:12 KJV).

III. LET THE CHURCH NOT DEPART FROM PREACHING JESUS CHRIST AND KEEPING HIM CENTRAL IN ALL OUR MISSION ENDEAVORS (Ac 10:36-43).
A. Today, there is increasing pressure on the church to emphasize everything else but Jesus Christ and Him crucified.
   1. We are tempted to forsake the centrality of the gospel.
   2. We must not allow our churches to become charitable organizations that fail to proclaim the message of Christ.
B. We must always "keep the main thing the main thing."
   1. We must ever maintain an eternal perspective.
   2. The preaching of the cross must be at the center of all we do.

IV. LET THE CHURCH RECOGNIZE WHY THE SPIRIT IS BEING POURED OUT (Ac 10:44-48; 11:15-16)
A. At Cornelius' house God surprised everyone by pouring out His Spirit in the middle of Peter's sermon (Ac 10:44-46).
   1. Like the Jews at Pentecost, these Gentiles needed God's power to take the gospel to "the ends of the earth" (Ac 1:8).
   2. Anyone capable of receiving the good news is also capable of sharing it with others.
   3. Every place the gospel goes *to,* it must go *from.*
B. We too must emphasis the empowering of the Holy Spirit.

V. FINALLY, LET THE CHURCH KNOW THAT GOD'S GLORY, AND NOT MAN'S, IS THE ULTIMATE GOAL
A. When the elders in Jerusalem heard Peter's report, they "praised God" and said…" (11:18; see Rev. 5:9-10).
B. We too must seek God's glory in all of our endeavors.
   1. Not caring who gets the credit, only that God gets the glory.
   2. Every church, no matter how large or small, has a significant contribution to make for the glory of God.

Conclusion and Altar Call
1. Let's all come and commit ourselves to God and His mission.
2. Let's come and be empowered by His Spirit.

[LC]

48 God's Will for You

Sermon in a Sentence: God wants all of His children to be baptized in the Holy Spirit and witnessing for Him.

Sermon Purpose: That God's people understand their privilege and responsibility of being empowered by the Holy Spirit.

Text: Matthew 8:2-3

Introduction
1. Every father has a loving desire for his children—He wants what is best for each of them.
2. In our text, Jesus demonstrates God's will for His children:
   a. The leper said to Jesus, "Lord, *if you are willing,* you can make me clean."
   b. Jesus answered, "I am willing…be clean!"
   c. God wills to do good for His children.
3. This message: "God's Will for You"
4. To understand God's will, we must know three things:

I. WE MUST KNOW THAT GOD IS A GOOD GOD
A. He is a loving heavenly Father (Lk 11:2).
   1. He desires what is best for His children.
   2. He does not want His children to live like orphans.
      a. Jesus: "I will not leave you as orphans…" (Jn 14:18)
      b. "The Father…will give you another Helper…" (v. 16).
   3. He wants to gives us "good gifts" (Mt 7:11).
B. God not only cares for His children—He cares for all people.
   1. He "causes his sun to rise on the evil and the good" (Mt 5:45).
   2. God is "not willing that any should perish, but that all should come to repentance" (2Pe 3:9).

II. WE MUST KNOW THAT GOD WANTS ALL OF CHILDREN TO BE FILLED WITH THE SPIRIT
A. Your being filled with the Spirit will do you good.
   1. The Holy Spirit will be your best friend and your guide.
   2. He will help you to go forward in your Christian walk.
   3. However, to be led by the Holy Spirit, we must first be baptized with the Spirit.
B. Also, your being filled with the Spirit will also result in good for the lost.

1. You will be empowered as Christ's witness (Ac 1:8).
2. God wants all of His children be Spirit-led witnesses.
3. We are empowered when we are baptized in the Holy Spirit (Ac 1:4-5; 2:1-4).
4. Through the Holy Spirit we can become powerful for ourselves and for the lost people around us.

III. WE MUST KNOW THAT JESUS CARRIES OUT THE WILL OF HIS FATHER

A. It is He who executes the Father's promise of the Holy Spirit.
 1. He is the One who promised the Spirit: "I am going to send you what my Father has promised…" (Lk 24:49)
 2. He prayed to the Father to send the Spirit: "I will ask the Father, and he will give you another Counselor" (Jn 14:16).
 3. He commanded us to be empowered by the Spirit: "He gave them this command: "Do not leave Jerusalem, but wait for the gift my Father promised…" (Ac 1:4-5).
 4. He poured out the Spirit at Pentecost: "…he has received from the Father the promised Holy Spirit and has poured out what you now see and hear" (Ac 2:32-33).
 5. In doing all of this, Jesus is fulfilling the will of the Father.
B. Now, God expects us to ask for the Spirit (Read Lk 11:9-10, 13).
 1. We must *ask in faith:* "Ask and it will be given…" (v.9)
 2. We must *receive by faith:* "Everyone who asks receives" (v.10). See also Mk 11:24: "believe that you have received"
 3. We must *speak in faith:* "All of them were filled with the Holy Spirit and began to speak in other tongues as the Spirit enabled them" (Ac 2:4).

Conclusion and Altar Call
1. The Heavenly Father wants what is best for each of us.
2. And He wants us to be powerful witnesses for Him.
3. Come now to be baptized in the Holy Spirit.

[JTG]

49 Empowered to Speak

Sermon in a Sentence: When God fills us with the Holy Spirit, He expects us to speak by the Spirit.

Sermon Purpose: That believers will be empowered by the Spirit with the sign of speaking in tongues and the result of Spirit-empowered witness.

Texts: Acts 1:8; 2:1-4

Introduction
1. Our first text is Jesus' final promise to His church; the second is the first fulfillment of that promise on the Day of Pentecost.
    a. (1:8) "You will receive power...you will be my witnesses"
    b. (2:4) "They were all filled...and began to speak..."
2. God empowers us by His Spirit so we can speak by the Spirit.
3. This message: Three compelling propositions concerning how and why the Spirit comes upon and fills believers:

I. WHEN THE HOLY SPIRIT COMES, HE FILLS THOSE WHO OF US WHO ARE SEEKING HIM

A. This is what happened at Pentecost.
   1. Jesus promised the Spirit (Lk 24:46-49; Ac 1:4-8).
   2. The disciples obeyed and began to ask for the Spirit (Lk 24:53; Ac 1:14).
   3. At Pentecost, God poured out His Spirit on them (Ac 2:1-4).
B. The same thing happened throughout the book of Acts.
   1. When disciples committed themselves to God's mission and opened their hearts to God's Spirit, He came upon them and filled them (Ac 5:32).
   2. At Pentecost (2:4), Caesarea (10:44-46); Ephesus (19:1-6)
C. God wants to do the same today.
   1. He wants to pour out and fill each of us with His Spirit.
   2. Jesus told His disciples how they could receive the Spirit:
      a. Ask in faith (Lk 11:9-13).
      b. Receive by faith (Lk 11:10; Mk 11:24).

II. WHEN GOD FILLS US WITH THE HOLY SPIRIT, HE EXPECTS US TO SPEAK BY THE SPIRIT

A. This is what happened on the Day of Pentecost (Ac 2:4).
B. The same thing happened throughout Luke-Acts; when people were filled with the Spirit, they began to speak by the Spirit.

1. Elizabeth (Lk 1:41-42); Zechariah (Lk 1:67)
2. Jesus (Lk 4:14-15; 18-19; 12:12-11)
3. Peter (4:8); the Jerusalem church (4:31); Saul (9:17-20); Cornelius' household (Ac 10:44-46); Paul (13:9); the Ephesian disciples (19:6)

C. The same thing should happen today.
1. When God gives us the Spirit, He expects us to speak by the Spirit.
2. This is the primary reason He fills us with His Spirit—that we might powerfully proclaim Christ to the lost (Ac 1:8).
3. When you come forward…
   a. Expect the Spirit to come upon you…
   b. Expect the Spirit to fill you…
   c. Expect to speak as the Spirit gives utterance…
   d. Expect to receive God's power to witness…

III. WHEN WE SPEAK BY THE SPIRIT, WE ARE ENABLED TO SPEAK GOD-INSPIRED WORDS.

A. On the Day of Pentecost, "[they] began to speak in other tongues *as the Spirit enabled them"* (Ac 2:4)
B. This Spirit-enabled speech occurred both in tongues and in the common language.
1. First, the Spirit enabled them to speak in tongues (2:4).
2. Then, the Spirit enabled Peter to speak in the common language and powerfully proclaim the gospel (2:14ff).
3. Both were a fulfillment of Jesus' promise in Ac 1:8.

C. We can expect the same thing to happen today.
1. When you are filled with the Spirit, you will speak in tongues as the Spirit gives the utterance.
2. Then, you will go out and share the gospel with others as the Spirit gives utterance.

Conclusion and Altar Call
1. Come, commit yourself to be Christ's Spirit-empowered witness.
2. Come and be filled with the Spirit.

[EML]

50 The Missionary Signs of Pentecost

Sermon in a Sentence: Each of the three signs of Pentecost has strong missionary implications.
Sermon Purpose: That believers will be filled with the Spirit with a clear understanding of the missional nature of the experience.
Texts: Acts 1:8; 2:1-4
Introduction
1. Describe the outpouring of the Spirit at Pentecost emphasizing the three signs of Pentecost: wind, fire, tongues.
2. It is critical that we understand that the events of Pentecost are a direct fulfillment of Jesus' words in Acts 1:8.
   a. They must therefore be interpreted in light of Acts 1:8.
   b. They therefore have strong missional implications.
3. Let's look at the three signs of Pentecost and their implications for missions:

I. **THE SPIRIT CAME INTO THEIR MIDST AS A "VIOLENT RUSHING WIND"** (Read v.2)
   A. Note how Luke describes the sign as a "sound *from heaven.*"
      1. "Heaven" speaks of its origin—it comes from God.
      2. The ascended Savior poured out the Spirit (Ac 2:32-33).
   B. Luke further describes this sign as a *"violent, rushing* wind."
      1. The Greek word translated *violent* literally means a powerful force that carries things along with it. (Like a mighty cyclone or hurricane.)
      2. The word *rushing* implies urgency, impatience, and determined movement. (Like a man rushing to a meeting.)
      3. This phrase points to the Spirit's determined movement throughout the earth to accomplish the mission of God.
      4. Jesus: "The wind blows wherever it pleases…" (Jn 3:8).
   C. Note what the wind did at Pentecost.
      1. It "filled the whole house where they were staying."
      2. The Spirit came, not only to fill the house, but to fill each of Christ's disciples and propel them to the ends of the earth.
      3. The wind of the Spirit "blows us" with power and purpose.

II. **THE SPIRIT CAME UPON THEM AS "TONGUES OF FIRE"** (Read v.3)
   A. Note how Luke describes the fire of Pentecost:
      1. First a great blazing ball of fire settled over them all.

2. The blaze then divided into 120 "tongues of fire" that "separated and came to rest on each of them."
   B. The tongues of fire at Pentecost have missional implications.
      1. Note that Luke does not refer to them as *"flames* of fire" but as *"tongues* of fire."
         a. This implies that the Holy Spirit had come to set the disciples' *tongues* aflame with the message of Christ.
      2. Note how a flame *"came to rest"* on each of them.
         a. Reminds us of Jesus' words in Acts 1:8: "You will receive power *when the Holy Spirit comes upon you...*"
      3. Note also how the flame came to rest on *"each of them"*
         a. All were empowered to be Christ's witnesses.
         b. Today the Spirit wants to set your tongue aflame…

III. THE DISCIPLES "BEGAN TO SPEAK TONGUES AS THE SPIRIT ENABLED THEM." (Read v.4)
   A. Luke says, they *"began to speak in other tongues as the Spirit enabled them."* (Four observations:)
      1. Unlike the previous two signs, their speaking by the Spirit came *after* (as a result of) their being filled with the Spirit.
      2. Their speaking in tongues was enabled by the Spirit (v.4).
      3. They spoke in Gentile tongues (vv. 5-11).
      4. They were *"declaring* the wonders of God" (v.11).
   B. Missional implications: Their speaking in tongues teaches us about the nature and purpose of baptism in the Holy Spirit:
      1. The baptism in the Holy Spirit is a powerful, God-given experience for all believers (vv. 2, 4).
      2. Its purpose is to empower believers for witness (Ac 1:8).
      3. When you are baptized in (empowered by) the Holy Spirit, you will speak by the Spirit:
         a. First in tongues (v.4; ref. 10:44-46; 19:6).
         b. Then you will speak by the Spirit in the common language proclaiming Christ to the lost.
         c. This is what Peter did at Pentecost (vv. 4, 14)

Conclusion and Altar Call
   1. The baptism in the Holy Spirit is a missional experience.
   2. Come and let the Spirit empower you as Christ's witness.

[DRM]

51 Dependence on the Spirit in Missions

Sermon in a Sentence: To accomplish the task of world evangelization we must depend on the Holy Spirit.

Sermon Purpose: That the people will commit to working together in the power of the Spirit to reach the nations for Christ.

Text: Revelation 3:17-18

Introduction
1. There is a danger of our becoming "self-dependent" in missions.
   a. ...of depending too much on human plans and strategies.
   b. ...of depending on marketing, research, technology, social sciences, and sophisticated fund raising to get the job done.
   c. We must guard against moving in the direction of the Laodicean church. (Read Re 3:17–18.)
2. More than ever in missions, we need the Holy Spirit.
3. We must, therefore, renew our dependence on the Holy Spirit and His empowerment.to fulfill the mission.
4. With this in mind, consider these three missionary proposals:

I. WE MUST SEEK A RENEWED DEPENDENCE ON THE HOLY SPIRIT

A. Many of us have become caught up in the complexities of life...
   1. ...and we have lost an awareness of the Spirit's presence.
   2. Paul exhorts us, "Do not put out the Spirit's fire" (1Th 5:19).
B. We can put out the Spirit's fire in several ways:
   1. ...by failing to recognize His presence.
   2. ...by ignoring His promptings to go or to speak a word.
   3. ...by going on with our plans before hearing His voice.
C. We must repent of our self-centeredness and self-absorption.
   1. We must open our ears to the Spirits voice (Read Is 30:21)
   2. We must surrender our wills to His will.
   3. We must trust the moving and direction of the Holy Spirit.
   4. We must realign with His purposes and priorities to His.
D. The empowering of the Holy Spirit must be at the core of our Pentecostal missions DNA.
   1. Dependence on the Spirit is what makes us what we are.
   2. We must seek a renewed dependence on the Holy Spirit.

II. WE MUST CULTIVATE A RENEWED INTERDEPENDENCE IN THE PENTECOSTAL CHURCH MISSION

A. Carrying out the Pentecostal mission also requires interdependence.
   1. In other words, we must partner with other like-minded people to achieve common goal of world evangelization.
   2. Paul understood the importance of partnership in missions.
      a. For example, he partnered with Apollos (1Co 3:6).
      b. He also partnered with Titus (2Co 8:23).
      c. He further with the Philippian church (Phi 1:3-6).
B. Above all, we must learn to partner with the Holy Spirit.
   1. The Holy Spirit is the impetus of all other partnerships.
   2. It is He who calls, empowers, and directs the mission.
   3. The repeated outpourings of the Spirit in the early years of the Pentecostal Movement created a tsunami of evangelistic efforts resulting in 600 million Pentecostal believers in the world today.
C. Pentecostal partnership builds on the promises of God:
   1. For instance… (Read Joel 2:28-29).
   2. Christ's final promise to the church (Read Ac 1:8.)
   3. We must continually emphasize the baptism in the Spirit as the means of missional empowerment (Ac 2:1-4).
   4. To leverage our mutual efforts for the advancement of the kingdom to the yet-to-be-reached peoples of our world, we must submit to the Spirit's strategy and empowerment.

III. WE MUST ACHIEVE AN INDEPENDENCE FROM THE DISTRACTIONS OF OUR AGE
A. A distraction is something that that amuses or entertains us so that we do not think about the task at hand.
B. Many things can distracts the mission of reaching the lost in the power of the Holy Spirit. (Including the following:)
   1. Satan (2Co 11:14–15)
   2. Judging one another (Mt 7:3-5)
   3. The lure of the world (1Jn 2:16-17; 2Ti 4:10)
   4. Lack of forgiveness (Mt 6:14-15)
   5. Works of the flesh (Ga 5:19-21)

Conclusion
1. The job of world evangelization is too big to do alone; we must depend on one another and on the Holy Spirit.
3. Come, and commit yourself to the mission and to one another.
2. Come and be filled with the Spirit.   [GM]

52 You Will Be My Witnesses

Sermon in a Sentence: We have each been called to be Christ's Spirit-empowered witnesses.

Sermon Purpose: That believers will be baptized in the Holy Spirit and become effective witnesses for Christ.

Text: Acts 1:8

Introduction
1. Our text reveals the Christian's primary vocation, that is, to be a witness for Christ.
2. Three important truths about being Christ's witnesses:

I. EVERY FOLLOWER OF CHRIST HAS BEEN COMMISSIONED AS CHRIST'S WITNESS
   A. Jesus has called each of us to be His witnesses (Ac 1:8).
   1. Being "His witnesses" means two things:
      a. We are witnesses *for* Christ.
         1) That is, on His behalf…as His agents.
         2) He is the one who sends us to witness.
      b. We are to witness *about* Christ.
         1) He is the subject of our witness (Ac 8:5).
   B. Spirit-empowered witness is a dominant theme in Acts.
      1. Christians are called "witnesses" ten times (e.g., 1:8, 22; 2:32; 3:15; 5:32; 10:39, 41; 13:31; 22:15; 26:16).
      2. The designation "Christian" (Ac 11:26) literally means "one whose vocation it is to bear witness to Christ."
   C. Jesus reveals the *extent* of our witness (Ac 1:8b):
      1. "In Jerusalem" (i.e., at home)
      2. "In Samaria" (i.e. to those "despised" and/or neglected ethnic groups around us)
      3. "To the ends of the earth" (see Mk 16:15; Mt 28:19-20)

II. AT THE HEART OF OUR WITNESS IS CHRIST'S DEATH AND RESURRECTION.
   A. Many today seem to be confused about what message they should be preaching.
      1. They are preaching about many trivial things.
      2. Some are even preaching a false gospel (Ga 1:6-9).
   B. In His command, Christ was clear about what we should bear witness (Read Lk 24:46-48).

1. We are to preach the gospel (Mk 16:15).
2. The gospel is the message Christ's death and resurrection (1Co 15:1-6).

C. The early disciples had no doubt about what they should preach; they preached Christ:
1. The apostles (Ac 2:32; 3:15; 4:33); Philip (Ac 8:4)
2. This message was accompanied by a call to faith and repentance (Ac 2:38-39; Ac 20:21).
3. Paul was determined to preach Christ (1Co 2:2-5).

C. We must not fail to preach this all-important message.
1. It is the only message that will prepare people for heaven (Ac 4:8-12).
2. If you have not repented of your sins and put your faith alone in Christ for salvation, do it now!

III. GOD HAS PROMISED US POWER TO BE HIS WITNESSES

A. He has promised us the power of the Holy Spirit.
1. "You will receive power when the Holy Spirit comes upon you and you will be my witnesses" (Ac 1:8).
2. God freely gives His power to anyone who will obey His command to be His witness (Acts 5:32).
    a. (Note that the context of this verse is obedience to Christ's command to be a witness—vv.27-32.)

B. This power to witness comes through an experience that both John the Baptist and Jesus described as a baptism in the Holy Spirit (Lk 3:16; Ac 1:4-5, 8).

C. You can receive the power to witness today (Acts 2:38-39).

Conclusion
1. Come now and commit yourself to be Christ's witness.
2. Come to receive the Spirit's power:
    a. Ask in faith (Lk 11:9, 13).
    b. Receive by faith (Lk 11:10; Mk 11:24).
    c. Speak in faith (Ac 2:4).
    d. Witness in faith (Ac 4:31).

[DRM]

53 The Spirit Says, "Go!"

Sermon in a Sentence: We must appropriate the Spirit's help as we go out to preach the gospel.

Sermon Purpose: That believers might be filled with the Spirit and dependent on Him as they go and witness for Christ.

Text: Acts 11:12-14

Introduction:
1. The Spirit directed Peter to go to Cornelius' house.
2. Today, the Spirit commands us to go and preach the gospel.
3. The good news is that the Spirit will go with us and help us.

I. TEN WAYS THE SPIRIT HELPS US IN MISSION
   A. The Spirit compels us to *"Go!"*
      1. The Spirit compelled Peter to go to the Gentiles (Ac 11:12).
      2. He still compels God's people to go to the lost.
   B. The Spirit tells us *where* to go.
      1. The Spirit told Peter where to go (Ac 10:19-20).
      2. The Spirit told Paul where to go (Ac 16:6-8).
      3. He will direct us where to go and preach the gospel.
   C. The Spirit tells us *when* to go.
      1. The Spirit told Paul and Barnabas when to go (Ac 13:1-4).
      2. The Spirit will tell us when it is best to start a new work.
   D. The Spirit gives us the *courage* to go.
      1. The Spirit filled the disciples with boldness to preach (Ac 4:31).
      2. The Spirit will give us boldness in face of threats.
   E. The Spirit fills us with *joy* as we go.
      1. He filled the disciples in Antioch, Pisidia, with joy (13:52).
      2. We are strengthened by the Spirit's joy (Ne 8:10).
   F. The Spirit tells us *what to say* when we get to where he sends us.
      1. Our message is "the message of salvation" (Ac 11:13-14).
      2. The Lord will give us the right words to say (Lk 12:11-12).
   G. The Spirit *anoints* the message.
      1. The Spirit anointed Jesus to preach (Lk 4:18-19).
      2. The Spirit anointed Stephen's words (Ac 6:10).
   H. The Spirit *speaks* through us.
      1. The Spirit spoke through the early Christians in tongues and in prophetic words (Ac 2:4, 18; 4:8; 10:46; 19:6).
      2. The Spirit wants to speak through us today.

I. The Spirit *warns* us of danger while in mission.
   1. He warned the church of a coming famine (Ac 11:28).
   2. He warned Paul of coming danger (20:23; cf. 21:4, 11).

II. FOUR WAYS WE CAN APPROPRIATE THE SPIRIT'S HELP IN MISSION
   A. We can be *filled and refilled* with the Spirit.
      1. Jesus has commanded us to be repeatedly filled with the Spirit (Lk 24:49; Ac 1:4-5)
      2. With this infilling comes power to witness (Ac 1:8).
      3. You can be filled and refilled today (Lk 11:9-13).
   B. We can *walk daily* in the Spirit's presence and power.
      1. It is not enough to be once filled with the Spirit—we must learn how to stay full of the Spirit and to daily walk in the Spirit (Ga 5:25).
      2. The early disciples remained full of the Spirit (6:3; 7:55; 11:24).
      3. We too must remain full of the Spirit at all times.
   C. We can *commit ourselves* to prayerful lives.
      1. Jesus and the apostles remained full of the Spirit because they lived prayerful lives.
      2. Jesus was a man of prayer (Lk 5:16; 6:12; 11:1).
      3. The early disciples were people of prayer (Ac 1:14; 6:4; 10:9).
      4. If we are going to remain full of the Spirit, we must commit ourselves to prayer.
   D. We can *remain sensitive* to and *obedient* to the Spirit's voice.
      1. We must keep our hearts open to the voice of the Spirit.
      2. Peter listened to the Spirit's voice (Ac 10:19-20)
      3. The Antioch church listened to the Spirit's voice (13:1-4)
      4. When we hear His voice, we must immediately obey.

Conclusion:
   1. Come now to commit yourself to Christ's mission and to be empowered by His Spirit.
   2. To be filled with the Spirit:
      a. Ask in faith Luke 11:9).
      b. Receive by faith (Luke 11:10; Mark 10:24).
   3. Speak in faith (Acts 2:4).

[DRM]

54 Keep the Fire Burning

Sermon in a Sentence: If we are to effectively participate in God's mission, we must keep the Spirit's fire burning in our hearts.

Sermon Purpose: To encourage believers to be daily filled with the Spirit to prepare themselves to participate in God's mission.

Texts: Leviticus 6:12-13 and 2 Timothy 1:6-7

Introduction
1. God has given us a mission to accomplish (Mk 16:15; Ac 1:8).
2. However, to fulfill that mission, we must keep the flame of the Spirit burning within our hearts.
3. Both the OT and the NT teach us this truth:
    a. In Le 6:12-23 Moses instructs the priests that "the fire on the altar must be kept burning; it must not go out."
    b. In 2Ti 1:6 Paul tells Timothy to "fan into flame the gift of God, which is in you."
4. Let's look more closely at these biblical injunctions to "keep the fire burning."

I. OBSERVATIONS FROM THE OLD TESTAMENT
A. Lessons from the *Tabernacle in the Wilderness*.
   1. When the Tabernacle was dedicated, fire came from God and consumed the burnt offering (Le 9:24, Ex 40:35).
   2. Note four things about this fire from God:
      a. It was a *spiritual* (or God-sent) fire (Le 9:24).
      b. It was a *consuming* fire (Le 9:24).
      c. It involved *sacrifice* (Le 9:18).
      d. It needed to be *maintained* daily (Le 6:8-13).
   3. If we are going to reach the lost for Christ, we too must keep the fire burning in our hearts.
      a. We must look to God as the source of the fire.
      b. We must offer ourselves as living sacrifices to God.
      c. We must let the fire consume our sin and selfishness.
      d. We must maintain the fire of the Spirit in our lives.
   4. The flame burned for 485 years until Solomon's Temple.
B. Lessons from *Solomon's Temple* (2Ch 7:1-2).
   1. At the dedication Solomon's Temple, fire came from heaven and consumed the offering and the glory of the Lord filled the place (2Ch 7:1-2).

2. Here we learn the same lessons as we learned with the Tabernacle: It was a *God-sent* fire, it was a *consuming* fire, it involved *sacrifice*, and it had to be *maintained*.
   3. The temple continued for about 374 years (960-586 BC).

II. OBSERVATIONS FROM THE NEW TESTAMENT
  A. Lessons from the *Day of Pentecost* (Ac 2:1-4):
   1. Tongues of fire sat on each of them (v 3).
   2. They all began to speak in other tongues (v 4).
   3. Notice three things about the fire of Pentecost:
      a. The fire was *from heaven*, that is, from God (v 2).
      b. It was *to empower* them for witness (Ac 1:8).
      c. It was given *again and again* (Ac 4:8, 31; 10:46; 19:6).
  B. Lessons from *Paul* (that he gave to Timothy)
   1. Timothy was Paul's young missionary associate.
   2. Paul told him to fan into flames the gift of the Holy Spirit that was in his life (2Ti 1:6-7).
   3. We still need to fan the flame of the Spirit in our lives.
      a. We must each *commit* ourselves to God's mission.
      b. We must each *be filled* with the Spirit (Ep 5:18).
      c. We must each *maintain* the Spirit-filled walk (Ga 5:25).
  C. How can we keep the flame of the Spirit burning in our lives?
   1. The early church serves as a pattern (Ac 2:42-47).
      a. They devoted themselves daily to God, to one another, to prayer, and to meeting together (vv.42, 44).
      c. They remained focused on the mission (Ac 1:8; 4:20).
      d. They were repeatedly filled with the Spirit (2:4; 4:8, 31).
   2. Look at how God responded to their devotion:
      a. He sent His Spirit upon them (Ac 4:31, 33).
      b. He made them into powerful witnesses (Ac 1:8).
      c. He gave them signs and wonders (Ac 2:43)
      d. The church grew and prospered (v.47).

Conclusion and Altar Call
1. Come, commit yourself to God's mission.
2. Come, be filled with the Spirit.
3. Come, commit yourself to maintaining the fire of the Spirit in your life.

[JN]

55 Compelled by the Spirit to Proclaim the Gospel

Sermon in a Sentence: We are compelled by Christ's love and God's Spirit to advance His kingdom in the earth.

Sermon Purpose: That people will commit themselves to advancing God's kingdom in the power of the Holy Spirit.

Text: Acts 20:17-25

Introduction
1. In our text, Paul declared that he was "compelled by the Spirit" to complete the task of "testifying to the gospel of God's grace."
2. Throughout his life, Paul had allowed the Spirit to work powerfully through him, enabling him to effectively proclaim the gospel to all (Ro 15:18-19).
3. Our text reveals three ways we, like Paul, must allow the Holy Spirit to work in our lives compelling us to proclaim the gospel:

I. THE SPIRIT COMPELS US TO PROCLAIM THE GOSPEL BY IMPARTING TO US THE LOVE OF CHRIST (Ac 20:19-20)

A. Because of the love of Christ he had experienced, Paul was moved to proclaim the gospel (1Tim 1:15-16).
   1. The cross convinced him of Christ's love (Ro 5:8).
   2. He never forgot how Christ had changed his life (Ac 26:19).
   3. The Holy Spirit amplified God's love in his heart (Ro 5:5).
   4. He thus proclaimed the gospel with deep gratitude and with love for Christ and people (Ac 20:19-20).
   5. We must do the same today.

B. Because of the love of Christ, Paul persevered even through great trials (Acts 20:19).
   1. The love of Christ compelled him (2Co 5:14).
   2. The love of Christ sustained him.
   3. Because of this, he never wavered in the face of difficulties.
   4. We, like Paul, must remain full of the Holy Spirit and conscious of the love Christ (Ro 5:5).

II. THE SPIRIT COMPELS US TO PROCLAIM THE GOSPEL BY MOTIVATING US TO FULFIL GOD'S MISSION (Ac 20:24-25)

A. God's mission is to redeem the nations and establish Christ's eternal kingdom in the earth.
 1. This is the hope of the whole world (Re 21:3-5).
 2. This is why the gospel of the kingdom must be proclaimed to all nations (Mt 24:14).
B. The Spirit powerfully motivated Paul to fulfil God's mission.
 1. Jesus gave Paul the task as testifying to the gospel (v.24).
 2. His main goal was to see God's kingdom established (v.25).
 3. He was even willing to give his life (Ac 20:24).
    a. Just as Jesus gave His life.
    b. God's kingdom is worth giving everything, even our lives if necessary.
 4. Like Paul, we must allow the Spirit to work in our lives until we fully commit ourselves to proclaim the gospel to all (Mt 13:44-45, Mk 8:34-35).
 5. Then, we must faithfully proclaim the gospel—and we must remain focused on the goal (Mt 6:33).

III. THE SPIRIT COMPELS US TO PROCLAIM THE GOSPEL BY FILLING US WITH HIS PRESENCE AND POWER
(Read Ac 20:22; Ac 1:8)
A Paul was compelled by the Spirit because he was full of the Spirit.
 1. He received the Spirit soon after his conversion (Ac 9:17).
 2. He immediately began to proclaim the gospel (9:20).
 3. Throughout his ministry Paul remained full of the Spirit and committed to preaching Christ (Ro 15:17-20).
 4. He made it his priority to encourage others to do the same.
 5. For instance, the twelve Ephesian disciples (Ac 19:1-6).
B. Like Paul, we must be empowered by the Holy Spirit in order to effectively proclaim the gospel of Christ (Ac 1:8).
 1. Jesus commanded His apostles not to begin the work until they had been baptized in the Holy Spirit (Ac 1:4-5)
 2. Today each us of can receive the Holy Spirit and be empowered and motivated to proclaim the gospel.

Conclusion and Altar Call
 1. Come, commit yourself to God's mission.
 2. Come and be empowered by the Spirit.

[MRT]

56 Your Power to Witness

Sermon in a Sentence: To fulfil our God-ordained purpose of witnessing for Christ, we must be empowered by the Spirit.

Sermon Purpose: That believers be filled with the Spirit and commit themselves to God's purpose for their lives.

Reading: Luke 24:45-49

Introduction
1. Our text is the Great Commission as presented by Luke.
2. Today, I will be asking four questions prompted by this passage.
3. Then I will call on you to respond.

I. WHAT IS THE PURPOSE FOR WHICH CHRIST HAS SAVED US AND GIVEN US THIS LIFE?
A. Note Jesus' four emphases in Luke 24:45-49:
  1. *Gospel* (v.46) "Christ will suffer and rise from the dead."
  2. *Nations* (v.47) "to all nations, beginning in Jerusalem."
  3. *Witness* (v.48) "You are witnesses of these things."
  4. *Empowerment* (v.49) "stay in the city until…"
  5. (We see the same four emphases in Acts 1:4-8)
B. The purpose for which God has saved us and given us life…
  1. …is that we might be His witnesses, declaring His message to all people everywhere in the power of the Holy Spirit.
  2. *In other words, w*e are called to use Spirit-empowered connections to move all people everywhere towards a relationship with Christ.

II. WHAT DANGER DO WE FACE IN REGARD TO OUR GREAT GOD-GIVEN PURPOSE?
A. The great danger we face is that we may fail to be a witness…*or* that our witness may fail to produce an effective result.
  1. We have been called to change the world by leading the lost to repentance and new life in Christ (2Co 5:17-20).
  2. You may say, "This job is too hard. I cannot do it."
B. However, we must realize that failure witness is, first of all, a failure to be empowered by the Holy Spirit.

III. HOW DOES THE BAPTISM IN THE HOLY SPIRIT HELP US TO WITNESS?
A. The book of Acts consistently presents two consecutive results to being baptized in the Holy Spirit:

1. They spoke in *tongues*—followed immediately by Spirit-*empowered witness.*
2. Throughout Scripture, Holy Spirit-empowerment has *always* resulted in Spirit-enabled speech.
   a. For instance, Moses, Saul, David, Isaiah, Jeremiah, Jesus, Peter, Paul, Stephen, Philip (and more).

B. When you are baptized in the Holy Spirit, you should expect to speak by the Spirit in two ways:
   1. First, you will be empowered to speak by the Spirit in a new language (Ac 2:1-4; 10:44-46; 19:7).
      a. This is a sign that God's Spirit is upon you.
      b. It is further a sign that God has empowered you to speak the message of Christ to the nations.
   2. Next, you will be empowered to speak about Jesus in the language(s) you *already know* (Ac 2:14-18; 4:31).

C. Once filled, Jesus' disciples were empowered by the Spirit.
   1. They were *in the world* (close enough to be seen, heard, admired, scorned, and questioned), yet they were *not of the world* (noticeably different, headed in a divergent direction, witnessing to the miraculous nature of Christ, calling men to faith, repentance, and Spirit-empowerment).

D. God wants to do the same with us today—He wants to empower us to proclaim Jesus' name "to the ends of the earth" (Ac 1:8).

IV. HOW MAY I BE FILLED WITH THE SPIRIT TODAY?
(To receive the Spirit today, do these three things:)
A. *Believe* the promise is for all of God's children—including you!
   1. The only requirements: Be saved…be hungry
B. *Receive* the gift of the Spirit by faith (Mk 11:24).
   1. Christ freely gives, now reach out by faith and take it.
C. *Choose* to speak in faith.
   1. Choose to let your spirit speak to God through you.
   2. Choose to speak the words He gives you.

Conclusion and Altar Call
1. Come now, to commit yourself to be Christ's witness.
2. Come, and be empowered by the Spirit.

[PY]

~ Section 5 ~
# The Call of God

57 Beautiful Feet

Sermon in a Sentence: We have all been called to take the message of salvation to those who are lost and without hope.

Sermon Purpose: To motivate Christians to get involved in reaching the lost at home and in unreached places.

Text: Romans 10:14-15

Introduction
1. Salvation by faith is a major emphasis of Paul's theology.
2. In this passage Paul lays out the doctrine of salvation by faith in chronological order. Salvation by faith requires...
   a. ... a proper *message:* There is no salvation without the gospel
   b. ... a proper *messenger:* The message must be proclaimed by those living in obedience to the faith.
   c. ... a proper *delivery:* The message must be preached with divine authority and in the power of the Spirit.
   d. ... a proper *reception:* The message must be understood.
   e. ... a proper *faith:* The message must be consciously believed and acted upon.
   f. ... a proper *name:* The name of Jesus, by whom alone comes salvation, must be believingly invoked.
3. The result will be redemption—that is, salvation from sin and misery resulting in a life of peace and joy.
4. In our text Paul speaks of three important issues in relation to this salvation by faith:

I. PAUL REVEALS THE UNIVERSAL STATE OF MANKIND—LOSTNESS

A. Lostness is most dreadful of human conditions.
   1. It is the only human condition that keeps people out of heaven.
   2. Throughout history human lostness has resulted in many horrible life situations, including poverty, and injustice.
      a. However, the most dreadful result is an eternity spent in hell separated from God and all goodness.
   3. In the world today, people are suffering in many ways, but these misfortunes will not keep them out of heaven.
      a. Millions of hungry people will die *and go to heaven.*
      b. Millions of sick will die—*and go to heaven.*
      c. Impoverished people will die—*and go to heaven.*
      d. But *no one* who is lost will ever make it to heaven.

B. The most unjust of all injustices is lostness without a choice.
1. Some will have made the choice not to follow Jesus.
2. However, others have never even been given that choice.
3. We have been called to right that injustice.

II. PAUL PROCLAIMS THE ONE SOLUTION TO LOSTNESS—THE GOSPEL
A. The gospel is the message of salvation through Jesus alone.
B. This message must be preached in all the world (Mt 24:14).
1. If people do not know, they cannot be saved (Ac 4:12).
2. Therefore, all must be told (Mk.16:15-16).
B. For the gospel to be preached, missionaries must be sent.
1. God Himself calls and sends (Ac.13:2, 4).
2. However, the church must also send (Ac 13:3; Ro 10:15).
C. Gospel proclamation is the world's greatest expression of justice.
1. It provides salvation for the eternal soul.
2. It also provides "redemptive lift" to a society.

III. PAUL DESCRIBES THOSE WHO GO AND PREACH THE GOSPEL—"BEAUTIFUL FEET"
A. Paul is quoting Isaiah the prophet (Is 52:7).
1. People see soiled, dusty feet as disgusting; God sees them as beautiful—when they are the feet of His messengers.
2. The image is of a herald hurrying toward a group of captive people. He comes with good news from a field of battle: "Deliverance has come!" It is a message of great joy.
B. The physical presence of a messenger of hope in a place of hopelessness is a powerful thing.
1. It represents deliverance and light and dispels darkness.
2. It brings hope and joy.
3. We are God's messengers of hope and life to a dying world.

Conclusion and Altar Call
1. God has called us to be His messengers to the lost.
2. Come now, and commit yourself to that mission.

[GB]

58 Jesus is Calling

Sermon in a Sentence: Just as Jesus called His first disciples to join Him in mission, He calls us today to do the same.
Sermon Purpose: That people might commit themselves to join Christ in His mission to reach the unreached with the gospel.
Text: Mark 3:13-15
Introduction
1. When we think of the call of God, we often think only about pastors, missionaries, and other ministers.
2. Christ, however, calls each of us to join Him in His mission to redeem the nations.
3. In our text today we learn three important lessons about the call of God and our response to that call:

I. JESUS CALLS US TO HIMSELF
A. In our text, Jesus called His disciples to Himself.
   1. v.13 "Jesus went up on the mountain and called to him those whom he desired, and they came to him."
   2. Note how He called them from the masses to Himself.
   3. To join Him, they had to leave where they were to go up the mountain to meet with Him at the top.
B. Today, Jesus calls us to draw near to Him.
   1. Note the phrase, "so that they might be with him" (v.14).
   2. Before Jesus sends us out, He calls us to Himself that so we may develop a deep, personal relationship with Him.
   3. As we draw near to Him, He fills us with His Word, His Spirit, and His vision for a lost world.
   4. This is where all ministry must begin…
   5. To change others, we must first allow God to change us.
C. Being with Jesus gives us a new perspective on life.
   1. We will begin to see the nations as He sees them—as hopelessly lost and in need of a Savior.
   2. Once we see them, we will weep with Him for the lost.
   3. We will gladly take up our cross to follow Him.

II. JESUS IS CALLS US TO JOIN HIM IN HIS MISSION
A. Jesus then appointed some to be "apostles" (v.14).
   1. An apostle is literally "one who is sent."

2. "Apostolic ministry" is therefore being sent to those who have never heard the good news of Christ.
   B. Today, Jesus is calling His followers to join Him in His apostolic mission.
   1. Are you prepared to fully surrendered your life to Christ?
   2. Are you willing to leave where you are and go where He sends?
   C. Jesus calls us that He might send us.
   1. "He appointed twelve…that he might send them" (v.14).
   2. He has blessed us that we might bless the nations.
      a. He has placed His Spirit among us.
      b. He has given us rest and prosperity.
   3 He has done these things so that we might make His name know among the nations.

III. JESUS EMPOWERS US TO ACCOMPLISH HIS MISSION
   A. Note how Jesus further "appointed twelve…to have authority to cast out demons" (v.15).
   1. Jesus did not send them out in their own strength.
   2. And neither will He send us out in our own strength.
   3. Jesus: "All authority in heaven and on earth has been given to me. Go therefore…" (Mt 28:18-20).
   B. Without His power and authority we will fail; however, in the power of the Spirit and the authority of Christ's name, the work will be accomplished (Mk. 3:15; Mt 12:28; Ac 1:8).
   C. We must now go to the battle fully armed and fully committed.
   1. We must commit ourselves to Christ and His mission.
   2. We must "put on the full armor of God" (Ep 6:11-13).
   3. We must be prepared to exercise our God-given authority over "all the power of the enemy" (Lk 10:19).
   4. We must appropriate the Spirit's power to be His witnesses (Ac 1:8).

Conclusion and Altar Call
   1. Today, Jesus is calling. Will you respond?
   2. Come now and say yes to Jesus' call.

[BD]

59 Christ's High Calling to be Fishers of Men

Sermon in a Sentence: Christ calls every Christian to the high calling of being "fishers of men."

Sermon Purpose: That the hearers commit themselves to winning the lost to Christ at home and around the world.

Text: Philippians 3:14; Matthew 4:18 (KJV)

Introduction
1. In our first text (Phi 3:14), Paul spoke of the "high calling" he received from Christ.
2. In our second text (Mt 4:18), Jesus defined that high calling as the call to become "fishers of men."
   a. In other words, we are to become people who will devote ourselves to the vocation of winning souls to Christ.
3. This message: Four reasons Christ's calling to be fishers of men is a "high calling":

I. IT IS A "HIGH CALLING" BECAUSE IT EXCEEDS OUR HUMANLY CHOSEN VOCATIONS

A. There is no higher vocation than winning people to Christ.
   1. This is why Jesus called the disciples from their nets.
   2. This is why they so willing left their nets to follow Him.
B. Today, God has called some to leave their "nets" (their current professions) and devote full time to fishing for men.
   1. Others He calls to remain in their current professions; however, they too must no longer allow that profession to be their great passion in life.
   2. Their great passion must be to become "fishers of men."
C. Either way, following Christ in His mission to redeem the lost must become our life's greatest vocation (Mt 16:24).

II. IT IS A "HIGH CALLING" BECAUSE IT EXCEEDS OUR COMMITMENT TO FAMILY

A. Not only did James and John leave their nets (their profession) to become fishers of men, they also left their father (their family).
B. We must be willing to do the same.
   1. Christ has commanded us to "Go into all the world and preach the good news to all creation" (Mk 16:15).

  2. On another occasion He said, "If anyone comes to me and does not hate his father and mother…" (Lk 14:26-27).
  3. Commitment to this high calling is why men and women leave all and go to the nations to share the message of Christ.
 C. Christ has promised to reward those who obey (Mk 10:29).

III. IT IS A "HIGH CALLING" BECAUSE IT EXCEEDS OUR OWN ASPIRATIONS
 A. Following the high calling of reaching the lost caused Paul to press forward to the very end. (Read Phi 3:12-14.)
  1. He forsook his own aspirations to follow Christ's (Phi 3:4-8)
 B. We too must abandon our "small ambitions" and follow Christ.
  1. Quotation: Francis Xavier, early Jesuit missionary to Asia wrote back to Europe, pleading, "Tell the students to give up their small ambitions and come eastward to preach the gospel of Christ."
  2. We too must be willing to give up our small ambitions to become fishers of men at home and around the world.

IV. IT IS A "HIGH CALLING" BECAUSE IT EXCEEDS OUR ABILITIES
 A. On one occasion Jesus showed His disciples how fishing for men can only be done through God's miraculous power.
  1. Tell the story of the miraculous catch of fish (Lk 5:4-10).
  2. Jesus then promised them, "Don't be afraid; from now on you will catch men" (v.10).
  3. However, they would not do it in their own abilities, but in God's power—as they obeyed Christ's command.
 B. Jesus' has promised us God's power to fish for men.
  1. Jesus' last promise (Ac 1:8): "But you will receive power…"
  2. We receive this power to witness for Christ when we are baptized in the Holy Spirit like the disciples on the Day of Pentecost (Ac 2:1-4).

Conclusion and Altar Call
 1. Come now and commit yourself to be a "fisher of men."
 2. Come now and be empowered by the Holy Spirit.

[JDE]

60. The Savior Who Sends

Sermon in a Sentence: The resurrected Christ empowers us and sends us to fulfill His mission in the earth.

Sermon Purpose: That believers be filled with the Spirit and commit themselves to God's mission.

Text: John 20:19-23

Introduction
1. This passage is John's "Great Commission passage."
2. The night of His resurrection Jesus appears to His disciples who were in hiding for fear of the Jews.
3. He speaks peace to them (vv.19-20).
    a. He is imparting to them God's supernatural *shalom.*
    b. They will need this peace to fulfill their mission.
4. Jesus then commissions His disciples (vv.21-23).
    a. Just as the Father had sent Him, He was sending them.
    b. Today Christ is calling and commissioning us.
5. From this passage we learn that Christ sends us to the world in three ways:

I. CHRIST SENDS US IN RESURRECTION POWER (vv.19-21)
A. Jesus appeared to His disciples on the night of His resurrection.
   1. He is the truth of the gospel revealed…He is alive!
   2. He is the "new and living way" (He 10:20).
B. The death and resurrection of Christ is the heart of the gospel we preach (Ro 10:9; 1Co 1:1, 3-4).
   1. Read 1Co 15:13-19
C. When we go out to preach the good news, we go in Christ's resurrection power.

II. CHRIST SENDS US IN THE SPIRIT'S POWER (vv.21-22)
A. Once Jesus had given His disciples His peace, He commissioned them:
   1. "As the Father has sent me I am sending you" (v.21).
   2. Then He empowered them: "He breathed on [into] them and said, 'Receive the Holy Spirit'" (v.22).
B. We too have been commissioned by Christ to preach the gospel to all creation (Mk 16:15-16; Mt 28:18-20).
   1. We must obey Christ's commission.
   2. He has also promised us His power (Ac.1:8).

- C. The Holy Spirit helps us in many ways:
    1. He awakens our hearts to see missions.
    2. He imparts compassion for those who are perishing.
    3. He causes us to be willing to obey Christ's command.
    4. He breaks down all social and tribal barriers and makes us love all people as Christ loves them (Ro.5:5).
    5. He opens closed doors for the gospel to go through.
    6. He builds our faith to proclaim the gospel with power.
- D. The Holy Spirit also empowers us in the following ways:
    1. He empowers our words to produce a strong effect.
    2. He confirms our words with supernatural manifestations.

III. CHRIST SENDS US OUT IN SALVATION POWER (vv.22-23)
- A. God alone can forgive peoples sins!
    1. Jesus has power to forgive sins (Mk 2:5).
- B. However, we can participate in God's mission of forgiveness.
    1. "If you forgive the *sins* of any, *they* are forgiven" (v.23).
    2. Note how the words "sins" and "they" are in the plural form—meaning the sins of people, not the sins of an individual person.
    3. Jesus sends His church in the power of His Spirit to declare "repentance and forgiveness of sins…in his name to all nations" (Lk 24:46-47).
- C. We must tell the nations that "Jesus saves!"
    1. The harvest is white, ready to be reaped (Jn 4:35).
    2. Let us arise and go!
    3. His presence is with us and His power will help us.

Conclusion and Altar Call
1. Christ sends us in His Power: Resurrection Power, Spirit Power, and Salvation Power.
2. Come now and commit yourself to go to the lost in God's power.

[SE]

61 Blessed to Obey

Sermon in a Sentence: God blesses and calls His people to participate in His mission to bless all nations through Jesus, the seed of Abraham.

Sermon Purpose: That the hearers will commit themselves to fulfilling God's destiny for their lives.

Texts: Genesis 12:1-4, 17:7

Introduction
1. It is a wonderful event when God speaks to a human being.
    a. When He does speak, He always has a purpose.
    b. He has a plan He wants to reveal.
2. In our text, God spoke to Abraham and made a covenant with him known as the "Abrahamic Covenant."
3. In this message we will to examine this covenant.
    a. More specifically we will examine how the obligation of obedience is embedded within the covenant.
    b. Like Abraham, we will learn that we are "blessed to obey."

I. BLESSED TO OBEY
A. God promised to bless Abraham—He also required him to obey.
    1. He told Abraham, "I will bless you" (4 times). (vv.2-3)
    2. He also told him to "Go from your country…" (v.1).
    3. Abraham obeyed and "went, as the Lord told him" (v.4).
    4. He chose to "trust and obey" God to lead him each step of the way.
B. Even today, God blesses His people that they may obey Him and do His will.
    1. Read and Explain Psalm 67:1-7. "God bless us…that your salvation might be known among all nations."
    2. If Abraham had not obeyed God, the Abrahamic Covenant would not have been fulfilled. (Read Ge 22:18 noting the phrase *"because you have obeyed me."*)
    3. God is pleased when we do what He asks us to do; He is displeased when we do not.
    4 Illustration: God was pleased with David (Ac 13:22).
C. When we obey a person, we honor them; when we disobey, we dishonor them.
    1. Abraham honored God by obeying him and "going."
    2. The apostles honored Christ by going to the nations.

3. We too must honor Christ by obeying the Great Commission (Mk 16:15-16) and the Final Command (Lk 24:49).

II. BLESSED WITH A DESTINY
A. Abraham was also blessed with a God-ordained destiny.
   1. He was to be the means through which God would send His Son to provide salvation for all mankind.
   2. In Abraham's "offspring,"—that is, Jesus (Ga 3:16)—"all nations on earth will be blessed" (Ge 22:18).
B. Each of us has been given a God-ordained destiny.
   1. God created each of us, and He has given to each of us a unique task to accomplish while on earth.
   2. We must never forget, however, that our individual destinies are joined to God's great destiny for the nations, that is, that "all peoples on earth will be blessed" (Ge 12:3).
D. We must each dedicate ourselves to fulfilling God's destiny for our lives.
   1. Abraham achieved God's tailor-made plan for his life.
      a. This was reaffirmed by God in Genesis 17:1-7.
      b. Hebrews 11 tells of Abraham's success. (Read vv.8-12.)
   2. As spiritual descendants of Abraham, we too must dedicate ourselves to achieving God's purpose for our lives.

III. BLESSED WITH RESPONSIBILITY
A. Abraham's blessing carried with it a responsibility.
   1. He was to "go to the land" God would show him (Ge 12:1).
   2. He was to share his faith in God with all peoples.
B. As spiritual children of Abraham, we too have been given the responsibility of trusting and obeying God.
   2. Paul wrote the Galatians, "[Christ] redeemed us in order that the blessing given to Abraham might come to the Gentiles through Christ Jesus" (Ga 3:14).
C. Today you are God's "Abraham," called with the responsibility of blessing all peoples and tribes with the good news of Christ.

Conclusion and Altar Call
1. Come now and commit yourself to Christ and His purpose for your life.

[JF]

62 Christ's Sent Ones

Sermon in a Sentence: As Christ's "sent ones," we must commit ourselves to fulfilling His mission in His way.

Sermon Purpose: That believers commit themselves to "go" in the Spirit's power to help fulfill Christ's mission of redeeming the lost.

Texts: John 20:19-21

Introduction
1. On the night of His resurrection, Jesus appeared to His disciples.
   a. They were hiding "for fear of the Jews" (Jn 20:19).
   b. Jesus said to them, "Peace be with you!"
2. He then commissioned them, saying "As the Father has *sent* me, I am *sending* you" (v.21). Then…
3. "He breathed on them and said, 'Receive the Holy Spirit" (v.22).
4. We will focus our thoughts on the small word "sent" in v.21.
   a. "Sent" implies a particular destination and objective.
   b. As Christ was the Father's "Sent One," we are Christ's "sent ones."
5. This message will focus on *how* Christ sends us. But first…

I. HOW DID THE FATHER SEND JESUS?
A. Jesus was sent by God the Father.
   1. "As the Father has sent me…" (v.21).
   2. Because He was sent by the Father…
      a. …Jesus represented His Father (Jn 6:57).
      b. …Jesus was committed to following the Father's instructions (He 10:7).
      c. …Jesus moved in and under the Father's authority and power (Jn 8:28).
   3. Jesus' testimony: "I tell you the truth, the Son can do nothing by himself; he can do only what he sees his Father doing" (Jn 5:19) (See also, Jn 8:42; 12:49; 14:31.)
      a. In Gethsemane: "Not my will, but yours…" (Lk 22:42).
B. The Father sent Jesus with a clear objective.
   1. That God might come near to people by being revealed as a human being (Jn 1:10, 14).
   2. God's plan for Jesus included His death on the cross which provided salvation for all who would put their trust in Him (Jn 3:16; 1Jn 4:14).

II. HOW DID JESUS SEND THE DISCIPLES?
A. God sent Jesus to *provide salvation* for the nations; Jesus sent His disciples to *proclaim salvation* to the nations.
   1. Only Jesus could provide salvation (Ac 4:12).
   2. However, He sent His disciples to proclaim the good news about that provision:
      a. "As the Father has sent me, I am sending you" (v.21).
      b. "Go…and preach the good news" (Mk 16:15).
B. The disciples were commissioned by Jesus and given power and authority to minister as He ministered:
   1. Jesus sent them to fulfill the *same mission* He had—the salvation of the lost at home and to the ends of the earth.
   2. Jesus sent them to proclaim the *same message* He proclaimed—the good news of salvation.
   3. Jesus sent them with the *same authority and power*—the authority of His Name and the power of the Holy Spirit.
C. The disciples then went out and preached the gospel with miraculous signs following (Mk 16:20; Ac 4:33).

III. HOW IS GOD SENDING US TODAY?
A. Jesus is sending us out just as the Father sent Him—and just as He sent His first disciples.
   1. We are to represent Him to everyone, everywhere—our families, friends, neighbors, towns, villages, and to the ends of the earth.
   2. We must obey and go immediately to the work.
B. We are to use the same methods He and His disciples used:
   1. We are to proclaim the gospel in the power of the Spirit.
   2. We are to trust God to confirm the word with signs following.
   3. We are to plant Spirit-empowered missionary churches.

Conclusion and Altar Call
1. Will you accept your commission as an honor from God?
2. Will you commit yourself to Christ and His mission?
3. Will you go, give, and send that all might know Christ?
4. Come now, and commit yourself to Christ and His mission.

[JF]

63 The God Who Calls

Sermon in a Sentence: God still calls His people to participate in His mission.

Sermon Purpose: That God's people will commit themselves to hearing and obeying God's call to go to the nations.

Text: Exodus 3:4-10

Introduction
1. Our text reading tells the story of God's call to Moses to liberate the people of Israel from Egyptian bondage. (Tell story.)
2. From this story, we can glean some important insights concerning God's missionary nature and the way He calls us to join Him in His redemptive mission.
3. Note five statements of intent spoken by God (vv.7, 8, 10).
   a. *"I have indeed seen* the misery of my people..." (v.7).
   b. *"I have heard* them crying out..." (v.7).
   c. *"I am concerned* about their suffering... (v.7).
   d. *"I have come down* to rescue them..." (v.8).
   e. *"I will send you..."* (to Egypt to deliver them) (v.10).
4. These five statements offer five vital insights into God's nature—and about of how and why He calls us today:

I. INSIGHT 1: GOD SEES—HE IS NOT BLIND
   — *"I have seen the misery of my people... "I have seen the way the Egyptians are oppressing them" (vv7-.9).*
   A. God saw the suffering of His people in Egypt (vv.7, 9).
      1. He looked down and saw their need of deliverance.
      2. Illustration: One time, Jesus saw His disciples struggling to survive—so He went to them (Mk 6:48-50).
   B. God still sees today.
      1. Read 2Ch 16:9: "For the eyes of the Lord range..."
      2. God sees the nations who need to be reached for Christ.
      3. He calls on us to do the same (Jn 4:35).

II. INSIGHT 2: GOD HEARS—HE IS NOT DEAF
   — *"I have heard them crying...because of their slave drivers" (v.7)*
   A. We must never forget that God always listens intently to the prayers of His people.
      1. In our text, God heard the cry or the Israelites in bondage.

2. David rejoiced in this truth: "Evening, and morning…will I pray, and cry aloud: and he shall hear my voice" (Ps 55:17).
B. We too must hear the cry of the lost people in our world.
1. They are crying, "Come over…and help us" (Ac 16:9).
2. Jesus' only prayer request: (Mt 9:37-38).

III. INSIGHT 3: GOD CARES—HE IS NOT INDIFFERENT
— *"I am concerned about their suffering…" (v.7)*
A. God not only hears when people cry out to Him, He is ready to answer their prayers.
1. He cared for the suffering Israelites.
2. No one cares more about hurting people than God.
3. He cares for each of the billions of lost people in the world.
B. We too must care for lost and suffering people.
1. We must be like Jesus (Mt 9:36).
2. The Holy Spirit will help us to care (Ro 5:5).

IV. INSIGHT 4: GOD COMES—HE IS NOT FAR
A. In our story, God cared enough to come down Himself.
1. He came to Moses in a burning bush (v.4).
2. The Son of God came down to rescue mankind (Lk 19:10).
3. Paul said, "He is not far from each one of us…" (Ac 17:27).
B. Today, we must follow Christ's example.
1. We must do more than care—we must "go" (v.10).
2. "As the father has sent me, I am sending you" (Jn 20:22).
3. Again: "Go into all the world and proclaim…" (Mk 16:15).

V. INSIGHT 5: GOD CALLS—HE IS NOT MUTE
— *"So now, go I am sending you…" (v.10).*
A. God called and sent Moses (v.10).
1. Throughout the Bible, God called and sent workers.
2. Jesus calls and sends His church (Jn 15:16).
B. Today, God is calling and sending us…
1. …to our neighbors …to the nations.
2. Will you say "yes" to God's call?

Conclusion and Altar Call
1. Come now, and commit yourself to God and His mission.

[JM]

64 Chosen for His Mission

Sermon in a Sentence: As with Paul, God has chosen each one of us to participate in His mission to redeem the nations.
Sermon Purpose: That the listeners be filled with the Spirit and commit themselves to God's mission.
Text: Acts 22:12-21 (Note especially vv.14-15)

Introduction
1. Paul's passion in life was to tell the Gentile nations about Jesus.
2. Tell the story of Paul's capture and message in the temple court in Jerusalem (Ac 21:27-22:21).
3. In the message, Paul speaks of his calling and God-given purpose in life (vv.14-15).
4. From Paul's testimony, we learn 3 important missionary lessons:

I. AS HE DID WITH PAUL, GOD HAS CHOSEN EACH OF US TO KNOW HIS WILL
   A. Paul addressed the mob and explained to them how God had revealed His will to him (vv.14-15).
      1. He told how Ananias had said to him, "The God of our fathers has chosen you to know his will..." (v.14).
      2. Jesus told Paul the same thing (Ac 26:15): "I have appeared to you to appoint you as a servant and as a witness..."
      3. Paul knew that God had chosen him, and he knew why.
         a. Jesus appeared to him in a vision and command Him, "Go; I will send you far away to the Gentiles" (22:21).
      3. This knowledge gave his life direction and purpose.
   B. God wants to do the same with you.
      1. He wants to show you His will for your life.
      2. He has shown you His will in His word—that you fully participate in Christ's mission (Mt 28:18-20).
      3. He will reveal His specific will for your life by His Spirit.
   C. How can you know God's will for your life?
      1. Commit yourself to God and His mission (Ac 9:6).
      2. Then, pray, listen, and obey the voice of the Spirit (Ac 5:32).
   D. It's not enough to *know* God's will, we must *do* God's will.

    1. Jesus said to Paul, *"Go,* I send you away to the Gentiles…"
    2. James 1:22 "Do not merely listen… *Do what it says."*

II. AS HE DID WITH PAUL, GOD HAS CHOSEN EACH OF US TO BE CHRIST'S WITNESS
  A. Paul testifies to how Ananias told him, "You will be [Christ's] witness to all men of what you have seen and heard" (Ac 22:15).
    1. Like Paul, we are called to be Christ's "servant and witness" (Ac 26:16).
    2. Christ commissions us all, "You will be my witnesses…to the ends of the earth (Ac 1:8).
  B. However, before we can be effective witnesses, we must first be empowered by the Holy Spirit." (READ: Ac 1:4-5)
    1. This happened at Pentecost (Ac 2:1-4, 14; 41).
    2. The same thing happened to Paul when Ananias laid hands on him:
      a. He was filled with the Spirit (Ac 9:17-18)
      b. He immediately began to preach Christ (v.20).
  C. You can be filled with the Spirit today; just do this:
    1. Ask in faith (Lk 11:9, 13).
    2. Receive by faith (Lk 11:10; Mk 11:24).
    2. Speak in faith (Ac 2:4).

III. AS HE DID WITH PAUL, GOD HAS CHOSEN EACH OF US TO GO QUICKLY TO THE MISSION
  A. Paul tells how in a vision, Jesus had commanded him to go quickly: "I fell into a trance and saw the Lord speaking. *'Quick!'* he said to me. 'Leave Jerusalem immediately…'" (Ac 22:18).
    1. Paul was to obey immediately and "Go!"
  B. We too must quickly obey and go to the nations (Mk 16:15).
    1. Jesus, "Do…not say for months…" (Jn 4:35).
    2. Jesus is coming; it is no time to *gaze* but to *go* (Ac 1:9-11).

Conclusion and Altar Call
    1. God has chosen each one of us to participate in His mission to redeem the nations.
    2. Come now and commit yourself to God's mission.
    3. Come to be empowered by the Spirit to participate in that mission.

[EG]

65 Deep Convictions about Missions

Sermon in a Sentence: We as Christ's messengers must have deep convictions about the proclamation of the gospel, the empowering of the Holy Spirit, and the second coming of Christ.

Sermon Purpose: To call on God's people to be filled with the Spirit and committed to Christ's mission.

Text: 1 Thessalonians 1:5-7

Introduction
1. In our Scripture passage, Paul reminds the Thessalonians of how he had preached the gospel to them.
2. Five ways: (1) "in words"… (2) "in power"… (3) "with the Holy Spirit"… (4) "with deep conviction"… and (5) out of a godly life style ("You know how we lived among you for your sake").
3. This message will focus on how Paul preached the gospel in Thessalonica with "deep conviction."
4. As we go about sharing the gospel with the lost, like Paul, we must also minister "with deep conviction."
5. We must have deep conviction about three things:

I. WE MUST HAVE DEEP CONVICTIONS ABOUT OUR PRIMARY RESPONSIBILITY AS DISCIPLES OF JESUS
   A. As Christ's disciples, our chief responsibility is to join Him in His mission to redeem the nations.
      1. Sadly, most Christians are not aware of why Christ has called them into His kingdom.
      2. He stated that mission in Mt 28:18-20 (Read).
   B. We are to be about fulfilling Christ's Great Commission.
      1. Jesus has shown us what to do: "Come, follow me…and I will make you fishers of men" (Mk 1:17).
      2. Paul clearly understood this his responsibility.
         a. He modelled how to spread the good news (1Th 1:5).
         b. The Thessalonians followed his example. (Read vv.6-8.)
      3. Like Jesus and Paul, we must dedicate ourselves to sharing the good news with the lost at home and abroad.

II. WE MUST HAVE DEEP CONVICTIONS ABOUT THE GOD-ORDAINED MEANS OF FULFILLING THE MANDATE
   A. We, like Paul and the Thessalonian Christians, must understand the absolute necessity of being empowered by the Holy Spirit.

      1. Paul told the Thessalonians, "Our gospel came to you… in power and in the Holy Spirit" (v.5).
      2. Then he reminded them, "You welcomed the word with the joy of the Holy Spirit" (v.6).
  B. Jesus had commanded His followers to be baptized in—and thus, empowered by—the Holy Spirit.
      1. First, He gave a command. (Read Ac 1:4-5.)
      2. Then, He gave a promise. (Read Ac 1:8.)
  C. We must share Jesus' and Paul's deep conviction about the necessity of every follower of Christ being empowered by the Holy Spirit.

III. WE MUST HAVE DEEP CONVICTIONS ABOUT THE LIMITED TIME WE HAVE TO FULFILL OUR MISSIONARY MANDATE

  A. Paul spoke of the Thessalonians' "work…and endurance inspired by hope."
      1. In other words, they worked and endured because they had hope that Jesus was coming soon.
      2. Later in 1Thessalonians Paul spoke with conviction about the soon coming of Christ (1Th 4:15-17).
      3. He and they were compelled to preach the gospel to all before Jesus came again.
      4. For example, during his trials in Caesarea, Paul told Felix about "the judgment to come" (Ac 24:25).
  B. We must share Paul's deep conviction that Jesus is coming soon and that people must be warned to "flee from the coming wrath" (Lk 3:7).
      1. This belief motived the early Pentecostals to go to the nations and announce, "Get ready, Jesus is coming soon!"
      2. Today, we must do the same.

Conclusion and Altar Call
1. We, as Christ's messengers, must have deep convictions about the proclamation of the gospel, the empowering of the Holy Spirit, and the soon coming of Christ.
2. Come now, and commit yourself to Christ's mission.
3. Come, and be filled with the Holy Spirit.

[DRM]

66. God is Calling! Are You Listening?

Sermon in a Sentence: God calls His people to join Him in fulfilling His mission.

Sermon Purpose: That the people might understand and respond to the call of God.

Texts: John 15:16; Acts 13:1-4

Introduction
1. We have here two texts about the call of God.
   a. Jesus explains the call to His disciples (Jn.15:16).
   b. The NT church implements the call (Ac 13:1-4).
2. We will examine both in our discussion about the call of God.
3. To mobilize the church for harvest, we need to preach and teach often on the call of God.
   a. People must understand God's call.
   b. And they must be given a chance to respond to His call.
3. This sermon will answer six questions about the call of God:

I. WHAT IS THE CALL OF GOD?
A. Definition: The call of God is God choosing and calling people unto Himself and to His purposes.
B. The call of God involves…
   1. God choosing (Jn.15:16).
   2. God appointing (Jn.15:16).
   3. God speaking (Acts 13:2).
   4. God setting apart (separating) (Acts 13:2).
   5. God sending (Jn 15:16; Acts 13:4).
   6. God empowering (Acts 1:8)

II. WHOM DOES GOD CALL?
A. God calls everyone!
   1. He calls sinners to repentance (Lk 5:31).
   2. He calls believers to discipleship and service (to "bear fruit").
B. However, there is also a special call from God.
   1. Some are "set apart" for special service (Ac 13:2; Ro1:1).
   2. Just as Jesus set apart His apostles (Mk 3:13-15).
   3. He sets apart pastors, evangelists, missionaries, church planters, intercessors, and others for special service.

II. WHY DOES GOD CALL?
A. That we might join Him in fulfilling His mission.
B. His desire is that none should perish (Jn 3:16; 2Pe 3:9).

IV. HOW DOES GOD CALL?
A. He calls us by His Word.
   1. He speaks to us through the Word of God—the Bible.
   2. He speaks to us through His "Great Commissions" (Mt 28:19; Mk 16:15; Lk 24:47; Jn 20:21; Ac 1:8)
B. He calls by His Spirit.
   1. He speaks to those with receptive hearts (He 4:7).
   2. He gives us specific assignments.
   3. He then empowers us for the work (Ac 1:8).
   4. We must be filled and remain full of the Holy Spirit.

V. WHEN DOES GOD CALL?
A. God calls when He has a job that needs to be done.
   1. Moses—to deliver God's people (Ex 3:1-10).
   2. Samuel—to bring national revival (1Sa 3:10-15).
   3. Isaiah—to pronounce God's judgment (Is 6:1-13).
   4. Jesus' Disciples—to usher in God's kingdom.
B. God is calling *now!*
   1. During this Decade of Pentecost (2010-2020) and beyond.
   2. Jesus is coming—the nations are waiting (Mt 24:14).

VI. HOW MUST WE RESPOND TO GOD'S CALL?
A. Like Samuel, we must open our hearts to God: "Speak Lord for your servant is listening" (1Sa 3:9).
B. Like Isaiah, we must offer ourselves to God: "Here am I Lord, send me" (Is.6:8).
C. Like the disciples at Pentecost, we must be empowered by the Holy Spirit (Lk.24:49: Ac.1:8: 2:4).

Conclusion
1. God is calling today. Who will respond to His voice?
2. Come now to be filled with the Holy Spirit.

[DRM]

67 The Call of God

Sermon in a Sentence: God is calling us to go to the nations and Preach the gospel.
Sermon Purpose: That God's people will commit themselves to obeying the Great Commission.
Text: 1 Samuel 3:1-11

Introduction
1. Tragically, more than half of the world's population have never been given an opportunity to respond to the gospel.
    a. God calls His church to go to these precious people.
2. The story of the call of Samuel clearly demonstrates how God calls His people into His service.
3. Missions is not sustained by personality, or education, or human initiative; missions is sustained by the call of God.
    a. The call causes people to leave home, friends, opportunity.
    b. I pray that God will call believers today—and that they will respond to His call to go to the nations.
4. This call of God can be characterized in 3 ways:

I. IT IS A CALL TO OBEDIENCE
A. The call to missions is not mere pity for the suffering people in the world (though that is certainly a good thing).
   1. It is not a desire to go new places and see new things.
B. The call of God is simple obedience to the command of Jesus.
   1. Jesus' clearly commanded, "Go into all the world and preach the good news to all creation" (Mk 16:15).
   2. Jesus has clearly commanded—we must simply obey.
   3. Such obedience is the foundation of all missions endeavor.
C. Unfortunately, there is resistance in the church.
   1. People are afraid of God, that He will demand their money, their lives, their time, their children.
D. But listen to what the Bible says:
   1. Jn 14:15: "If you love me, you will obey what I command."
   2. 1Jn 3:5: "This is love for God: to obey His commands."
   3. Ac 5:29: "We must obey God rather than men!"
   4. We must be willing to give all to fulfill His command.

II. IT IS A CALL TO OPPORTUNITY
A. It is a call to walk through open doors.

1. Col 4:3: "Pray for us, too, that God may open a door for our message, so that we may proclaim the mystery of Christ…"
2. Rev 3:7: "What He opens no one can shut."
3. Eph 5:16: "…making the most of every opportunity…"
B. Opportunities to fulfill the Great Commission are everywhere.
 1. Jesus: "Open your eyes and look at the fields!" (Jn 4:35).
 2. Look around you and see the near opportunities:
  a. Unsaved friends and neighbors.
  b. Unreached communities and villages.
 3. Look farther to the unreached tribes and nations.
C. This is truly the day of the open door.
 1. Open doors demand response—we must go now.
 2. The job is doable.
  a. We have more workers today than ever before.
  b. We have new technologically.
 3. Pr 10:5: "He who sleeps during harvest is a disgraceful son."

III. IT IS THE CALL OF PENTECOST
A. To be Pentecostal is to be missionary.
 1. From its beginning, the Pentecostal Movement has been a missionary movement.
 2. Missionaries went out from Azusa Street to the nations.
 3. This is still true today, for the Spirit is still moving.
B. Our true "missionary distinctive" is Pentecostal power to go to the ends of the earth.
 1. This is the true evidence that the Spirit is among us (Ac 1:8).
 2. God said, "In the last days I will pour out my Spirit on all flesh" (Ac 2:17)
 3. And Jesus said, "You will be my witnesses…to the ends of the earth" (Ac 1:8).
 4. These two promises are inseparably connected.
C. Jesus promised: "If you will go, I will give you signs following." (Read Mk 16:15-16.)

Conclusion and Altar Call
1. God is calling us to empowered obedience.
2. Come now, and say "Yes!" to God's call to go to the nations.

[LT]

68 Called to Work for the Kingdom

Sermon in a Sentence: God has given each of us life, and He expects us to invest that life in advancing His kingdom in the earth.

Sermon Purpose: That God's people will commit themselves to advancing His kingdom in the power of the Holy Spirit.

Text: Luke 19:11-27

Introduction
1. Jesus began His ministry by declaring, "Repent, for the kingdom of heaven is near" (Mt 3:2).
   a. This declaration set the theme for His entire ministry.
   b. The King came to bring the kingdom of God to humanity.
2. Our text is one of Jesus' "Kingdom Parables" (v.11).
   a. (Note: A *mina* is equal to about 3 month's wages.)
3. This parable teaches us about 3 important kingdom issues:

I. THE CURRENT REALITY OF THE KINGDOM
A. Jesus told this parable to correct a Jewish misconception.
   1. "The people thought that the kingdom of God was going to appear at once…" (v.11).
   2. However, Jesus intended a delay in the final fulfillment of His kingdom until later:
      a. Note v.2: "…the king went away to a distant country"
   3. He is teaching that there will be a period of time between the kingdom's *inauguration* (at Jesus' first coming) and its *consummation* (at Jesus' second coming).
B. Jesus' main point is that, during this interval, we must be about God's business of building His kingdom.
   1. This is the current reality of the kingdom.
   2. The kingdom of God is active and advancing (Mt 11:12).

II. OUR RESPONSIBILITY IN THE KINGDOM
A. While we wait for Christ's return, we must work for the advancement of His kingdom in the earth (v.13).
   1. The King's instructions are clear—and they are not optional.
   2. We must make "disciples of all nations" (Mt 28:18-19).
   3. We must preach "the gospel of the kingdom…in the whole world as a testimony to all nations…" (Mt 24:14),
B. Jesus called us to be *servants* of His kingdom.
   1. Jesus uses the word "servant" four times (vv.12, 15, 17, 20).
   2. We are to be faithful to *His* kingdom work (1Co 4:2).

3. The first two servants acknowledged that they were investing *His* mina (vv. 16, 28). The third servant didn't:
   a. He admitted, "I kept *your* mina" for myself (v.20).
   b. He worked for his own profit, not the kingdom's (21).
   c. Because of this, the Master calls him "wicked" (v.22).
4. As servants, we must put the work of the kingdom first.
   a. Read Mt 6:33: "Seek first the kingdom of God…"
   b. Read Mt 16:24 "If anyone would come after me…"

C. We must act in faith for the advancement of God's kingdom.
  1. The faithful servants acted in faith.
     a. They took a risk and invested the king's mina.
     b. And they succeeded (vv.16-18).
     c. We can expect to succeed when we invest in the KOG.
  2. Jesus has promise power to advance His kingdom:
     a. Read Ac 1: 8: "You will receive power when…"
     b. Paul: "The KOG is…a matter of…power" (1Co 4:20).
     c. We receive kingdom power when we are baptized in the Holy Spirit (Ac 2:1-4).

III. THE REWARD FOR FAITHFUL SERVICE IN THE KINGDOM

A. We will all give an account of our kingdom work. (Read v. 15.)
  1. This should make us think about how we live our lives.
  2. The wicked servant was condemned because he refused to invest in the kingdom—As a result, he lost everything.
B. The faithful servants obeyed and were rewarded. (See vv.16-19).
  1. The point is not how much each servant gained—it is rather that they were faithful—and that they used what they had been given for the benefit of the King and His kingdom.
  2. When the king returned, He rewarded them generously.
C. This parable is about us:
  1. The *mina* represents the life God has given us.
  2. We must invest that life in advancing God's kingdom.
  3. Our reward or loss will depend on how we spend the life God has given us.

Conclusion and Altar Call
1. Come now, and commit yourself to advancing Christ's kingdom until He comes again.
2. Come and receive kingdom power (Ac 1:8). [MRT]

~ Section 6 ~
Mobilizing for Missions

69 Following the Example of Jesus

Sermon in a Sentence: We must follow Jesus' example of going everywhere and calling disciples to follow Him.
Sermon Purpose: That Christians commit themselves to reaching the lost and making disciples for Christ.
Text: Matthew 4:17-25
Introduction
1. The four gospels tell us about Jesus' ministry.
2. In our text, we learn that He called people to repentance and told them about the kingdom of God (v.17).
3. He further called people to follow Him and become His disciples and His representatives to others (vv.18-25).
4. In this message, we will learn how Jesus set an example for us that we must follow.
5. Notice first how…

I. JESUS CALLED DISCIPLES TO FOLLOW HIM
A. He called Peter and Andrew (vv.18-20).
   1. He called them unto himself: "Come follow me…" (v.19).
   2. He promised to make them "fishers of men" (v.18).
   3. They left everything and followed Him (v.20).
   4. Today he calls us to do the same.
B. However, Jesus did not stop there, He went further…
   1. …and called James and John to follow Him (vv.21-22).
   2. He then went throughout Galilee ministering to the people and calling them to follow Him (vv.23-34).
C. Today, Jesus calls us to go further to call people to Him.
   1. Further than our church buildings, cities, provinces…
   2. And ultimately to the ends of the earth (Mk 16:15; Ac 1:8).
   3. Not only did Jesus call disciples to follow Him…

II. JESUS' DISCIPLES FOLLOWED HIS EXAMPLE BY CALLING OTHERS TO FOLLOW HIM
A. During His final days on earth, Jesus commanded His disciples to "go and make disciples of all nations." (Read Mt 18:19-20.)
   1. This command is known as the Great Commission.
   2. In other words, just as Jesus had done with His disciples, they were to do with others.

B. But, how did the disciples go about obeying Jesus' command?
1. They began while Jesus was still on earth. (Two examples:)
   a. Philip led Nathaniel to Jesus (Jn 1:45-46).
   b. The disciples "went from village to village, preaching the gospel and healing people everywhere" (Lk 9:6).
2. After the Day of Pentecost they continued the work (Three examples:)
   a. Ac 4:33 "With great power the apostles continued to testify to the resurrection of the Lord Jesus…"
   b. Ac 8:4 "Those who had been scattered preached the word wherever they went."
   c. Sent out by the Holy Spirit, Barnabas and Saul went to Salamis, where "they proclaimed the word of God in the Jewish synagogues…" (Ac 13:5)

III. TODAY WE MUST FOLLOW THE EXAMPLE OF JESUS AND THE EARLY DISCIPLES

A. Like Jesus' first disciples, we are under divine orders.
1. The Great Commission still applies.
2. Like Paul, we are under obligation to preach the gospel to all. (Read Ro 1:14-15.)

B. However, today our task is more urgent that ever,
1. For death does not wait for anyone (He 9:27).
2. Because, "today is the day of salvation" (2Co 6:2).
3. Because Jesus could come at any moment (Mt 24:27).

C. We must therefore not be ashamed to proclaim His name anywhere and everywhere we go.
1. Jesus said, "If anyone is ashamed of me and my words in this adulterous and sinful generation, the Son of Man will be ashamed of him when he comes in his Father's glory with the holy angels" (Mk 8:38).
2. Paul declared, "I am not ashamed of the gospel…" Ro 1:16).

Conclusion and Altar Call
1. We must imitate the example of Jesus and His disciples of going everywhere and calling disciples to follow Him.
2. Come and commit yourself to the work of calling people to Christ.

[EYA]

70 Five Important Elements of Missions

Sermon in a Sentence: In doing missions, we are to follow the example of Jesus and the early church.
Sermon Purpose: That Christians will understand and apply five important elements to their missionary work.
Text: Acts 10:34-43
Introduction
1. In out text, Peter tells the people of Cornelius' household about how Jesus carried out His ministry.
2. Jesus has called every disciple to continue His mission.
   a. He has given us the task of making disciples of all nations (Mt 28:19-20).
   b. We must fail in our responsibility.
3. Five elements are needed for us to accomplish the mission Christ has given us:

I. ELEMENT 1: STRONG CONVICTION (Ac 10:15, 34-35)
   A. We must have a conviction that Christ is for all people.
      1. Peter spoke of his strong conviction: "I now realize how true it is that God does not show favoritism but accepts men from every nation who fear him and do what is right (vv. 34-35).
   B. Such conviction comes when we encounter God.
      1. On the Damascus road Paul encountered the resurrected Christ
         a. This encounter changed him from a persecutor of Christians to a proclaimer of Christ (Ac 9:1-20).
      2. Now, Peter encounters God in a vision.
         a. This encounter caused him to begin to respect people of other races and tribes (Ac 10:28).
         b. It caused him to go to Cornelius' house (Ac 10:9-17).
   C. We, too, must have an encounter with Christ that will change the way we think about people.

II. ELEMENT 2: EMPOWERMENT OF THE HOLY SPIRIT
   A. Our text tells how Jesus was anointed by the Holy Spirit (v.38).
      1. So was Peter as he preached the message.
   B. If Jesus was anointed, how much more we need to be anointed and empowered by the Holy Spirit.

1. Cornelius' household received the Spirit, thus preparing them to be Christ's witnesses too (vv.44-46).
2. The Holy Spirit gives us the power we need to be witnesses and to fulfill the mission God has given us (Ac 1:8).

III. ELEMENT 3: THE TESTIMONY OF OUR LIFESTYLES
A. Our text says that "Jesus went around doing good" (v. 38).
   1. Early Christians were known for doing good (Ac 5:13).
B. We too must have good testimonies.
   1. We witness with our lives as well as our words (2Co 3:2)
   2. What do people say about you?
   3. How does your life witness for Christ?

IV. ELEMENT 4: AN UNCHANGEABLE MESSAGE
A. Peter told the people about Jesus. (Read vv. 36-43.)
   1. He told the about Jesus' death, burial, and resurrection (Ac 10:39-40).
   2. He called on them repent and follow Christ (vv.42-43).
B. We must do the same.
   1. We must declare the unchangeable message—the gospel.
   2. No matter where God may lead us, or in what circumstances we may find ourselves, our message remains the same—"Repent and put your faith in Jesus!"

V. ELEMENT 5: THE COMMISSION OF CHRIST
A. In his sermon Peter refers to the Great Commission:
   1. "He has command us to preach to the people…" (v. 42).
B. We have been given the same commission.
   1. Mk 16:15: "Go into all the world and preach the good news to all creation."
   2. We are to go, not in our own authority, but in His authority.

Conclusion and Altar Call
1. We must all commit ourselves to God and His mission.
2. Come now and be filled with the Spirit and commit yourself to God's mission.

[DB]

71 Three Strategic Functions of Missions

Sermon in a Sentence: We must work together to reach the lost at home and around the world.
Sermon Purpose: That the people might commit themselves to the missions program of the church.
Text: John 3:16
Introduction
1. Missions involves Spirit-led strategies integrating at least three functions: outreach, networking, and serving.
2. Let's look at each of these 3 strategic functions of missions:

I. MISSIONS IS OUTREACH
A. "Missions outreach" is sharing the gospel with the lost.
 1. It requires that we go and pray.
 2. It also requires that we give generously to the work.
B. God the Father set the example by giving His only begotten Son (John 3:16).
C. Jesus exemplified the attitude of giving as He gave the bread at the Lord's Supper (Lk 22:19).
D. Peter possessed no silver or gold, but through the power of the Holy Spirit he gave what he had (Ac 3:6).
E. We too must give so that others may know Christ.

II. MISSIONS IS NETWORKING
A. "Missions networking" is working together to send people to build relationships with those who have never heard the gospel.
B. The believers in the church at Antioch worked together to send out Barnabas and Saul to reach the lost (Ac 13:4).
C. John taught that, if we are to become most effective in our witness, we must deepen our fellowship in 3 ways (1Jn 1:3):
 1. We must deepen our fellowship with *God*.
 2. We must deepen our fellowship with *Jesus*.
 3. We must deepen our fellowship with the *Holy Spirit*.
 4. We do this through prayer, worship, and proclamation of the gospel.
D. Unity is essential in missions.
 1. Unity gives us power to accomplish our God-given goals.

2. David spoke of the importance of unity (Ps 133:1).
   3. We must forget our petty differences and move forward with a common purpose to reach the lost.
   E. Some of us are called to go to our neighbors; others of us are called to go to distant places and other cultures.
      1. We must all be willing to go, give, and pray.
      2. Remember, when we go, we do not go alone (Mt 28:20).

III. MISSIONS IS SERVING
   A. "Missions serving" is committing ourselves to serve others.
   B. We can only fulfill the Great Commission together.
      1. Jesus employed His disciples to help Him feed the five thousand (Jn 6:1-14).
      2. Mark tells the story of four men who worked together to bring a paralytic to Christ (Mk 2:1-12).
         a. They were concerned about their friend.
         b. They had faith that Christ could heal him.
         c. They were burdened enough to do something about it.
      3. Moses felt unqualified to serve God and his people (Ex 3:11)
         1. Yet, God used him because he was willing to be used.
   C. God turns our inabilities into His possibilities.
      1. With the Spirit's help, we who are weak and meek can make a difference in the lives of others (1Co 1:26-29).
      2. F.B. Meyer said, "I used to think, that God's gifts were on shelves, one above another, and the taller we grow, the easier we can reach them. Now I find that God's gifts are on shelves, one beneath another, and the lower we stoop, the more we get!"
      5. Will you humble yourself to serve others who have never heard the gospel?

Conclusion and Altar Call
   1. Together, we must commit ourselves to the work of missions.
   2. Come, and commit yourself today.

[AC]

72 The "World of Unless"

Sermon in a Sentence: The work of missions cannot succeed *unless* we pray, give, go, and send.
Sermon Purpose: That God's people will commit themselves to fulfilling God's mission by praying, giving, going and sending.
Text: 2 Corinthians 1:8-11
Introduction
1. Missions exists in a "World of Unless."
2. Let me explain what I mean by that statement.
   a. Imagine a nation of millions of people living on the edge of the Sahara Desert. These people live and die with no hope of eternal life.
   b. This is because there is no one in their midst to share with them the good news about Christ.
   c. *Unless* we send someone to them they will die without hope.
3. This message will focus on our role in the mission of God.
   a. The Creator of the universe has called us, His people, to partner with Him in His mission to redeem all nations.
   b. However, *unless* we pray, *unless* we give, *unless* we go, and *unless* we send, the work of redeeming the nations will not happen.
4. Let's look at each of those four elements:

I. UNLESS WE PRAY...
A. God calls on us to partner with Him is through prayer
B. In our text, Paul requested prayer from the Corinthian believers.
   1. Read 2 Corinthians 1:8-11.
   2. Paul tells of his struggles in Asia: "We were...burdened beyond our strength...we despaired of life itself" (v.8).
   3. He then asks for prayer: "You...must help us by prayer."
C. *Unless* we pray, the lost will remain unreached.
   1. Missions involves spiritual warfare (Ep 6:12).
   2. Spiritual battles require spiritual weapons (2Co 10:4).
   3. Prayer is a powerful spiritual weapon.
D. How we can pray for missions?
   1. We can pray for the missionaries (2Co 1:11).
   2. We can pray for open doors (Col 4:3).
   3. We can pray to the Lord of the Harvest (Mt 9:37).

II. UNLESS WE GIVE...
A. A second way we partner with God in missions is through giving.
B. Many Christians seek peace and security in their finances.
   1. They base their self-worth on their financial bottom line.
C. However, we must understand why God has given us wealth.
   1. He gives you money so "you can be generous" (2Co 9:11).
   2. He blesses us so we can bless the nations (Ps 67:1-2).
D. We must know how God wants us to give (Ex 25:1-9; 35:20-22).
   1. We are to give out of a willing heart as the Spirit of God stirs our Spirits (25:2; 35:21).
   2. Three ways you can give to missions.
      a. You can make a monthly commitment to missions.
      b. You can give when you see a need.
      c. You can give as the Spirit prompts you to give.
   3. *Unless* we give the lost will remain unreached.

III. UNLESS WE GO AND SEND...
A. A third and fourth way we partner with God in missions is through going and sending.
   1. Read Romans 10:13-15.
   2. Notice how some must go, while others must send.
B. *Unless we go,* the unreached will never hear the gospel and be saved.
   1. Some must be willing to leave home and family and go to the unreached peoples and places of the world.
   2. If they will not go, people will not hear and be saved.
C. *Unless we send,* those willing to go will not be able to go.
   1. Some must commit themselves to sending those who are willing to go.
   2. If the senders refuse to send, the goers will not be able to go.

Conclusion and Altar Call
1. We must partner with God in His mission by praying, giving, going, and sending.
2. Come, commit yourself to God's mission today.

[BD]

73 The Power of One
~ The Difference One Person Can Make in God's Mission ~

Sermon in a Sentence: God can use one person to make a huge difference in his or her world.
Sermon Purpose: That listeners will commit their *one life* to serving God and His redemptive mission.
Text: Ezekiel 22:23-31 (Emphasize v.30)
Introduction
1. We live in perilous times. Our nation and world are in rebellion against God. God's judgment must surely be imminent.
2. What then should be our stance as God's missionary people? What does God expect of us?
3. Today's Scripture text gives us some clues:
    a. In Ezekiel's day, God looked for an intercessor, "a man to stand before me in the gap on behalf of the land" (v.30).
    b. God sought for one man to intercede for all—but sadly, He found no one.
4. Today, God seeks individuals who will "stand in the gap..."
    a. This message: The Power of One"—how God can use one person to make a difference in his or her world.
5. Let's explore three powerful insights about the Power of One:

I. THE POWER OF ONE PERSON WHO WILL "STAND IN THE GAP" BETWEEN GOD AND LOST PEOPLE
A. In our text, God looked for a man to "stand in the gap."
   1. All of Israel had turned their backs on God: the princes, the priests, the rulers, the prophets—and even the people themselves (vv.24-29).
   2. So, God sought for an intercessor—*but He found none.*
B. However, on other occasions, He did find those who would stand in the gap between judgment and deliverance.
   1. For instance, Abraham stood in the gap for immoral Sodom.
   2. He called on God to spare the rebellious city (Ge 18:20-33).
   3. As a result, part of his family was saved (19:29).
C. Today, God calls on us to "stand in the gap" between Him and lost humanity. (In two ways:)
   1. By praying for the lost at home and around the world.
   2. By pointing them to Christ and His salvation (Ro. 10:13-15).
D. One man, one woman, one child, one church can make all the difference in a lost and dying world.

II. THE POWER OF ONE SINNER COMING TO CHRIST
A. When a sinner comes to Christ, it makes a powerful difference in that one person's life.
 1. God's wrath is withheld; the person's life is transformed.
    a. "If anyone is in Christ, he is a new creation..." (2Co 5:17).
 2. Paul's personal testimony: (Ac 26:8-26; 1Co 15:9-10)
B. One person's conversion can also make a powerful difference in the lives of many others.
 1. The conversion and empowering of Saul (Paul), resulted in the door of faith being opened to the Gentiles (Ro 15:17-18).
 2. It also resulted in his writing about 1/3 of the New Testament.
C. It is a powerful thing to lead just one soul to Christ.

III. THE INFINITE POWER OF ONE SAVIOR DYING ON THE CROSS
A. The death of *One* resulted in the salvation of *many* (Ro 5:19).
 1. Jesus' died for the whole world (1Jn 4:14).
 2. Now, anyone who calls on His name can be saved (Ro 10:13).
B. Christ does not only love the whole world, He loves each *one*.
 1. John 3:16 speaks of both "the world" (all) and "whoever believes" (each person in the world).
 2. Illustration: The Parable of the One Lost Sheep (Lk 15:4-7).
 3. Illustration: The Parable of the Lost Coin (Lk 15:8-10).
 4. The moral to both stories is that God loves individuals and seeks to save them.
C. Like Jesus, we must seek every lost person (Lk 14:23).
 1. We must each follow Jesus' example of seeking and saving the lost (Lk 19:10).
 2. And, we must obey His command to "Go into all the world and preach the good news to all creation" (Mk 16:15).

Conclusion and Altar Call
 1. God is still searching for individuals who will "stand in the gap" on behalf of lost humanity.
 2. Come now and dedicate your one life to God and His mission.

[JDE]

74. Two Great Missionary Challenges

Sermon in a Sentence: The gospel must be advanced in the world using spiritual means.
Sermon Purpose: That God's people will commit themselves to advancing God's kingdom in the earth using spiritual means.
Texts: Ephesians 6:12; 2 Corinthians 10:3-4
Introduction
1. In our first text, Paul describes a great spiritual warfare that we the church are involved in.
2. In the second text, he tells how spiritual battles can only be fought using spiritual weapons.
2. In this message I want to apply these principles to the work of missions.

I. TODAY THE CHURCH FACES TWO GREAT MISSIONARY CHALLENGES:
A. The first challenge is *secularism*.
   1. Secularism is a denial of the supernatural.
   2. It is the belief that everything can be understood through human reason—and that man has the ability to solve his own problems.
   3. Therefore, belief in God should play no role in government, education, or any other part of society.
   4. Secularism is pervading society—even in Africa.
B. A second challenge is *Islam*.
   1. How Islam began: Tell the story of Muhammad.
   2. The practice of Islam is based on "five "pillars":
      a. *The confession:* "There is no god but Allah, and Muhammad is the messenger of Allah."
      b. *Prayer:* Ritual prayer 5 times a day
      c. *Alms:* Giving to the poor
      d. *Fasting:* Occurs mainly during Ramadan
      e. *Pilgrimage:* To Mecca once in a lifetime
   3. Muslims also believe in *Jihad:* Holy war, the struggle of believers against nonbelievers
   4. Islam is expanding rapidly in many parts of the world.
      a. 1.6 billion Muslims in the world (2010 statistics)
      b. 250 million Muslims in Sub-Saharan Africa.
      c. 322 million Muslims in N Africa and Middle East.

II. HOW IS THE CHURCH TO RESPOND TO THESE TWO GREAT CHALLENGES?
   A. We must respond in *love*.
      1. We must not fight evil with evil (Mt 5:43-48).
      2. We must become an evangelistic community (Mk 16:15-16).
   B. We must not compromise *the gospel*.
      1. Salvation is found in Christ alone (Ac 4:12).
      2. We must therefore boldly go in the Name of Jesus.
         a. We must pray in His Name.
         b. We must proclaim salvation in His Name.
   C. We must respond *spiritually*.
      1. We are involved in spiritual warfare (Ep 6:12).
      2. Therefore, we must be empowered by the Spirit (Ac 1:8).
      3. We must let our faith overcome our fear of the unknown.
   D. We must go, give, and pray.

Conclusion and Altar Call
   1. Come now and commit yourself to advancing God's kingdom using spiritual means.
   2. Come and be filled with the Spirit.

[JLE]

75 God's Missionary Plan

Sermon in a Sentence: We must all get involved in reaching the unreached by going, praying and giving.
Sermon Purpose: That God's people commit themselves to get involved in reaching the unreached for Christ.
Text: Romans 10:12-14
Introduction
1. In our text Paul sets out God's strategy to build his church.
2. This message will address three critical missions issues which Paul raises:

I. THE CONTEXT OF GOD'S STRATEGY—LOSTNESS
A. In our text Paul is concerned about people who have never heard the good news about Jesus Christ.
B. The Bible describes lost people as living in "thick darkness" (Is 60:2, NIV) or "darkness as black as night" (NLT).
   1. Imagine yourself in complete, utter darkness.
C. Thousands in the world live in such utter spiritual darkness.
   1. They live with no light, no hope, no chance of eternal life.
   2. They live in places where there are no churches, no Bibles, and the name of Jesus is never spoken.
   3. For instance, the Beja of eastern Sudan:
      a. 2.5 million Beja, stretching through 3 countries.
      b. Less than 30 known believers.
      c. Their lives are filled with violence, treachery, and fear.
   4. In our text, Paul has in mind people who have never had an opportunity to know Christ.
      a. Not because they have rejected Him, but because they have never been given the opportunity to know Him.
   5. We have been given the responsibility of telling them.

II. GOD'S DESIRE FOR HUMANKIND—REDEMPTION
A. In our text, Paul also reveals God's intent for humankind.
   1. Paul says "For *everyone* who calls on the name of the Lord will be saved" (v.13).
      a. God's desire is for everyone to hear about Jesus and be given a chance to call on His name.
      b. In Revelation, John gives us a glimpse of where God's plan is heading (Rev 5:9; ref. Mt 24:14).

2. God is not only concerned about us and our people, He is concerned about people from every tribe and nation.
  B. May God's passion for those who have never heard the story of Jesus consume our hearts and minds.

III. GOD'S STRATEGY TO CARRY OUT HIS MISSION—GOING AND SENDING
  A. Paul frames the solution with two challenging questions:
   1. *Question 1: "How can they hear without someone preaching to them?"*
      a. God is looking for those who will leave their homes and people and go to places where the name of Jesus has never been proclaimed.
      b. This is the only way millions will ever hear the gospel.
      c. Who will go with the gospel to these people if not us?
   2. *Question 2: "How will they preach unless they are sent?"*
      a. The only way people can *go* is if they are *sent*.
      b. The call to send is one of the foundations on which work of missions is built.
  B. What then does it mean to send?
   1. Sending means *praying*.
      a. God works through our prayers.
      b. Not everyone can go, but all can pray.
   2. Sending means *giving*.
      a. Giving to missions is investing in God's kingdom.
      b. Giving to mission is a privilege that God has given us to participate in His mission to reach the nations.
   3. Are you ready to participate in proclaiming Christ to the lost around the world by giving to missions?

Conclusion and Altar Call
   1. As we each do our part, Christ's church will be built of people from every tribe and nation… Then, Jesus will come!
   2. Will you join me in committing yourself to God's mission?

[SH]

76 A Missionary Psalm for Everyone

Sermon in a Sentence: God blesses us that we may participate in His mission to reach all the tribes of the earth.

Sermon Purpose: To convince God's people to participate in God's mission to reach the unreached with the good news of salvation.

Text: Psalm 67:1-7

Introduction
1. The Psalmist wants all people to know the true God.
2. This amazing psalm was written hundreds of years before Christ; and yet, the writer understood the implications of God's covenant with Abraham: "All peoples on earth will be blessed through you" (Ge 12:3).
3. From this psalm we learn four important principles concerning God's mission and how we should participate in it:

I. BLESSING IS FOR MISSION (vv.1-2)
  A. The psalm begins with a blessing (v.1).
    1. This blessing is similar to Aaron's blessing in Nu 6:24-26.
      a. It speaks of God's "shalom" blessing.
      b. *Shalom* means wholeness in all areas of life.
    2. While Aaron's blessing focuses on Israel, the Psalmist's blessing extends to all nations (or people groups).
    3. In the Psalms, the shining of God's face speaks of deliverance, redemption, or salvation.
  B. The Psalmist knows that God's blessing comes for a reason:
    1. To bring salvation to the nations.
    2. God blesses us so that we may all participate in His plan.
  C. Consider this: When God blesses you…
    1. …do you think about those who haven't heard? The lost?
    2. …do you realize how your being blessed must be used to bring salvation to the nations?

II. SALVATION BRINGS JOY TO THE NATIONS AND PRAISE TO GOD
  A. Note the repeated phrase: "May the peoples praise you, O God; may all the peoples praise you" (v.3).
    1. In the Bible repetition often indicates emphasis.
    2. The psalmist's hope (expectation) is that all peoples of the earth will join Israel in praising God.
  B. The result of God's salvation reaching all peoples is twofold:
    1. God's salvation will bring joy to the nations (v.3).
    2. In their joy all the tribes of the earth praise God (v.4).

    C. As the church goes out in the power of the Spirit, many unreached tribes are experiencing the joy of salvation.
       1. It happened in Samaria (Ac 8:8)
       2. It happened in Antioch (Pisidia) (Ac 13:52).
       3. It happened to the Philippian jailer (Ac 16:14)

III. ALL PEOPLES ARE TO GIVE PRAISE, HONOR AND GLORY TO GOD

    A. The refrain of v.3 in is repeated in v.5: "May *all*...praise you!"
       1. Every people group is important to God.
       2. Everyone needs the opportunity to know the joy of salvation.
    B. There still is room for others to join the choir.
       1. Many unreached tribes who are waiting to experience the joy of salvation and to sing praises to God.
       2. We *must* keep participating in God's plan until the divine vision of this psalm is accomplished!

IV. OUR LOCAL HARVEST DEPENDS ON OUR PARTICIPATION IN GOD'S MISSION

    A. The psalmist directly connects our local harvest with our participation in God's mission (vv.6-7).
       1. He is saying that, when we share the blessing of salvation with the nations, God will, in turn, abundantly bless us.
       2. It is all made possible through our prayers and gifts.
       3. In other words, if a person, family, church, or nation has made it possible for the unreached to experience salvation, God will bless their endeavors at home.
    B. The psalm ends with a declaration that "all the ends of the earth" will someday fear God. Hallelujah! (v.7).
       1. And we have been given the privilege of participating.

Conclusion and Altar Call
    1. Will you join me as we together commit ourselves to participate in God's mission to take His salvation to all peoples?
    2. Come now and commit yourself to God's mission to redeem the nations.

[JL]

77 The Gospel Spread Unhindered

Sermon in a Sentence: For the gospel to spread unhindered, we must each pray, be empowered by the Spirit, and commit ourselves to proclaiming Christ to the lost.

Sermon Purpose: That people be filled with the Spirit and commit themselves to prayer and proclamation of the gospel.

Text: Acts 28:30-31

Introduction
1. The book of Acts closes with these words. "For two whole years Paul…proclaimed the kingdom of God and taught about the Lord Jesus Christ—with all boldness and without hindrance!"
2. This message: Three keys to an unhindered spread of the gospel:

I. KEY #1: PRAYER
A. Pentecostal revival can only come and be sustained by prayer.
B The book of Acts is saturated with prayer.
   1. Prayer is mentioned 32 times.
   2. For example: Acts 1:14; 24; 2:42; 3:1; 4:24, 31; 6:4, 6; 7:59; 8:15; 9:11, 40; 10:2, 9, 30-31; 11:5; 12:5, 12; 13:3; 14:23; 16:13, 25; 20:36; 21:5; 22:17; 27:29; 28:8.
C. Because the church prayed, they were filled with the Spirit, and because they were filled with the Spirit, the mission progressed.
D. We, too, must commit ourselves to prayer:
   1. "When we work, *we* work. When we pray *God* works."
   2. Acts 1:8 was—and will be—fulfilled only by people who pray.

II. KEY #2: POWER
A. The power of Pentecost was not just for personal blessing, it was for missional witness.
   1. Acts 2 was a fulfilment of Jesus promise in Acts 1:8.
   2. We too must believe that the Spirit's power will help us.
   3. We must allow the Holy Spirit to control our lives.
B. The power of the Spirit in Paul's life was the secret to the gospel proceeding unhindered in Rome (Ac 28:31).
   1. He was first empowered in Damascus (Ac 9:17-18).

      2. Now, many years later, Paul is still full of the Spirit.
      3. Because of this, the gospel proceeded—even in the face of persecution.
  C. Jesus has told us how we can receive the Spirit (Lk 11:9-13):
      1. We must ask in faith (Lk 11:9, 13).
      2. We must receive by faith (Lk 11:10; Mk 10:24).
      3. We must speak in faith (Ac 2:4).

III. KEY #3: PROCLAMATION
  A. The gospel was meant to be proclaimed.
      1. Jesus said, "This gospel of the kingdom *shall be proclaimed* in all the world…" (Mt 24:14).
      2. Again, "Go into all the world and *proclaim the gospel* to the whole creation (Mk 16:15 ESV).
  B. Like Paul, we have all been commissioned as "servants and witnesses" (26:16).
      1. Jesus, "You will be *my* witnesses" (Ac 1:8).
      2. Jesus is the *purpose* and *subject* of our witness.
  C. We are called to proclaim the gospel—the message of Jesus
      1. Mk 16:15; Lk 24:46-49; 1Co 15:1-4.
      2. We must stop preaching nonessentials, and start telling everyone that "Jesus saves!"

Conclusion
    1. We want the gospel to proceed unhindered here in this place.
    2. For that to happen, we must pray, we must be empowered by the Spirit, and we must boldly proclaim the gospel.
    3. Come now and commit yourself to these principles.

[DM]

78 God's Great Destiny for Africa

~ Africa Shall Quickly Stretch out Her Hands to God ~

Sermon in a Sentence: God has a great missionary destiny for the African church.

Sermon Purpose: That African Christians commit themselves to God and His great missionary destiny for the African church.

Texts: Acts 1:8; 2:1-4
Psalm 68:31; then 28, then 34-35 (NIV)

Introduction
1. Does God have a plan for the African church?
2. Yes, our texts seem to indicate that He does.
3. Ps 68:28-35 highlights three amazing facts about this plan:

I. GOD DOES INDEED HAVE A GREAT DESTINY FOR AFRICA (v. 31) *"Envoys will come from Egypt; Ethiopia will stretch out her hands to God"* (NASB).
   A. The meaning of the word "Ethiopia" (Hebrew: *Kush*).
      1. To the ancients, "Ethiopia" meant "Africa south of Egypt."
      2. Ethiopia is a Greek word meaning "people with dark faces."
      3. Therefore, Egypt + Ethiopia = all of Africa.
      4. It would thus be correct to translate v 31, "*Africa* will quickly stretch out her hands to God!"
      5. *Question:* When will this amazing prophecy be fulfilled —and how?
   B. It has been fulfilled throughout church history:
      1. In the book of Acts:
         a. African languages were spoken at Pentecost: "Egypt and the parts of Libya near Cyrene…" (Ac 2:10)
         b. God sent Philip to the Ethiopian nobleman (Ac 8:26-40).
         c. African missionaries helped bring missional revival to the church in Antioch (Ac 11:20-21).
      2. In church history:
         a. In the 2nd century the church flourished in North Africa.
         b. In the following centuries the church declined.
         c. In the 19th century, missionaries entered Africa with the good news.
         d. In the 20th century Pentecost came to Africa.
   C. However, today as never before, Africa is *quickly* stretching out her hands to God in repentance and faith.

1. The church is growing exponentially in Africa.

II. GOD'S GREAT DESTINY FOR AFRICA INVOLVES THE NATIONS
A. Look again at verses 31 and 32:
   1. (v. 31) "Envoys will come out of Egypt, Africa will quickly stretch out her hands to God..." *Then...*
   2. (v. 32) "Sing to God, O kingdoms of the earth..."
   3. In other words, once Africa stretches out her hands to God, the nations will hear the gospel and rejoice.
B. Today, Africa is stretching out her hands to God in obedience to the Great Commission.
   1. In OT missions, the nations flowed to Jerusalem
      a. This has been called "centripetal missions."
      b. (v.29) "Because of your temple at Jerusalem kings will bring you gifts..."
      c. (v.31) "Envoys will come from Egypt..."
   2. Since Pentecost, the church goes to from Jerusalem to the "ends of the earth" (Ac 1:8)
      a. This has been called "centrifugal missions."
C. Today, Africa is mobilizing itself to fulfill her Great Missionary Destiny.
   1. What was once a missions field is quickly becoming a missions force.

III. GOD'S GREAT DESTINY FOR AFRICA IS INTRINSICALLY LINKED TO PENTECOST.
A. Note the context of our text is a prophecy of Pentecost.
   1. Note the language of Pentecost: (Ps 68:28) "Summon your power O God..." (v.34) "Proclaim the power of God... whose power is in the sky..." (v.35) "God gives power...to his people." (See Ac 1:8; 2:2).
B. Amazingly, in the midst of all of these Pentecostal references is our prophecy concerning Africa: "Envoys will come out of Egypt; *Africa will quickly stretch out her hands to God."*
C. Today, I invite you to stretch out your hands to God.
   1. Commit yourself to Him and His mission.
   2. Ask Him empower yo with His Spirit.

Conclusion and Altar Call
1. Come now, and quickly stretch out your hands to God.
2. Come and commit yourself to His mission   [DRM]

79 The Measure of a Missionary Church

Sermon in a Sentence: We should strive to ensure that our church is a missionary church like the church in Antioch.

Sermon Purpose: That the people commit themselves and their church to fulfilling God's mission.

Text: Acts 11:19-30

Introduction
1. The birth of a child is an exciting event—and so is the birth of a new church.
2. Our text tells of the birth of the church in Antioch, Syria.
3. This church will emerge as a powerful missionary church.
   a. It was the home base for Paul's missionary journeys.
   b. It is a great example of what our church should look like.
4. By observing the Antioch church, we discover seven essential characteristics of a great missionary church:

I. THE PRESENCE AND POWER OF THE SPIRIT
A. Luke says that "the Lord's hand was with them…" (v. 21).
   1. This is another way of saying that the Holy Spirit was powerfully working among them (2Kg 3:13; Ez 3:14).
B. As a result of the Spirit's powerful working through them, "a great number of people believed and turned to the Lord" (v.21).
C. We too must ensure that our church is full of the Holy Spirit and that God's Spirit is moving powerfully in our midst.

II. ANOINTED, FAITH-FILLED LEADERSHIP
A. The church in Antioch was led by men who were full of the Holy Spirit and faith, such as Barnabas and Saul (vv.22-26).
   1. Barnabas "a good man, full of the Holy Spirit and faith" (24).
   2. Paul was also full of the Holy Spirit and faith (Ac 13:9).
B. We too must ensure that our church is led by men and women who are full of the Holy Spirit and faith.

III. VISIONARY OUTWARD FOCUS
A. The church in Antioch aggressively reached out the residents of its city (vv.19-21).
   1. They reached out to both Jews and Gentiles.
   2. They would soon send missionaries to the nations (Ac 13:1-4).

    B. Our church must have the same outward focus.

IV. SPIRIT-EMPOWERED PROCLAMATION
    A. Luke says that the members of this church proclaimed "the good news about the Lord Jesus" (v. 20).
    B. This is a characteristic of disciples throughout Acts: (Ac 8:4-5; 16:30-31; 28:31).
    C. We, like them, must faithfully tell everyone about Jesus.

V. DELIBERATE, SYSTEMATIC MISSIONAL TRAINING
    A. Luke says that "for a whole year Barnabas and Saul met with the church and taught great numbers of people" (v.26).
        1. They surely taught the basics of Christian living.
        2. They must have also taught about God's mission and how they could effectively participate in that mission.
    B. We must do the same in our churches.

VI. THE FREE OPERATION OF SPIRITUAL GIFTS
    A. They encouraged the gifts of the Spirit to operate in their gatherings, enabling and guiding them to do God's will.
        1. The prophet Agabus spoke by the Spirit (Ac 11:27-28).
        2. Later in Acts, another prophecy launched Paul and Barnabas onto their First Missionary Journey (Ac 13:1-4).
    B. We too must cultivate and encourage the manifestation of Spirit gifts in our church today.

VII. SPIRIT-PROMPTED GENEROSITY
    A. They gave generously to advance the work of the kingdom.
        1. They responded to Agabus' prophecy by giving (11:29).
        2. This reminds us of what happened at Pentecost (Ac 2:44-45).
    B. Like them, we too must give generously to missions.

Conclusion and Altar Call
    1. We must strive to ensure that each of these seven traits are found in our church today.
    2. Let's all come together and commit ourselves to having a truly Spirit-empowered missionary church.

[DRM]

80 A Motto for Missions
"Think Globally—Act Locally"

Sermon in a Sentence: Any Christian or local church can impact the nations—if they will "think globally and act locally."

Sermon Purpose: That Christians will commit themselves to become involved in global missions by thinking globally and acting locally.

Text: John 3:16-17

Introduction
1. The phrase, "Think globally—act locally" is a phrase used in various contexts: business leaders, environmentalists
2. It is a great motto for missions mobilization.
3. Those who have advanced the gospel to the nations have implemented this strategy—often unconsciously.

I. EXAMPLES OF THOSE WHO IN THE PAST WHO THOUGHT GLOBALLY AND ACTED LOCALLY

A. Our text demonstrates how *God* himself thought globally and acted locally (Jn 3:16).
   1. God had a global vision: "For God so loved the world…"
   2. Yet, He acted locally: "He gave his only Son…"
B. *Jesus* also thought globally and acted locally.
   1. Like His Father, Jesus had a global vision of the world.
      a. He came to give His life as "a ransom for many" (Mt 20:28), that is, for all humanity (see 1Ti 2:6).
      b. The woman at the well recognized that He was "Savior of the world" (Jn 4:42).
   2. Yet, He acted locally.
      a. He was born in Bethlehem and never left His country.
      b. Nevertheless, He acted deliberately and decisively: "He gave himself as a ransom for all" (1Ti 2:6).
      c. That local act became the basis of redemption for all humanity.
C. Another young man, named *William Carey*, thought globally and acted locally
   1. He was an impoverished shoemaker who lived in England in the mid 1800's.
      a. He began to read the Bible and concluded, "We are all obligated to send missionaries to the nations."
      b. He read another book, *The Journeys of Captain Cook,* which talked about distant lands and strange people.

2. He began to think globally.
3. Then, he acted locally—he wrote a book: *An Inquiry into the Obligation of Christians to Use Means in the Conversion of the Heathens.*
   a. He then founded the Baptist Mission Society.
   b. He became their first missionary and went to India.
   c. He became known as the "Father of Modern Missions."
4. Carey thought globally, then acted locally.

II. WE TOO MUST LEARN TO THINK GLOBALLY AND ACT LOCALLY
A. We must learn to think globally.
   1. Jesus: "Open your eyes and look on the fields…" (Jn 4:35).
   2. In another place He said, "The field is the world" (Mt 13:38).
   3. How can we learn to *think globally*?
      a. We can make ourselves aware of what the Bible says about God's love for the nations and our responsibility to reach them (for instance Jn 3:16; Mk 16:15-16).
      b. We can become students of geography, including maps, foreign lands, and world need.
      c. We can cultivate an interest in other peoples & cultures.
B. Then, we must *act locally*.
   1. We must do something and we must do it now.
      a. Any Christian, any pastor, any church can do something significant for missions—*if they will act!*
   2. What we can do locally that will have a global impact:
      a. We can preach and teach on missions.
      b. We can systematically receive missions offerings.
      c. We can organize ourselves to pray for missions.
      d. We can invite missionaries to speak in our churches.
      e. We can faithfully support missionaries.

Conclusion and Altar Call
1. We will think globally—and we will act locally.
2. Come and commit to do your part for world missions.

[DRM]

81 Nine Steps to the Mission Field

Sermon in a Sentence: You can get to the mission field, if you will take these nine steps.

Sermon Purpose: To make the listeners aware of the step that may be required to get to the mission field.

Text: John 15:16; Romans 1:1

Introduction
1. In our first text (Jn 15:16), Jesus tells His disciples that He has personally chosen and appointed them to go out and to bear fruit.
2. In the second (Ro 1:1), Paul speaks of his call to be an apostle.
3. Jesus still chooses and appoints missionaries today.
4. Possibly, you are sensing a call to mission work, but you are wondering, "How do I get from here to the mission field?"
5. This message: Nine important steps to the mission field:

I. ENSURE THAT YOU HAVE BEEN TRULY BORN AGAIN
A. Jesus: "No one can see the kingdom of God unless he is born again" (Jn 3:3).
B. Missions begins with a personal encounter with God.
C. One cannot give what he or she does not possess (2Ti 2:6, KJV).

II. CONSECRATE YOURSELF FULLY TO GOD AND HIS PURPOSES
A. Jesus: "If anyone would come after me, he must deny himself and take up his cross and follow me..." (Mk 16:24-25).
B. Like Peter and the disciples, the missionary must be willing to leave everything and follow Christ (Mk 10:28).

III. BE EMPOWERED BY THE HOLY SPIRIT
A. Jesus commanded His disciples to "Go!" (Mk 6:15), but first they were to "stay in Jerusalem" until they had been empowered by the Holy Spirit (Lk 24:46-49; Ac 1:4-5).
B. Jesus has promised us that same power to witness (Ac 1:8).
C. We must "not leave home without it!"

V. ENSURE THAT GOD IS CALLING AND THAT THE SPIRIT IS SENDING YOU
A. In out text Jesus said, "You did not chose me, but I chose you… (Jn 16:15).
B. He also said, "As the Father has sent me, I send you" (Jn 20:21).
C. Illustration: The Holy Spirit sent out Barnabas and Saul (Ac 13:2, 4).

IV. ACQUIRE A THOROUGH KNOWLEDGE OF SCRIPTURE
A. This is of upmost importance for any missionary.
B. Jesus told us to "make disciples of all nations…" (Mt 28:19-20).
C. We must gain a broad knowledge of the Bible (Ac 20:27).
D. This must include a clear understanding of God's mission.

VI. CULTIVATE A STRONG DEVOTIONAL LIFE
A. Ministry flows out of one's growing relationship with Christ.
B. Illustration: Like Peter and John (Ac 4:13).
C. Your devotional life will sustain you on the field.

VII. GET DIRECTION FROM THE SPIRIT
A. The Spirit directed Jesus (Lk 4:1, 14).
B. The Spirit directed Paul (Ac 16:6-10).
C. Listen to the Spirit, and He will direct you.

VIII. ASSOCIATE WITH AND SUBMIT TO A REPUTABLE MISSIONS AGENCY
A. Barnabas and Saul were also sent out by the church (Ac 13:3).
B. Become part of a team of committed senders and goers.
C. You will need a strong support base (Ro 10:15).

IX. GO IN FAITH TRUSTING GOD FOR PROVISION
A. In God's time, take the step of faith and go.
B. All preparation is for naught if you refuse to go.
C. Remember, you will not go alone (Mt 28:20b).

Conclusion and Altar Call
1. Come and consecrate yourself to the Lord of the Harvest.
2. Come and be empowered by the Spirit.   [DRM]

82. Reaping the Nations: What It Will Take

Sermon in a Sentence: If we are going to effectively reap the nations, we must adopt the NT missions strategy presented by Luke in Acts.

Sermon Purpose: That the people will commit themselves to the New Testament strategy of missions.

Text: Acts 1:1-11

Introduction

1. We have been called by Christ to "reap the nations" (Ac 1:8).
    a. …to take the gospel to the lost worldwide. (Mt 24:14)
    b. But what will it take to reap the nations?
2. We are amazed by the success of the church in Acts.
    a. However, today this NT strategy has been largely dismissed.
    b. We have sought other "more contemporary" strategies.
3. Luke wrote Acts to answer the question, "How can a church become a powerful missionary force in the earth?"
4. In Acts, Luke emphasized four essential elements necessary for any church to become truly effective in missions:

I. THOSE INVOLVED IN REAPING THE NATIONS MUST THEMSELVES HAVE A CURRENT, LIVING RELATIONSHIP WITH CHRIST

A. Luke presented the New Testament witnesses as people having such a relationship with Christ.
  1. A relationship was born out of a life-transforming experience Jesus called being "born again" (Jn 3:3-7).
     a. Those who met Jesus were transformed.
     b. Luke gives the example of Paul (Ac 9:1-17).
B. Jesus' disciples understood that only those in a living relationship with Christ can lead others into such a relationship with Him.
C. Therefore, if we are to reap the nations, we must honestly examine our own relationship with Christ.
D. And, we must ensure that our people are truly born again.

II. THOSE INVOLVED IN REAPING THE NATIONS MUST HAVE A CLEAR UNDERSTANDING OF GOD'S MISSION

A. Unfortunately, many today do not understand God's mission.
B. Jesus' disciples clearly understood God's mission.
  1. For three years, Christ had taught them the mission.

2. He further exhibited God's mission with His life, His ministry, and ultimately with His death on the cross.
   3. As a result, they understood their role and responsibility.
C. We too must understand and teach God's mission.
   1. The ignorance in our churches must be remedied.
   2. We must teach and preach often on the mission of God.

III. THOSE INVOLVED IN REAPING THE NATIONS MUST HAVE A RADICAL COMMITMENT TO CHRIST AND HIS MISSION

A. Not only must we understand the mission, we must totally commit ourselves to that mission.
   1. Jesus taught us what it will take. (Read Jn 12:24-26.)
   2. With His life and death on the cross, Christ demonstrated for us the kind of commitment it would take.
B. In Acts, we read about people who were ready to suffer and even to lay down their lives for the sake of the gospel.
   1. Stephen was martyred (Ac 7:54-60)
   2. Paul was stoned (Ac 14:19-20; 2Co 11:25-28).
   2. Tertullian, "The blood of the martyrs is seed."
C. If we are to reap the nations, we too must commit ourselves totally to Christ and His mission.
   1. And yet, one final thing is needed...

IV. THOSE INVOLVED IN REAPING THE NATIONS MUST BE EMPOWERED BY THE HOLY SPIRIT

A. Jesus' final command to His disciples was not to leave Jerusalem until they were empowered by the Holy Spirit.
   1. He was saying, "Don't leave home without it!"
B. This empowering comes through an experience called the baptism in the Holy Spirit
   1. It is a command for every Christian (Ac 1:4-5, 8; Ep 5:18).
   2. An essential element in reaping the nations (Lk 24:47-49).
C. You need to be empowered by the Spirit to participate in God's mission of reaping the nations.

Conclusion and Altar Call
   1. Come now to commit yourself to God's mission.
   2. Come to be empowered by the Holy Spirit.

[DRM]

83 Seedtime and Harvest

Sermon in a Sentence: We must commit ourselves to the kingdom principles of sowing and reaping.
Sermon Purpose: That the people will commit themselves to God's harvest.
Text: Mark 4:26-29
Introduction
1. It is harvest time in Africa and around the world.
   a. It is God's time for sowing and reaping.
2. Mark 4:26-29 is especially applicable.
   a. It is one of Jesus' "kingdom parables."
   b. It is known as the Parable of the Growing Seed.
3. This is one of nine parables found in Mk 4, Mt 13, and Lk 8.
   a. They begin with the phrase, "The kingdom of God is like…"
   b. They reveal "principles of the kingdom," that is, how the kingdom of God works.
4. In the Parable of the Growing Seed, Jesus reveals…
   a. …four principles of sowing in the kingdom,
   b. …and two principles of reaping.

I. FOUR PRINCIPLES OF SOWING IN THE KINGDOM
   A. *Principle #1:* The primary task of the church is sowing the seed.
      1. "A man scatters seed on the ground" (v 26).
      2. This is what Jesus did (Lk 8:1).
      2. So did the disciples of Jesus (Lk 9:6; Ac 8:1, 4).
      3. And so must we!
   B. *Principle #2:* The seed has within itself the power to reproduce a harvest.
      1. "Night and day, whether he sleeps or gets up, the seed sprouts and grow, though he does not know how" (v.27).
      2. The power of reproduction is in the seed—not in the sower!
         a. It does not matter *who* sows—it matters *what* you sow.
      3. The gospel is "the power of God unto salvation" (Ro1:16).
   C. *Principle #3:* The soil also has hidden power.
      1. "All by itself the soul produces grain…" (v.28a).
      2. Within the heart of every person is the power of to receive the gospel and be saved.
   D. *Principle #4:* We should expect to see growth in stages.

1. "...first the stalk, then the head, then the full kernel in the head" (v.28b).
2. We must be patient in the work of sowing and reaping.
   E. Implications and applications for us today:
      1. We must be zealous about sowing the seed.
      2. There are two ways we must sow:
         a. We must sow *in abundance*—at every opportunity and in every place.
         b. We must sow *in faith*—we must believe in the power of the seed (the gospel) to produce a harvest.
      3. We must believe in the people we are preaching to.
         a. Like all people, they have been created in the image of God.
         b. They therefore have the ability to receive the gospel and produce a harvest.

II. TWO PRINCIPLES OF REAPING IN THE KINGDOM
   A. *Principle #1:* We must realize that the harvest has come.
      1. "As soon as the grain ripens...the harvest has come" (v.29).
      2. It harvest time across Africa and around the world!
      3. Worldwide, 70,000 become Christians each day
      4. The church in Africa, and other parts of the world, is mobilizing for missions as never before.
      5. God wants to use us in His great harvest.
   B. *Principle #2:* Harvest time is a time of urgency.
      1. "As soon as the grain is ripe, he (*immediately,* KJV) puts the sickle to it, because the harvest has come" (v.29).
      2. Harvest time is a time of urgency!
   C. Implications and applications for us today:
      1. We must be about harvesting.
      2. We must not delay.

Conclusion and Altar Call:
1. The harvest is now.
2. Come and commit yourself to God's harvest.

[DRM]

84 The Sending Mission of the Church

Sermon in a Sentence: The church must mobilize itself to send missionaries to the nations.
Sermon Purpose: That churches and Christians commit themselves to sending and supporting missionaries.
Texts: Romans 10:13-15; Acts 13:1-4
Introduction
- A. To fulfill the Great Commission will require that some obey Christ's command to "Go!"
  1. Jesus commanded, "Go into all the world and preach the gospel to all creation" (Mk 16:15).
  2. Many are saying, "Yes, I will go."
- B. But that is not enough; others must be willing to send.
  1. An unescapable fact: The success of the work of missions rises or falls on the church's commitment to sending.
- C. This message will emphasize the sending mission of the church.
  1. It is the responsibility of every Spirit-filled Christian to be involved in sending missionaries into the harvest.
  2. We will examine two texts to discover what they say about the sending mission of the church.

I. THE NEED TO SEND (Ro 10:13-15)
- A. Before missionaries can go to the nations, there must be those who will send them.
  1. Paul speaks of this in Ro 10:13-15 (Read).
  2. First, he states a wonderful promise. (v.13): "Everyone who calls on the name of the Lord will be saved."
  3. And yet, in vv.14-15 he reveals certain other critical things must happen first:
     - a. First, they must *hear* and *believe* the good news.
     - b. Before that, someone must *preach* the gospel to them.
     - c. But even before that, someone else must *send* them.
- B. For every goer, there must be an army of senders standing behind them and supporting them with their love, prayers, and finances.
  1. Illustration: Just as in the military: for every soldier on the front line, there must be hundreds behind them supporting them.

II. THE ONES WHO SEND (Read Acts 13:1-4)
A. Our text in Acts 13 speaks of two "senders":
 1. The *Holy Spirit* sends:
    a. v.2: "The Holy Spirit said, 'Set apart for me Barnabas and Saul for the work to which I have called them.'"
    b. v.4: "The two of them, sent on their way by the Holy Spirit, went down to Seleucia and sailed from there…"
 2. The *Church* sends:
    a. v.3 "So after they had fasted and prayed, they placed their hands on them and sent them off."
B. God Himself is the first and primary sender:
 1. The Father sends (Jn 1:6; 20:21).
 2. The Son sends (Mt 9:38; Mk 16:15; Jn 20:21).
 3. The Spirit sends (Ac 13:2).
 4. Every true missionary is sent by God (Jn.1:6).
 5. God sends because He has a missionary God. He is on a mission to redeem the nations.
C. The Church joins God in sending.
 1. When the church sends, we simply become partner with God who is the primary sender of missionaries.
 2. This is what we see happening in Ac 13:1-4.

III. OUR COMMITMENT TO SEND
A. We must commit ourselves to joining the Father, Son, and Holy Spirit in sending missionaries to the nations.
B. This commitment to sending involves two essential tasks:
 1. We must *hear* and *obey* the voice of the Spirit!
 2. We must lovingly *care* for those we send (1Ti 5:18).
C. We must care for those we send in at least two ways:
 1. We must faithfully *pray* for them.
 2. We must faithfully *support* them financially.

Conclusion and Altar Call
 1. Come and commit yourself to sending missionaries to God's harvest fields.
 2. Commit yourself to pray.
 3. Commit yourself to give.

[DRM]

85 How Can They Hear?

Sermon in a Sentence: God calls His church to send messengers to the world preaching the gospel of Jesus Christ.

Sermon Purpose: That Christians commit themselves to sharing the gospel in their own sphere of influence and to sending others to where they themselves cannot go.

Text: Romans 10:13-15

Introduction
1. This passage is one of the great missionary passages of the Bible.
2. It compels us to go beyond our current efforts to send missionaries to take the message of Jesus Christ to the unreached people of the world.
3. The central truth of this message is that God calls His church to send messengers to the world preaching the gospel to all.
4. From our text, we glean three compelling missionary facts:

I. Missionary Fact #1: **THOSE WHO HAVE NOT HEARD OF JESUS ARE LOST AND WITHOUT HOPE**
   A. Paul wrote, "Everyone who calls on the name of the Lord will be saved" (v.13).
      1. By implication, those who do not call are not saved.
      2. Jn 3:18: "Whoever does not believe is condemned already..."
   B. Notice Paul's logical progression:
      1. *Calling on the name of the Lord requires faith:* "How, then, can they call on the one they have not believed in?"
      2. *Faith requires hearing:* "And how can they believe in the one of whom they have not heard?"
      3. *Hearing requires preaching:* "How shall they hear without a preacher?"
      4. *Preaching requires sending:* "And how can anyone preach unless they are sent?"
   C. Christ has given His church the responsibility of sending missionaries to the lost people of world.
      1. If we do not, they will die without Christ and without hope.

II. Missionary Fact #2: **JESUS IS GOD'S ONLY ANSWER FOR THIS LOST WORLD**

- A. Some falsely teach there are many pathways to heaven.
    1. To them, all roads lead to heaven—any path you choose will get you there.
    2. That is like saying any airplane will take you to your desired destination.
- B. There is only one way to heaven and only one Savior who gives eternal life—and His name is Jesus.
    1. Jesus: "I am the way and the truth and the life. No one comes to the Father except through me" (Jn 14:6).
    2. Peter: "Salvation is found in no one else, for there is no other name under heaven by which we must be saved" (Act 4:12).
    3. Paul: "For there is one God and one mediator between God and men, the man Christ Jesus" (1Ti 2:5).
- C. This sobering truth compels us to share the message of salvation in Christ with all people everywhere.

III. Missionary Fact #3: **WE MUST COMMIT OURSELVES TO SEND PREACHERS TO TELL THE LOST ABOUT JESUS**
- A. Our text's six key words, put in the reverse order, summarize God's plan for taking the message of salvation the world:
    1. Send… Preach… Hear… Believe… Call… Saved.
- B. Note how the action that starts the chain of events leading to souls being saved is the word "send."
    1. We must personally tell those within our sphere of influence.
    2. And, we must also send others to go where we cannot go.
- C. We, as God's missionary people, must be in the sending business—we must send preachers to the lost people of our world.
    1. Sending involves praying.
    2. Sending involves giving.

Conclusion and Altar Call
1. Come now and commit yourself to sharing the gospel with those around you.
2. Commit yourself to sending others to the nations by giving and praying for missions.

[JO]

86 By All Possible Means
Win the Lost to Christ

Sermon in a Sentence: We must do everything possible to reach the lost for Christ.

Sermon Purpose: That the people of God commit themselves to winning the lost to Christ "by all possible means."

Text: 1 Corinthians 9:22

Introduction
1. In our text Paul spoke of his passion to win people to Christ *"buy all possible means."*
    a. He was excited about missions.
    b. His one great desire in life was to see people saved.
    c. He would therefore do whatever it took to win the lost.
2. We should imitate Paul in His strategies to win people to Christ.

I. **LET'S THINK ABOUT WHAT "BY ALL POSSIBLE MEANS" MEANT TO PAUL** (It meant four things:)
   A. First, it meant that Paul was *willing to invest* his entire life into the work of winning people to Christ.
      1. From the moment Paul met Christ on the Damascus Road, he was ready to give all for Christ and His mission.
      2. He asked Jesus, "What do you want me to do?" (Ac 9:6 KJV).
      3. From that time forward, he sought to do God's will.
   B. Second, it meant that Paul was *willing to adapt* to other peoples' cultures in order to win them to Christ.
      1. In our text he said, "To the weak I became weak, to win the weak. I have become all things to all people so that by all possible means I might save some" (1Co 9:22).
      2. Paul was not afraid to adopt to the customs of others in order to win them to Christ, so long as those customs did not transgress Scripture.
   C. Third, it mean that Paul was *willing to suffer* and endure hardship for the sake of the lost.
      1. Paul described some of his sufferings in 2Co 11:25-27.
      2. Ro 8:18: "I consider that our present sufferings are not worth comparing with the glory that will be revealed in us."

D. Finally, it meant that Paul *focused his ministry* on both people's present needs and their eternal needs.
   1. He sought to see people as God sees them.
   2. He prayed for the sick, cast out demons, fed the hungry—and he presented Christ to them as Savior.

II. **WHAT, THEN, SHOULD "BY ALL POSSIBLE MEANS" MEAN TO US TODAY?** (It means five things:)
   A. First, it means that *we too must become excited* about—and committed to—missions.
   B. Second, it means that *we must commit all* to reach the lost at any cost.
      1. We must pray, give, and go.
   C. Third, it means that *we must reach out to all people*—people of all tribes, races, and cultures.
      1. Paul was committed to reaching "all men" (1Co 9:22).
      2. Since God loves all people, and Jesus died for all, we must not exclude anyone from our missions outreach,
      3. We must identify with people who are different from us.
   D. Fourth, *it means that we must mobilize* ourselves and our churches to reach the lost at home and in distant places.
      1. We must instill missionary vision in our people.
      2. Missions must be done by every believer, every time, and in every place.
   E. Finally, *we must seize every opportunity* to share Christ with the lost.
      1. Paul never missed an opportunity.
      2. We must sow the gospel by all available means.

Conclusion and Altar Call
   1. What are you doing to keep sinners from going to hell?
   2. Will you give, go, and pray?
   3. Come and commit yourself to reaching the lost "by all possible means."

[MO]

87 Four Principles of the Harvest

Sermon in a Sentence: We must obediently commit ourselves to Christ's mission to "feed" the nations.

Sermon Purpose: That the people give themselves to God and His mission.

Text: Matthew 14:13-21

Introduction
1. It is vital that we understand the nature of God's kingdom.
2. The story of Jesus' feeding of the 5,000 reveals *four key principles* concerning the nature and expansion of the kingdom:

I. THE PRINCIPLE OF DIVINE EXPECTATION
A. Jesus expected His disciples to attempt the impossible: "You give them something to eat" (v.16).
   1. They wanted to send them away, but Jesus commanded them to do the impossible.
   2. He told them to feed 5,000 men plus women and children.
B. Today, Christ has given the church an impossible task—to take the bread of life [the gospel) to the nations.
   1. He is telling us, "You do the impossible. You give them something to eat."
C. To do this, God expects to be like Christ.
   1. God commissioned His Son to "go and give."
   2. Now, He expects us to do the same (Jn 3:15; Mk 16:15).
   3. We can do this because we have been infused with the very nature of God (2Co 5:17).

II. THE PRINCIPLE OF DIVINE POSSIBILITY
A. Jesus wants His disciples to understand that "with God all things are possible" (Mk 10:27).
   1. He taught them this principle a few days earlier.
   2. Now, He shows them how the principle operates.
   3. He would use a little boy's faith-filled obedience to do it.
B. The boy's obedient gift became the catalyst for a miracle.
   1. But first, notice the disciples' faithless response:
      a. They emphasized the smallness of the boy's lunch.
      b. They had fallen prey to the "deception of perception."
      c. In other words, our perception of reality often hinders what God is able to do in and through us.

2. In contrast with the disciple's unbelief, the boy's faith-filled obedience prepared the way for a miracle.
   a. When Jesus saw the boy's lunch, He said, "It is enough."
   b. Give what you have to Jesus; *it is enough!*
C. We are living in the time of divine possibility.
   1. The nations can be reached with the gospel.
   2. However, with such possibility comes great responsibility.
   3. We must act in faith and obedience to Christ's commands (Mk 16:15-16; Ac 1:8).

III. THE PRINCIPLE OF DIVINE POWER
A. Jesus wants us to know that apart from Him, and His divine power, we can do nothing (Jn 15:5).
   1. Unless Jesus acts, nothing happens.
   2. As with them, our God-given task is beyond human ability.
   3. Like the broken bread continued feeding the multitude, Christ's broken body continues to "feed" the nations.
B. We, like the disciples in our story, must look to Christ as our source of divine power and provision.
   1. He is the Lord of the Harvest.
   2. He is the Savior, the Healer, and Holy Spirit Baptizer.

IV. THE PRINCIPLE OF DIVINE INTENTION
A. Christ wants everyone to be given an opportunity to eat the Bread of Life.
   1. "They *all* ate and were satisfied" (v.20).
   2. He wants all peoples to have the opportunity to hear the gospel and be saved (2Pe 3:9; see Ps 34:8).
   3. True "satisfaction" can only be found in Jesus.
B. We must share in Christ's desire for everyone to hear the gospel.
   1. We must pray, give, and go.
   2. We must believe that He will work a miracle through us.

Conclusion and Altar Call
1. Come now and commit yourself to Christ's mission.

[SP]

88   Seventy-two Plus You

Sermon in a Sentence: Those who commit themselves to God's purposes and mission are truly blessed.

Sermon Purpose: To call God's people to commit themselves to God's mission of saving the lost.

Text: Luke 10:1-2, 9, 17-20, 23-24

Introduction
1. Our text speaks to us about God's Great Purpose, His Promise of Great Power, and a Great Privilege He offers to us.
2. Let's look at how Jesus offers all three to those who will commit themselves to fulfilling God's mission in the earth.

I. JESUS REVEALS GODS GREAT PURPOSE (vv. 1-2, 9)
A. Jesus appointed 72 disciples and sent them on a mission.
   1. He was transferring His mission to His followers.
      a. He sent them with the same message He proclaimed—the gospel of the kingdom of God (v.9; Mk 1:14).
      b. He sent them to perform the same works that He did—healing the sick (v.9), casting out demons (v.17).
   2. Still today, Jesus is our model for ministry.
   3. Why did Jesus choose and send these men on this mission?
B. Christ sent them because saving people is God's priority.
   1. Nothing is more important to God than His mission.
   2. That is why Jesus came to earth (Lk 19:10).
   3. God's mission is so great that it is worth dying for—and that is exactly what Jesus did.
C. Christ sent them because "the harvest is plentiful" (v. 2).
   1. He sent them because multitudes need to be saved.
   2. Jesus often talked about the harvest (Jn 4:35; Mt 9:36-37).
   3. The problem is not with the harvest—it is plentiful. The problem is rather with the lack of harvesters.
   4. Therefore, Jesus sends out workers
   5. Aand He instructs us to pray for even more workers (v.2).
D. Jesus now calls us to choose His purpose.
   1. Will you make God's purpose your priority?
   2. For everyone who chooses His purposes...

II. JESUS PROMISES GOD'S GREAT POWER (vv.17-20a)
A. This text reminds us that we need God's power to do His work.

1. This is because we are fighting against a strong enemy.
2. Jesus sent out the 72 to set people free from Satan.
3. He therefore gave them authority over all the *power* of the enemy (v.19).
4. The 72 *rejoiced* because Satan could not stand against them.

B. Today Christ promises the same power and authority to those who commit themselves to His great purpose (Jn 14:12; Ac 1:8).
C. Jesus also gives us a word of warning (v.20).
1. Rejoicing in power is dangerous (vv.13-15).
2. We should rejoice in the salvation of souls more than power to work miracles.
3. This will keep us humble and pleasing to God.
4. If we commit ourselves to God's purpose—and we are filled with His power…

III. JESUS OFFERS TO US A GREAT PRIVILEGE (vv.23-24)
A. Jesus' disciples were *blessed* because of what they were seeing.
1. They saw two marvelous things:
   a. They saw the kingdom of God manifested in power.
   b. They saw people responding in faith and being brought into the kingdom.
2. True blessing is related to the fulfillment of God's mission of saving the lost and advancing his kingdom.

B. This privilege can be ours today.
1. Jesus said "blessed are the eyes that see what you see" (v.23).
2. Many today are preoccupied with getting God's blessing.
3. However, true blessing comes when we commit ourselves to God's mission and seek the power of His Holy Spirit.
4. Then we will see what others have longed to see, and our eyes will be the blessed ones to see it.

Conclusion and Altar Call
1. Will you join the 72 and many others who have committed themselves to God's mission?
2. Come now, be filled with the Spirit and commit yourself to God's mission.

[MRT]

89 Becoming a Global Christian
~ Finding Your Strategic Role in World Evangelization ~

Sermon in a Sentence: If we are to achieve "world evangelization in our generation," we must all become Global Christians.
Sermon Purpose: That every listener find their role in God's mission as Global Christians.
Texts: Genesis 12:1-4; Matthew 28:18-20; Revelation 7:9
Introduction
1. Our three verses speak of God's global mission.
2. *This message:* How you can find your strategic role in God's mission of world evangelization.
3. We will address four strategic issues:

I. OUR GOAL—WORLD EVANGELIZATION
A. The goal of the global church is world evangelization.
1. World evangelization is the global distribution of the gospel in all the world so that every person on earth has an opportunity to hear the gospel in their own language and cultural context and be given a chance to make an informed decision on whether or not follow Jesus Christ.

B. Our texts give us an overview of God's plan of world missions:
1. His mission was announced to Abraham (Ge 12:1-3).
2. It was re-emphasized by Jesus (Mt 28:18-20).
3. It will ultimately be fulfilled (Mt 24:14; Rev 7:9).

II. OUR CHALLENGE—REACHING THE WORLD'S UNREACHED BILLIONS
A. According to the Joshua Project
1. *7.25 billion* people live on earth today.
2. *3 billion* of those have little or no access to the gospel.

B. Every person on earth deserves a chance to hear the gospel.
1. Illustration: Imagine a country where the people in the rural areas are starving, while those in the city have many times more to eat than they need. This illustrates the world's situation in regards to the gospel.
2. Our job is to ensure that every person on earth has access to the gospel in their own language and cultural context.

3. Missionary pastor Oswald J. Smith once said, "No one has the right to hear the gospel twice, when some have never heard it even once."

III. OUR SOLUTION—GLOBAL CHRISTIANS
A. God's method of evangelizing the world is to use people…
   1. …and *we* are the people He has chosen to use.
   2. Someone, "The world is not yet fully evangelized because the church is not yet fully missionized."
B. The way to world evangelization is for every Christ-follower to become a Global Christian.
   1. We must not only be *Jerusalem Christians,* we must also be *Judea Christians, Samaria Christians*, and *Ends-of-the-Earth Christians.* (See Ac 1:8.)
C. We must all become Global Christians with a Global Vision.
   1. We must be ready to do whatever it takes to ensure the completion of the Great Commission in this generation.

IV. OUR RESPONSE—WE MUST JOIN THE GLOBAL CHRISTIAN MOVEMENT
A. Missions is not only the work of missionaries—it is the job of all Christians.
   1. Illustration: A soccer team needs more than *strikers.* They also need *goalkeepers, defenders*, and *midfielders.*
   2. The same is true in missions—the work needs more than missionaries, it needs many other Global Christians.
B. Five strategic roles in a Global Christian Team:
   1. *Intercessors* are needed. (Ps. 2:8; Mt 4:37-38)
   2. *Goers* are needed. (Mk 16:15; Is 6:8)
   3. *Senders* are needed. (Ro 10:15; Phi 4:15-16). Sending is supporting the goers through prayer, finances, etc.
   4. *Welcomers* are needed. (Lev 19:34). "Welcomers" show hospitality to the internationals who live in their countries, and they introduce them to Jesus.
   5. *Mobilizers* are needed. "Mobilizers" work to see others awakened, trained, and released into missional ministry.

Conclusion and Altar Call
1. God has a place for you in His global missions team.
2. Come now, and commit yourself to be a Global Christian.

[RSK]

90. The Greatest Story Ever Told

Sermon in a Sentence: We must each become part of God's story (His-story) and His mission to redeem fallen mankind.
Sermon Purpose: That God's people will commit themselves to doing their part to participate in God's mission to redeem the nations.
Text: Matthew 28:18-20; Acts 1:8

Introduction
1. The Bible is the greatest story ever told.
2. It is His-story—the story of God and His redemptive mission.
3. In this message we will look at how God has written His own story in the Bible and how we may each participate in His-story.

I. THE BIBLE IS HIS-STORY
A. The Bible is *one story.*
  1. It is the story of God carrying out His mission to redeem fallen humanity.
  2. Let's look quickly at five highlights of that story:
B. Early in the story God chose *one man.* (Read Ge 12:1-3)
  1. God later promised Abraham, "Through your offspring all nations on earth will be blessed" (Ge 26:4).
  2. He was talking about Jesus. (Read Ga 3:16.)
C. Then, God appointed *one nation* to carry out His mission.
  1. He raised up the nation of Israel, "a great nation."
  2. He told them, "The whole earth is mine, you will be for me a kingdom of priests and a holy nation" (Ex 16:5-6).
  3. In other words, Israel would represent God to the nations.
D. Then, God established *one eternal kingdom.*
  1. He promised David, "Your throne will be established forever" (2Sa 7:16).
  2. God would carry out His mission to redeem all nations through a king and an eternal kingdom.
E. Eventually, God sent *one King* to set on the throne of David.
  1. Jesus, "the son of David, the son of Abraham" (Mt 1:1).
  3. He will reign from the throne of David forever (Lk 1:32).
  4. He is the "Savior of the world" (Jn 4:42).
F. Now, God has *one missionary people.*
  1. He has chosen us to proclaim His name to the nations.
  2. "Go and make disciples of all nations…" (Mt 28:18-20).
  3. He has given us power to accomplish the mission (Ac 1:8).

II. HIS-STORY HAS BECOME OUR STORY
   A. The Pentecostal Church has become part of HIS-story.
      1. It began in with a mighty outpouring of the Holy Spirit in a small mission on Azusa Street in Los Angeles, California, USA, in 1906.
      2. The revival has spread around the world.
      3. Now, 350 million Pentecostals worship in 1 million local congregations worldwide.
      4. Pentecostal churches are bringing 50,000 people to Christ every day.
   B. Revival was born in the crucible of prayer and hunger for God.
      1. We must commit ourselves wholly to God.
      2. We must call on His Spirit to fill and empower us.

III. NOW, HIS MISSION MUST BECOME OUR MISSION
   A. At the heart of the early Pentecostal movement was the message of missions.
      1. Missionaries went directly from Azusa to Liberia, Angola, South Africa, and other parts of the world.
      2. At its second General Council in 1914, the newly-formed Assemblies of God committed itself to "the greatest evangelism in the world has ever seen."
      3. Today, the AG reports 68 million believers meeting in 366,000 churches in 252 countries around the world.
   B. This is our moment in history to participate in HIS-story.
      1. 3 billion people in the world have never heard of Jesus.
      2. There remain more than 850 unreached tribes in Sub-Sahara Africa.
   C. How shall we respond?
      1. We must understand our role in fulfilling God's mission.
      2. We must be empowered by the Spirit (Ac 1:4-8).
      3. We must commit ourselves to give, go, and pray.

Conclusion and Altar Call
   1. Come now and commit yourself to God and His mission.
   2. Come and be filled with the Spirit.

[BVW]

91 The Holy Spirit the Director of Missions

Sermon in a Sentence: We must allow the Spirit to direct us in the work of missions.

Sermon Purpose: To encourage Christians to pray, and then listen to and obey the Spirit's voice directing them in missions.

Text: Act 8:26-40

Introduction
1. The book of Acts tells the story of how the Spirit empowered and directed the church to spread the gospel (Ac 1:8).
2. Chapter 8 tells of how "Philip went down to the city of Samaria, and preached Christ unto them" (v.5).
3. He later went to Gaza and led an African man to Christ (Tell the story: vv.26-40.)
4. From Philip's ministry, we learn four powerful lessons that will help us to be more effective in missions:

I. LIKE PHILIP, WE MUST OBEY THE SPIRIT'S VOICE
A. When the Spirit spoke, Philip quickly obeyed.
 1. An angel appeared to Him and told him to go to Gaza (v.26).
 2. The Spirit then directed him to the Ethiopian's chariot (29).
 3. Both times Philip immediately obeyed (vv.27, 30).
B. Like Philip, we must hear and obey the voice of the Spirit.
 1. We must seek God's face and listen to His voice.
 2. Then, when He speaks, we must immediately obey.
 3. The Spirit knows best where and when the gospel needs to be preached.

II. LIKE PHILIP, WE MUST BE WILLING TO BREAK SOCIAL AND CULTURAL BARRIERS
A. Philip went to a Gentile African.
 1. Gentiles were considered "unclean" to the Jews.
 2. Nevertheless, the Spirit told Philip to approach the man.
 3. In doing this, Philip broke ethnic and social barriers.
B. Racial prejudice is a major hindrance to missions work.
 1. Some Christians shun particular tribe or people because of their history, customs, and racial prejudices.
 2. This is wrong, as the Spirit showed Peter (Ac 10:28; 11:8-9).

C. We, like Jesus and the apostles, must be willing to cross social and cultural barriers to preach the gospel to all people.
  1. Philip crossed the walls that segregated the Jews from the Samaritans and the African nobleman.
  2. He was following the example of Jesus who went to the Samaritan woman (Jn 4:9).
  3. We too must be willing to cross any social, racial, cultural or tribal barriers to preach the gospel to all.

III. LIKE PHILIP, WE MUST SEIZE THE OPPORTUNITY
A. The Ethiopian nobleman was ripe for harvest.
  1. The Lord had prepared his heart to receive the gospel.
     a. He was reading from the Bible, seeking the truth.
     b. His heart was open ready to receive the gospel.
  2. Then God arranged a "divine appointment" between Philip and the man.
  3. Philip seized the opportunity, obeyed the Spirit, went to the man, and told him about Jesus.
B. Today is a day of great opportunity.
  1. Jesus said that "the fields are ripe for harvest" (Jn 4:35).
  2. We must quickly put in the sickle and reap (Mk 4:29).
  3. Today's great need is laborers for the harvest.
C. We must seize the opportunity.

IV. LIKE PHILIP, WE MUST ACCOMPLISH OUR MISSION
A. Philip's mission was to reach a lost man for Christ.
  1. He preached Christ to the African man (v.35).
  2. He then baptized the man in water according to Christ's command in Matthew 28:19 (v.36-38).
  3. The Ethiopian Eunuch went home rejoicing (v.39).
  4. He became the first missionary to take the gospel to Africa.
B. We too must accomplish our God-given mission.
  1. We must lead people to Christ, baptize, and disciple them
  2. Then, we must lead them into the baptism in the Spirit and mobilize them to reach others for Christ.
  3. Until we so these things work remains incomplete.

Conclusion and Altar Call
1. Come now and commit and be filled with the Spirit.
2. Come, and commit yourself to God's mission.   [PFM]

92 Everywhere!

Sermon in a Sentence: Every follower of Jesus Christ must fully participate in God's mission to reach the lost in every place.

Sermon Purpose: That believers might be filled with the Spirit and fully commit themselves and their churches to fulfilling the Great Commission of Christ.

Text: Matthew 16:13-18

Introduction:
1. In our text Jesus declares, "I will build My church!" (v.18).
    a. As the church of Jesus Christ, we are His *ekklesia,* which means, we are His "called-out ones."
    b. We have been called out of the world unto Him for His purposes.
2. Jesus has thus commissioned *every believer, to go everywhere to reach everyone* with the gospel.
3. He declared that His church will be built on His life, His death, and His resurrection power.
4. With these things in mind, let's look at three biblical principles through which Christ builds His church:

I. PRINCIPLE 1: EVERY CHURCH IS A MISSION OUTPOST
A. Jesus has given His church a clear mission:
   1. To preach the gospel to all creation (Mk 16:15-20).
   2. To disciple all nations (Mt 28:18-20).
   3. To obey Him as He obeyed the Father (Jn 20:21-22).
   4. To be His empowered witnesses to the ends of the earth (Ac 1:8).
B. Therefore, every church must be an outpost from where the gospel spreads to the village, city, region, and the world.
   1. This includes both national and local churches.
   2. The more churches we plant, the more outposts we have.
C. No power in hell can prevail against the church—because it moves in the power of the Holy Spirit and in the authority of Jesus' name.
   1. Jesus has given us the power of binding and loosing (v.19).

II. PRINCIPLE 2: EVERY PASTOR IS A MISSIONS MOBILIZER

A. Every local pastor is responsible for mobilizing his or her church to reach the lost at home and around the world.
B. We mobilize the church in these ways:
   1. By teaching them about God's mission.
   2. By leading them into the baptism in the Holy Spirit.
   3. By teaching them to give, pray, and go.
   4. By going with them to win the lost and plant churches.
C. We must not neglect this great responsibility.
   1. We must be like Jesus: "Come, follow me…and I will make you fishers of men" (Mt 4:19).
   2. The wise man said, "He who sleeps during harvest is a disgraceful son" (Pr 10:5).

III. PRINCIPLE 3: EVERY BELIEVER IS A MISSIONARY
A. The call to reach the lost is not for pastors only.
   1. Every believer in Jesus Christ has been called to participate in God's mission of redeeming the lost (Lk 14:23).
   2. Philip was a deacon but he went and preached Christ to the people of Samaria (Ac 8:5-13).
B. We must each do our part to evangelize the nations.
   1. We must all *go* to our world and share Christ with the lost.
   2. We must all *pray* for the success of God's mission.
   3. We must all *give* our time, talent, and treasure to reach the lost at home and around the world.
C. But first you must be empowered by the Holy Spirit.
   1. Jesus' last command: ""Do not leave Jerusalem, but wait for the gift my Father promised, which you have heard me speak about. For John baptized with water, but in a few days you will be baptized with the Holy Spirit" (Ac 1:4-5).
   2. Jesus' last promise: "But you will receive power when the Holy Spirit comes on you; and you will be my witnesses in Jerusalem, and in all Judea and Samaria, and to the ends of the earth" (Ac 1:8).

Conclusion and Altar Call:
1. Every church must be a missions station, and every believer must be a Spirit-empowered missionary.
2. Come and commit yourself to God's mission today.
3. Come, and be empowered by the Spirit.

[SE]

93 The Cost of Missions

Sermon in a Sentence: We must all be willing to pay the cost for reaching the world for Christ.
Sermon Purpose: That the people will give themselves completely to Christ and His mission.
Text: Luke 14:25-33
Introduction:
1. How much does it cost to do missions?
2. In our text Jesus answers that question:
   a. He said that we must count the cost of following Him.
   b. To follow Him in missions we must "take up [our] cross and follow Him," and we must "love Him more than we love our own lives" (vv. 26-27).
3. In other words, to do missions we must surrender all that we have to the One who calls us to follow His example.
4. We often sing, "I surrender all," but do we really know what that means?
5. This message will discuss both obvious costs and hidden costs of missions:

I. THE OBVIOUS COSTS OF MISSIONS
A. We could call this our "intentional payments to missions."
   1. When we purchase something, we make an intentional choice— and then we make intentional payment.
   2. We know what we are getting into.
   3. In missions, we must know what we are getting into.
B. In our text, Jesus gave two illustrations of counting the cost:
   1. A *builder* counting the cost before building a tower.
   2. A *general* counting the cost before or going into war.
   3. Likewise, we must count the cost of doing missions.
C. Every disciple of Christ is required to participate in fulfilling the Great Commission in three ways:
   1. Every disciple must *pray* for missions:
      a. For our lost family, friends, and neighbors.
      b. For those around the world who have never heard.
      c. For the missionaries we send.
   2. Every disciple must *give* to missions.
      a. Including one-time donations and monthly support.
      b. We can give donations of clothing and produce.

       c. However we give, we must all give sacrificially.
  3. Every disciple must *go* to missions.
       a. Some will leave the country to go to other lands.
       b. Some will go to an unreached people inside the country.
       c. Others will go to their family, friends, neighbors, schoolmates, or coworkers.
       d. We are all required to share the gospel with others.

II. THE HIDDEN COSTS OF MISSIONS

  A. While there are the more obvious costs to doing missions, there are other "hidden costs" that most people never see.
    1. Illustration: It's like when you purchase a vehicle. You see the cost of vehicle itself, but you don't see the hidden costs of fees such as taxes, fuel, maintenance, etc.
  B. What are some of the "hidden costs" of missions?
    1. The cost of being misunderstood by your family and friends.
    2. The cost of being misjudged by your ministerial colleagues.
    3. The cost of being unappreciated by the people you have been sent to minister to.
    4. The cost of living without the conveniences of life.
    5. The cost of being far away from family.
    6. The cost of living in dangerous situations.
    7. The cost to one's health of living far from medical services.
    8. The cost of enduring persecution.
  C. We must be willing to pay both the visible and hidden cost of doing missions.

Conclusion and Altar Call
1. Is missions worth the cost?
2. Yes, it is worth it, for what price can we place on a soul?
3. Hear the words of Jesus: "If anyone comes to me and does not hate his father and mother, his wife and children, his brothers and sisters—yes, even his own life—he cannot be my disciple. And anyone who does not carry his cross and follow me cannot be my disciple" (Lk 14:26-27).
4. Come and commit your all to missions today.

[LE]

94 Missionary Lessons from Elijah

Sermon in a Sentence: We must all be empowered by the Spirit, and then we must go boldly to proclaim Christ to the lost.

Sermon Purpose: To see the people empowered by the Holy Spirit and actively witnessing for Christ.

Texts: 1Kings 17:2-3; 18:1 (ESV). Emphasize the phrases "hide yourself" and "show yourself."

Introduction
1. Our text tells us part of the exciting story of Elijah the prophet. (Briefly tell the story of chapters 17-18.)
2. From two commands that God gave to Elijah, we can learn some important missionary lessons.

I. GOD COMMANDED ELIJAH, "HIDE YOURSELF"
A. Read and explain 1Kings 17:2-3 (ESV).
   1. God told Elijah to *hide himself* by the brook Cherith.
   2. Why did God want Elijah to hide himself?
   3. God had a work *for* Elijah to do—but first, He had a work to do *in* Elijah.
B. Elijah needed to learn some important lessons:
   1. That God would *provide* for him (17:4-6; 8-9).
   2. That God would *project* him.
   3. That God would *guide* him.
C. Like with Elijah, there are times when God wants us to hide ourselves.
   1. We must seek Him in prayer and fasting.
   2. We submit ourselves to Him and His mission.
   3. We must receive His power and guidance.

II. THEN, GOD COMMAND ELIJAH, "SHOW YOURSELF"
A. Read and explain 1Kings 18:1 (ESV)
   1. God had a work for Elijah to do.
   2. The time had come for Elijah to leave his place of solitude and deliver the message God had given him.
B. Notice how Elijah responded to God's command.
   1. He obeyed and went (18:2).
   2. He boldly delivered God's message (vv.15-18; 21).
   3. He demonstrated God's power (18:23-38).

4. He brought a nation to its knees (v 39).
   5. He was an agent of God's blessing (rain). (18:41-46).
  C. Like with Elijah, there are times when God expects us to show ourselves.
   1. We must go out and boldly proclaim Christ to the world.
   2. We must demonstrate Christ's love and power.

III. JESUS HAS GIVEN TO US THE SAME TWO COMMANDS THAT GOD GAVE TO ELIJAH
  A. As Jesus was about to return to heaven, He left His church with two parting commands:
   1. First, He told them that "repentance for the forgiveness of sins will be preached in his name to all nations" (Lk 24:46-47).
    a. Like Elijah, they were to show themselves.
    b. They were to go and proclaim the gospel to all nations.
   2. Then, he told them, "Stay in the city until you have been clothed with power from on high" (v.48).
    a. Before they showed themselves, they would need to hide themselves.
    b. They would need to be empowered by the Holy Spirit. (Read and discuss Acts 1:4-5, 8).
    c. They received the Spirit's power at Pentecost (Ac 2:1-4).
    d. They immediately began to call people to repentance and faith in Christ (Ac 2:14; 38-39, 41)
  B. Jesus has given us the same two commands:
   1. First, we must first *hide ourselves*.
    a. We must commit ourselves to God and His mission.
    b. We must be empowered by the Holy Spirit.
   2. Then, we must *show ourselves*.
    a. We must boldly proclaim Christ.
    b. We must demonstrate His power.
    c. We must go to the nations in the power of the Spirit.

Conclusion and Altar Call
 1. Come and commit yourself to proclaiming Christ to the lost.
 2. Come and be empowered by the Holy Spirit.

[DRM]

~ SECTION 7 ~
PRAYER AND SPIRITUAL WARFARE

95 Motivated for Mission

Sermon in a Sentence: Like Paul, we must be motived for mission through intercession, impartation, and proclamation.

Sermon Purpose: That the hearers understand the true motivators for mission and that they commit themselves to doing God's work.

Text: Romans 1:9-17 (NIV)

Introduction
1. What kind of compelling motivation must one have to be an effective servant of the Lord today?
2. In our text, Paul spoke of his motivation (or inner drive) for mission: "I serve *with my whole heart* in preaching the gospel of his Son" (v.9).
3. Our text further reveals what motivated Paul—and how that same motivation will help us to effectively carry out God's mission today.
4. Consider with me the importance of *Intercession, Impartation,* and *Proclamation* in motivating us for mission today.

I. PAUL WAS MOTIVATED BY INTERCESSION
   A. Intercession was the underlying source of Paul's service to God.
      1. Note vv.9-10: "I constantly I remember you in *my prayers.*"
      2. Paul literally lived in prayer (1Th 5:17).
      3. Prayer was what urged him to go to the Romans.
   B. Authentic passion for *going* is the product of *prayer*.
      1. Passion born of anything but prayer is little more than a profession or job.
      2. However, when one's heart is linked by prayer to God and people, their going will be divinely motivated.
      3. Paul testified: "I pray that now at last *by God's will* the way may be opened for me to come to you" (v.10).
      4. Authentic desire for going starts with impassioned prayer.
   C. We must commit ourselves to fervent intercession for the lost.

II. PAUL WAS MOTIVATED BY IMPARTATION
   A. Impartation was a primary reason for Paul's missionary journeys.
      1. Paul told the Roman Christians, "I long to see you *so that I may impart* to you some spiritual gift…" (v.11).
      2. Paul wanted to share what he had received from God.

B. Paul's desire to be an agent of impartation drove him to go.
   1. Hear his impassioned words: "I long to see you..." (v.11).
   2. Understand his reason "...that I may impart to you..."
C. Paul wanted to impart what was most needed:
   1. "I long to see you so that I may impart to you *some spiritual gift* to make you strong" (v. 11)
   2. Paul's chief desire was not to give the buildings, or goods, or programs, or methods but something spiritual.
   3. Christians are engaged in spiritual ministry and warfare, and they needed to be strong—Only *some spiritual gift* will do!
D. Paul's ultimate desire "that I might have a harvest among you" (v.13).
   1. Only spiritual impartation will result in a spiritual harvest.
   2. We cannot give what we do not possess.

III. PAUL WAS MOTIVATED BY PROCLAMATION (vv.14-16)
A. Proclamation of the gospel of Christ was the overarching purpose of Paul's life. (See Ac 9:15; 1Co 9:16-17.)
B. This noble purpose is summed up in Paul's three "I am's":
   1. *"I am obligated* to both Greeks and non-Greeks..." (v.14). (Paul was not motivated primarily by need or opportunity, but rather by God's love [see 2Co 5:14].)
   2. *"I am eager* to preach the gospel..." (v.15). (The harvest needs technicians and specialists—but more than anything else, it needs anointed preachers of the gospel.)
   3. *"I am not ashamed* of the gospel..." (v.16). (Paul had ultimate faith that the message of Christ is "the power of God unto salvation to everyone who believes.")
C. We must share in Paul's confidence in the gospel—and His passion and commitment to share the good news about Christ with all people.

Conclusion and Altar Call
1. Come now and commit yourself to God's mission.
2. Ask God to fill you fill you with His Spirit and give you the right motivations for doing His work.

[DC]

96 Prayer and the Mission of God
~ Doing God's Work in God's Way ~

Sermon in a Sentence: If we are to do God's work in God's way, we must commit ourselves to prayer.
Sermon Purpose: That God's people will commit themselves to fervent prayer for God's mission.
Text: Acts 6:3-4
Introduction
1. E. M. Bounds wrote, "What the Church needs today is not more machinery or better, not new organizations or more and novel methods, but men whom the Holy Ghost can use—men of prayer."
2. Our text is one example of how the early Christians prayed.
    a. The apostles were committed to prayer and proclamation.
    b. They understood the importance of prayer to advancing the kingdom of God.
3. This message: "Prayer and the Mission of God: Doing God's Work in God's Way."
    a. For God's mission to progress with speed to the ends of the earth, we must give ourselves to fervent prayer.
    b. Transition: Let's begin by discussing…

I. THE MEANING OF MISSIONS
A. What do we mean by the word "missions"?
   1. *Missions is* proclaiming the gospel to the lost so they can be rescued from the dominion of darkness and brought into the kingdom of God through faith in Christ Jesus.
   2. Further, *missions is* God working through His Church in the power of the Holy Spirit so that His redemption will be extended to all.
B. Missions is the plan of God.
   1. Missions was not created by the Church—on the contrary, God's mission created the Church.
   2. The Church is simply the means through which God works to execute His mission.
   3. However, we must never think that we can accomplish God's mission in our own ability and by our own means.
       a. We will never have enough intelligence, money, equipment, or technology to get the job done.

II. SPIRITUAL NEEDS REQUIRE SPIRITUAL MEANS
   A. We must never forget that missions is a work of the Spirit.
      1. The great need of humanity is spiritual.
      2. Mankind's great problem is sin and separation from God.
   B. Therefore, the solution must also be spiritual.
      1. Only the Spirit can change the heart of man.
      2. The Holy Spirit works through the Church to call people to repentance and faith in Christ.
      3. He works through those who give themselves to prayer.
      4. When we fail to pray, we chose to rely on ourselves; when we give ourselves to prayer, we choose to rely on God.
   D. The mission of God requires His people to be women and men of prayer so that the Spirit can work His purpose through us.

III. THE USE OF SPIRITUAL MEANS RESULTS IN SPIRITUAL FRUIT (For instance…)
   A. Prayer strengthens our relationship with God.
      1. The main purpose for praying is to discover God—to get to know Him.
      2. As we get to know Him, we become like Him.
   B. Prayer brings down the power and presence of God.
      1. This what happened at Pentecost.
         a. Before Pentecost they prayed ten days (Ac 1:14).
         b. Then, God's Spirit was poured out, and 3,000 people were added to the church (Ac 2:1-4; 41).
      2. When prayer is directed to God, it ascends to heaven empowered by the promises of and presence of God.
   C. Prayer will result in the church advancing in the power of the Spirit.
      1. In Acts every forward thrust of the church was immersed in prayer.

Conclusion and Altar Call
   1. We must do God's work in God's way, that is, we must saturate the work with prayer.
   2. Come and commit yourself to praying for God's mission.
   3. Come and be empowered by the Holy Spirit.

[DMc]

97 Overcoming the Enemy
~ Insights for Spiritual Warriors ~

Sermon in a Sentence: In advancing God's kingdom, we must engage and overcome spiritual powers.

Sermon Purpose: That believers commit themselves to advancing God's kingdom in the power of the Holy Spirit.

Texts: Revelation 12:7-12; Ephesians 6:12-13

Introduction
1. Our texts are two examples of spiritual warfare in Scripture.
    a. The first, *in the heavenlies:* Michael and his angels fighting against the dragon and his angels.
    b. The second: *on earth:* Our spiritual warfare against "the rulers, against the authorities, against the powers…"
2. This message will talk about some missional implications and tactics of spiritual warfare.

I. THE SCRIPTURES DESCRIBE FOUR KINDS OF SPIRITUAL WARFARE
A. *Cosmic* spiritual warfare
   1. In the heavenlies between angelic and demonic warriors.
   2. Described in our first text (Rev 12:7-12)
B. *Strategic* spiritual warfare
   1. On earth against spiritual "principalities and powers"
   2. Described in second text (Ep 6:12)
C. *Tactical* spiritual warfare
   1. On the earth (Ground level spiritual warfare).
   2. Described in Mk 16:17: "they shall cast out demons."
D. *Internal* spiritual warfare
   1. The battle for the mind (2Co 10:5).
   2. The battle against temptation and carnal attitudes.
   3. Transition: The rest of this message will discuss two missional issues concerning spiritual warfare.

I. THE OBJECTIVES OF SPIRITUAL WARFARE
A. We must understand *why* we engage in spiritual warfare.
   1. It is more than just beating up on the devil—or "showing off" in the Spirit—or "being Pentecostal."
   2. The purpose of spiritual warfare is to advance God's kingdom in the earth. (Read Lk 4:18-19.)

B. Four objectives of spiritual warfare:
   1. To bring God's salvation to the nations.
   2. To demonstrate God's great power and glory.
   3. To advance the kingdom of God in the earth.
   4. To bring ourselves, and others, into full submission to the authority of Christ.
C. Christ has commissioned us to engage in such spiritual warfare (Mk 16:15-18).

II. THREE SPIRITUAL TACTICS WE MUST USE TO DEFEAT SATAN (John spoke of these three tactics in Revelation 12:11. They are…)
A. Appropriating the provisions of Christ's work on the cross.
   1. "They overcame Him by the blood of the Lamb" (v.11).
   2. Those provisions include *salvation* from sin, *holiness* of life, and the *empowering* of the Spirit (Ac 2:33).
   3. All are appropriated by faith.
B. Courageously proclaiming the gospel of Christ (v.11).
   1. "They overcame him by…the word of their testimony."
   2. This speaks of the proclamation of the gospel.
      a. That is, "the testimony of Jesus" (Rev 1:9; 12:17; 20:4).
   3. Our primary responsibility as disciples of Jesus is to testify for Him, that is, to be His witnesses (Ac 1:8).
C. Totally committing ourselves to God and His mission.
   1. "They overcame him… [because] they loved not their lives even unto death" (v.11).
   2. In other words, they were totally committed to Christ and His mission.
      a. Jesus calls us to total commitment (Lk 14:26-27).
      b. We see that commitment lived out by Jesus (He 10:7; Lk 22:42).
      c. We also see it lived out by the disciples in Acts.

Conclusion and Altar Call
1. We have been called to engage in spiritual warfare to advance God's kingdom in the earth.
2. We can to it—if we will appropriate the provisions of Christ's work on the cross, boldly proclaim the gospel to the lost, and totally commit ourselves to Christ and His mission.
3. Come now and make those commitments.

[DRM]

98 Help Them with Our Prayers

Sermon in a Sentence: Your prayers can make a huge difference in the lives and ministries of our missionaries.
Sermon Purpose: That Christians will commit themselves to pray for their missionaries.
Text: 2 Corinthians 1:8-11
Introduction
1. In our text, Paul asks the Christians in Corinth to pray for him.
2. He first shared with them his difficulties (Read v.8).
    a. In Asia, he had lived and ministered under great stress.
    b. He even "despaired of life."
3. He then confessed faith in God and in their prayers: "On him we have set our hope that he will continue to deliver us, as you help us *by your prayers*" (vv.10-11).
4. Our missionaries need our financial support…
5. …they also need our prayer support.
    a. Your prayers for missionaries makes a huge difference in their lives and ministries.
    b. This message will discuss why and how we can pray for our missionaries.

I. MISSIONARIES OFTEN FACE CHALLENGING CIRCUMSTANCES IN THEIR LIVES AND MINISTRIES
A. Paul faced great challenges in the Roman province of Asia.
   1. He wrote, "We suffered hardships in the province of Asia… We were under great pressure, far beyond our ability to endure…We despaired of life" (v.8).
   3. Later in 2 Corinthians, Paul lists some of the great challenges he faced in ministry. (Read 2Co 11:23-28.)
B. Missionaries experience the same difficulties we all face…
   1. …however, because of their circumstances, these difficulties are often amplified.
   2. For instance family, health, and financial issues.
   3. Imagine having to deal with these problems while thousands of miles away from home.
C. Missionaries also face unique difficulties. (For instance…)
   1. Living in a strange culture, learning another language.
   2. Dealing with hostile governments and religions.

   3. Lack of adequate health and educational services.
   4. Challenges from demonic spirits.
  D. In the midst of these challenges, they seek to fulfill their ministries (Bible school, church planting, building, etc.)
  E. Our missionaries really need our prayers.

II. YOUR PRAYERS CAN MAKE A HUGE DIFFERENCE IN THE LIVES OF OUR MISSIONARIES.
  A. In our text, Paul shared how the saint's prayers sustained him.
   1. Paul relied on God and their prayers.
   2. As a result, "God delivered us from…deadly peril."
  B. Scripture teaches us the awesome power of prayer, for instance…
   1. Moses prayed—and the Red Sea opened…
   2. Joshua prayed—and the walls of Jericho fell…
   3. The Corinthian church prayed—and Paul was delivered.
   4. And when we pray for our missionaries—God moves and meets their needs.

III. WE MUST NOT FAIL TO PRAY FOR OUR MISSIONARIES.
  A. Here are some specific ways you can pray for missionaries:
   1. Pray for them by name.
   2. Pray for their ongoing needs (health and protection; children's education; care and provision; emotional needs; spiritual well-being; victory over evil spirits)
   3. Pray for their success of their ministries.
   4. Pray for them as the Spirit leads and prompts.
  B. Let's be generous and faithful in praying for our missionaries.

Conclusion and Altar Call
  1. Only in heaven knows the effect our prayers had on the lives and ministries of our missionaries.
  2. Come now and commit yourself to praying for our missionaries.

[JO]

99 Opening Prayers

Sermon in a Sentence: We must pray that God will open the way for effective gospel witness.

Sermon Purpose: To encourage God's people to pray for the work of evangelism and mission.

Text: Acts 4:31

Introduction
1. In our text, the disciples prayed a missionary prayer. They asked God to empower them—and embolden them—to proclaim Jesus to the lost in the power of the Holy Spirit.
2. Every stage of kingdom advance is founded on prayer.
3. Only God can make the way; however, as we go, we must pray "opening prayers."
4. This message: Three ways we can pray "opening prayers":

I. WE MUST PRAY FOR OPEN DOORS
A. It is better to walk through a door God has opened than to try to force our way through a closed and locked door.
B. Satan seeks to keep doors closed.
  1. He blinds the eyes of unbelievers (2Co 4:4).
  2. He hinders us from going to the work (1Th 2:18).
C. Jesus, however, is the "Lord of the Open Door."
  1. He has all authority in heaven and earth (Mt 28:18).
  2. He opens and closes doors (Re 3:8).
  3. He opened doors for Paul (1Co 16:9; 2Co 2:12).
D. We must pray for open doors:
  1. Paul often asked for prayer that God would open doors.
  2. Once while in prison (Col 4:3).

II. WE MUST PRAY FOR OPEN MOUTHS
A. Once God opens the door, we must walk through it, open our mouths, and proclaim the good news.
  1. This is how the disciples prayed in our text (Ac 4:28-31).
B. We too must pray that we will be ready to preach the gospel when the opportunities come.
  1. Pray that God will give us words (Ep 6:19).
  2. Pray that God will fill us with the Holy Spirit and empower our words (Ac 1:8; 4:31, 33).

C. Then we will be able to preach with power and conviction (1Th 1:5).
      1. With "words taught by the Spirit" (1Co 2:13).
      2. The Spirit will make our words effective (Ac 14:1).
      3. None of us really knows how to preach; we need our mouths to be opened by God.
   D. We must therefore pray that we may "speak the word with great boldness" (Ac 4:29).
      1. God will answer our prayer (Ac 4:31a).
      2. He will open our mouths to speak with power:
         a. He did it with the apostles (Ac 4:31, 33).
         b. He did it with Stephen (Ac 6:10).
         c. He will do it for us today!

I. **WE MUST PRAY FOR OPEN HEARTS**
   A. As we go to preach the gospel, we must pray that God will open the hearts of those who hear the word.
   B. Paul often asked people to pray to this end (2Th 3:1).
   C. If we will pray, the Spirit will open people's hearts to receive the good news.
      1. Jesus opened the hearts of the disciples on the Road to Emmaus (Lk 24:31).
      2. He also opened the disciples' hearts to understand the Scriptures (24:27, 45)
      3. The Spirit opened Lydia's heart to the gospel (Ac 16:14).
      4. The Spirit will open unbelievers' hearts (1Co 14:24-25).
   D. But we must pray for open hearts.

Conclusion and Altar Call
   1. Come and commit yourself to pray for open doors and open hearts.
   2. Then join me in walking through those open doors.

[PW]

100 Prayer and the Missionary Task

Sermon in a sentence: If we will seek the Lord in prayer, the Spirit will show us the right people and the right moment to send missionaries.

Sermon Purpose: To challenge the church to send missionaries in a truly Spirit-directed manner.

Text: Acts 13:1-4

Introduction
1. In Acts, the Holy Spirit is the Director of Missions.
2. We have an example of this in Acts 13:1-4.
3. With this event, the church in Acts launches its mission to "the ends of the earth" as Jesus had instructed (Ac 1:8).
4. From this story, we learn four important missionary lessons:

I. THE IMPETUS FOR MISSION: THE HOLY SPIRIT
A. The Holy Spirit is force behind all true missions.
   1. He is the one who compels us to go and tell others.
   2. The Holy Spirit ordered, "Set apart for me Barnabas and Saul for the work to which I have called them" (v.2).
   3 They were "sent on their way by the Holy Spirit" (v.4).
B. The Holy Spirit always disturbs the status-quo.
   1. He leads to the next phase of church growth and advance.
   2. He pushes us to missions beyond our comfort zones.
C. In Acts, we see the Holy Spirit directing missions in three ways:
   1. The Holy Spirit *initiates mission.*
      a. After receiving the Spirit at Pentecost, Peter immediately began to declare Christ to the lost (Ac 2:4, 14, 41).
      b. In Antioch, the Spirit initiated Paul and Barnabas' first missionary journey (Ac 13:1-4).
   2. The Holy Spirit *guides mission.*
      a. Philip was guided by the Spirit to go to the Ethiopian nobleman (Ac 8:29).
      b. Step-by-step the Holy Spirit guided Paul and his missionary colleagues into Europe (Ac 16:6-10).
   3. The Holy Spirit *universalizes mission.*
      a. The Holy Spirit pushed Peter across the impossible chasm between Jew and Gentile (Ac 10:1-48; 11:12).
      b. Opened the door for missions to the "ends of the earth."

II. THE PERSONNEL FOR MISSION: BARNABAS AND SAUL
A. The Holy Spirit prepares the right people for mission.
B. Barnabas and Saul had proved themselves through faithful service in the Antioch church (11:22-26; 13:1).
   1. They had gained the confidence of the people (11:30).
C. The experience that Barnabas and Saul had gained prepared them for more effective missionary work.

III. THE TIMING OF MISSION: WAITING ON GOD
A. Saul had known from the time of his conversion that he was called to go to the Gentiles (Ac 9:15-16; 22:21; 26:14-18).
   1. Years of preparation had passed since Saul's conversion.
   2. This day came as no surprise to Barnabas and Saul (v.2).
   3. It was a moment they had been anticipating.
B. Waiting is sometimes part of preparation for missions.
   1. Jesus ordered His disciples to wait for Pentecost (Ac 1:4).
   2. While waiting, Paul and Barnabas involved themselves in prayer and local church ministry (Ac 11:26).
   3. While waiting for your moment, keep busy by serving God in every way you can.

IV. THE SUPPORT OF MISSION: THE CHURCH
A Not only were the two missionaries sent out by the Spirit, they were also sent out by the church (v.3).
B. This is the proper way to deploy missionaries to the work:
   1. God calls, then the church recognises their calling and gifts.
   2. Then, the Spirit chooses and reveals the right moment for them to go to the field.
   3. Then the church immediately moves into action (Mk 4:29).
C. Guidelines and lessons learned:
   1. We should look to God to identify those who are being prepared for special service.
   2. We should anticipate moments when the Holy Spirit witnesses that people are being set apart for the ministry.
   3. We should encourage and support those whom God calls.

Conclusion and Altar Call
1. Come and commit yourself to God and His mission.

[PW]

Scripture Text Index

Sermon Text	Sermon Number
Genesis 1:26-27	32
Genesis 3:6-9, 15	39
Genesis 12:1-4	61, 89
Genesis 17:7	61
Exodus 3:4-10	63
Leviticus 6:12-13	54
1 Samuel 3:1-11	67
1Kings 17:2-3; 18:1	94
Psalm 67:1-7	76
Psalm 68:31	78
Psalm 96:1-13	4
Psalm 126:4-6	2
Jeremiah 17-21	30
Jeremiah 32:1-9	30
Ezekiel 22:23-31	73
Matthew 1:1	28
Matthew 4:17-25	69
Matthew 4:18	59
Matthew 8:2-3	48
Matthew 9:35-38	12, 33, 40
Matthew 13:44	44
Matthew 14:13-21	87
Matthew 16:13-18	92
Matthew 21:28-31	13
Matthew 24:3-14	8
Matthew 24:14	12, 24
Matthew 28:16-20	19

Sermon Text	Sermon Number
Matthew 28:18-20	13, 17, 18, 20, 21, 22, 23, 24, 25, 26, 28, 41, 42, 89, 90
Mark 3:13-15	58
Mark 4:26-29	83
Mark 16:15-18	1, 3, 5, 21, 22, 25
Luke 4:40-44	43
Luke 5:17-25	37
Luke 14:25-33	90
Luke 10:1-24	88
Luke 19:11-27	68
Luke 24:33-48	7
Luke 24:46-49	15, 21, 22, 25, 56
John 3:16	71
John 3:16-17	80
John 4:4-10	38
John 4:4-42	6
John 4:27-35	45
John 4:27-42	34, 45
John 4:34-38	33
John 15:16	66, 81
John 20:19-23	60, 62
John 20:21	21, 22, 25
Acts 1:1-11	82
Acts 1:4-8	25
Acts 1:8	15, 16, 21, 22, 41, 49, 50, 51, 52, 78, 90
Acts 2:1-4	49, 50, 78
Acts 4:1-20	9
Acts 4:31	99
Acts 6:3-4	96
Acts 8:26-40	91
Acts 10:9-48	47
Acts 10:34-43	70
Acts 11:1-18	47
Acts 11:12-14	51, 53
Acts 11:19-30	79

Sermon Text	Sermon Number
Acts 13:1-4	66, 84, 100
Acts 17:22-27	35
Acts 19:1-10	46
Acts 20:17-25	55
Acts 22:12-21	64
Acts 28:17-31	16
Acts 28:30-31	77
Romans 1:1	81
Romans 1:9-17	31, 95
Romans 9:1-4	36
Romans 10:12-14	75
Romans 10:14-15	57, 85
Romans 13:11-14	29, 84
Romans 15:15-21	10
1 Corinthians 1:17-25	11
1 Corinthians 1:18	27
1 Corinthians 1:21	12
1 Corinthians 9:22	86
1 Corinthians 12:12-14	17
1 Corinthians 12:27-31	17
2 Corinthians 1:8-11	72, 98
2 Corinthians 10:3-4	74
Ephesians 6:12	74
Ephesians 6:12-13	97
Philippians 3:14	59
1 Thessalonians 1:5-7	65
2 Timothy 1:6-7	54
Revelation 3:17-18	51
Revelation 7:9	89
Revelation 12:7-12	97

Other Decade of Pentecost Books
~ Available from the Acts in Africa Initiative ~

Proclaiming Pentecost: 100 Sermon Outlines on the Power of the Holy Spirit (2011) (Available in French, Spanish, Portuguese, Swahili, Mooré and Amharic)

Power Ministry: How to Minister in the Spirit's Power (2004) (also available in French, Portuguese, Malagasy, Kinyarwanda, and Chichewa)

Empowered for Global Mission: A Missionary Look at the Book of Acts (2005)

From Azusa to Africa to the Nations (2005) (also available in French, Spanish, and Portuguese)

Acts: The Spirit of God in Mission (2007)

In Step with the Spirit: Studies in the Spirit-filled Walk (2008)

The Kingdom and the Power: The Kingdom of God: A Pentecostal Interpretation (2009)

Experiencing the Spirit: A Study of the Work of the Spirit in the Life of the Believer (2009)

Teaching in the Spirit (2009)

Power Encounter: Ministering in the Power and Anointing of the Holy Spirit: Revised (2009) (also available in Kiswahili)

You Can Minister in God's Power: A Guide for Spirit-filled Disciples (2009)

The Spirit of God in Mission: A Vocational Commentary on the Book of Acts (2011)

Globalizing Pentecostal Missions in Africa (2011)

The 1:8 Promise of Jesus: The Secret of World Harvest (2012)

Walking with the Apostles: Forty-five Days in the Book of Acts (2016)

All of the above books are available from AIA Publications
580A Central Street, Springfield, MO, 65802, USA
E-mail: ActsinAfrica@agmd.org

www.ingramcontent.com/pod-product-compliance
Lightning Source LLC
Chambersburg PA
CBHW071659090426
42738CB00009B/1586